RETIREMENT GUARDRAILS

Scores of lawsuits have pushed retirement plan sponsors to shorter, easier-to-navigate menus, but – as Ian Ayres and Quinn Curtis argue in this work – we've only scratched the surface of retirement plan design. Using participant-level plan data and straightforward tests, Ayres and Curtis show how plan sponsors can monitor plans for likely allocation mistakes and adapt menus to encourage success. Beginning with an overview of the problem of high costs and the first empirical evidence on retirement plan fee lawsuits, they offer an overview of the current plan landscape. They then show, based on reforms to a real plan, how streamlining menus, eliminating pitfalls, and adopting static and dynamic limits on participant allocations to certain risky assets or "guardrails" can reduce mistakes and lead to better retirement outcomes. Focusing on plausible, easy-to-implement interventions, *Retirement Guardrails* shows that fiduciaries need not be limited to screening out funds but can design menus to actively promote good choices.

IAN AYRES is a lawyer and an economist. They are Deputy Dean and the Oscar M. Ruebhausen Professor at Yale Law School and Professor at Yale's School of Management.

QUINN CURTIS is Professor of Law and an economist at the University of Virginia School of Law. His work focuses on the regulation of retirement plans and investments.

T0384494

RETIREMENT GUARDRAILS

How Proactive Fiduciaries Can Improve Plan Outcomes

IAN AYRES
Yale Law School

QUINN CURTIS
University of Virginia School of Law

CAMBRIDGE
UNIVERSITY PRESS

Shaftesbury Road, Cambridge CB2 8EA, United Kingdom

One Liberty Plaza, 20th Floor, New York, NY 10006, USA

477 Williamstown Road, Port Melbourne, VIC 3207, Australia

314–321, 3rd Floor, Plot 3, Splendor Forum, Jasola District Centre,
New Delhi – 110025, India

103 Penang Road, #05–06/07, Visioncrest Commercial, Singapore 238467

Cambridge University Press is part of Cambridge University Press & Assessment,
a department of the University of Cambridge.

We share the University's mission to contribute to society through the pursuit of
education, learning and research at the highest international levels of excellence.

www.cambridge.org
Information on this title: www.cambridge.org/9781316518632

DOI: 10.1017/9781009001007

© Ian Ayres and Quinn Curtis 2023

This publication is in copyright. Subject to statutory exception and to the provisions
of relevant collective licensing agreements, no reproduction of any part may take
place without the written permission of Cambridge University Press & Assessment.

First published 2023

A catalogue record for this publication is available from the British Library.

Library of Congress Cataloging-in-Publication Data
Names: Ayres, Ian, 1959– author. | Curtis, Quinn, 1979– author.
Title: Retirement guardrails : how proactive fiduciaries can improve plan
outcomes / Ian Ayres, Yale Law School; Quinn Curtis, University of
Virginia School of Law.
Description: Cambridge, United Kingdom ; New York, NY : Cambridge
University Press, 2023. | Includes bibliographical references and index.
Identifiers: LCCN 2022048439 | ISBN 9781316518632 (hardback) | ISBN
9781009001007 (ebook)
Subjects: LCSH: Pension trusts – Finance – Law and legislation – United
States. | Trusts and trustees – United States.
Classification: LCC KF3512 .A997 2023 | DDC 344.7301/252–dc23/eng/20230403
LC record available at https://lccn.loc.gov/2022048439

ISBN 978-1-316-51863-2 Hardback
ISBN 978-1-009-00984-3 Paperback

Cambridge University Press & Assessment has no responsibility for the persistence
or accuracy of URLs for external or third-party internet websites referred to in this
publication and does not guarantee that any content on such websites is, or will
remain, accurate or appropriate.

CONTENTS

v

FIGURES

vi

TABLES

ACKNOWLEDGMENTS

This book grew out of a number of projects over several years dealing with participant choice in retirement plans. The authors are particularly grateful to the University of Virginia Human Resources Department and Dave King for access and help with data.

We have benefited from the superb work of numerous RAs. Substantial contributions to the empirics were made by Zachary Shelley, Eni Iljazi, and Pranjall Drall. Data collection and cleaning efforts were supported by Jeremey Kass, Chase Smith, Jeremy Iacavou, Albert Lee, David Zhou, Juanita Castenada, Sindi Daci, Wei Bao, Adam Sola, Victory Lee, Sophia Nam, Adam Solar, Sean Guyton, Eli Mekonen, Eric Dement, Kyle Connors, Robert Gunn, Samuel Cordle, Sebastien Brunot, Shannon Brooks, Taylor Mitchell, Trevor Quick, and William Vieth.

We are grateful to Jon Ashley and the University of Virginia Law School Legal Data Lab for supporting data collection. For financial support, we are grateful to the Mayo Center for Asset Management at the University of Virginia Darden School of Management.

Finally, we are sincerely grateful for the support of our families and colleagues over the course of this project.

~

Introduction

Many Americans bear responsibility for managing their own retirement savings by choosing from menus of investment options provided through their employer's retirement plan. This book is about how the law can help them make better allocation decisions while preserving their freedom to choose among reasonable investment options.[1]

While employers have a fiduciary responsibility to include only prudent options in their plan menu, they enjoy a safe harbor from liability for inappropriate participant choices over those menus. A wave of recent lawsuits has challenged plans for including options with imprudently high fees, but neither courts nor scholars have grappled in depth with the nature of employer's fiduciary duty in menu construction. This book fills this gap by arguing that prudent menu design shouldn't stop at eliminating high-fee options from the plan menu. Using real plan data, we show that employers can identify options that are highly likely to have been misused by investors. When reviewing their menu design, fiduciaries should learn more and do more. Prudent fiduciaries should (i) assess on an ongoing basis the likelihood and extent to which participants are misusing their plan's menu and (ii) where appropriate, take corrective action to reduce the likelihood of menu misuse. We show in this book how fiduciaries can take action to become better informed in ways that they heretofore have never been. We also show how they can take new actions to remedy menu misuse. Specifically, we argue that the streamlining approach to menu design, where fiduciaries eliminate some underperforming or problematic funds

---

[1] We are not the first to tread these paths. See, e.g., Richard H. Thaler and Shlomo Benartzi, *Save More Tomorrow: Using Behavioral Economics to Increase Employee Saving*, 112 J. POLITICAL ECON. 164, 187 (2004); RICHARD H. THALER & CASS R. SUNSTEIN, NUDGE: IMPROVING DECISIONS ABOUT HEALTH, WEALTH, AND HAPPINESS (2008); James Kwak, *Improving Retirement Savings Options for Employees*, 15 U. FA. J. BUS. L. 483, 483 (2013). At the outset, we should disclose that we have served as amici in ERISA cases and one of us has served as a compensated, expert witness in several cases for plaintiffs alleging fiduciary imprudence in the management of retirement plans.

from the plan menu, is not always the best remedy to the problem of menu misuse. Instead, drawing on plan data, this book shows that allocation errors can often be better mitigated by adopting "guardrails" that constrain but maintain choice.

The Employee Retirement Income Security Act of 1974 (ERISA) requires that participant-directed retirement plans, such as 401(k) plans, give participants (i.e., employees participating in their job's retirement plan) the ability to diversify their portfolios over a menu of options. If plan fiduciaries provide a prudently designed menu, they are protected from liability for participant choice by a safe harbor under ERISA § 404(c). As an empirical matter, many fund menus succeed at giving plan participants substantial diversification opportunities,[2] but many of these same menus create opportunities for participants to make grievous allocation mistakes. How should the fiduciary duty of prudence in menu design be reconciled with predictable, observable participant mistakes over that menu? We argue that plan fiduciaries should do more than simply provide a menu and hope for the best. Prudent menu design requires an understanding of how investors use and misuse choices. Regulations under ERISA, and courts interpreting 404(c), should be attuned to the realities of menu misuse. Increased vigilance could improve retirement outcomes for millions of investors.

There are three core allocation errors that plague retirement plan investments: fee errors, diversification errors, and exposure errors.[3] Fee errors occur when fund level or plan expenses are excessive. Supra-competitive fees reduce portfolio returns and can substantially shrink participants' ultimate accumulation. Diversification errors occur when the portfolios of participants/employees fail to be sufficiently invested in diverse asset classes to eliminate idiosyncratic risk. Because capital markets don't compensate investors for idiosyncratic risk, undiversified portfolios needlessly erode portfolio performance by reducing risk-adjusted return. And finally, exposure errors occur when participant portfolios are exposed to too little or too much market (or systemic) risk. While there are different views on how much exposure is appropriate for particular types of investors, there is a general consensus that it is mistaken for young workers

---

[2] Ian Ayres and Quinn Curtis, *Beyond Diversification: The Pervasive Problem of Excessive Fees and Dominated Funds in 401(k) Plans*, 124 YALE L.J. 1346 (2015).

[3] The possibility of these three allocation mistakes is also discussed in Ian Ayres & Edward Fox, *Alpha Duties: The Search for Excess Returns and Appropriate Fiduciary Responsibilities*, 97 TEXAS L. REV. 445 (2019).

to invest all of their retirement savings in money markets, and for older workers to invest all of their retirement savings in stocks.

When thinking about allocation errors, it is important to distinguish the allocation errors that are hard-wired into the plan versus those that are affirmatively chosen by individual participants. In the first category, fee errors are particularly prominent. Chapter 2's analysis of 2009 data shows that the average plan forced participants to pay 48 basis points (0.48%) annually in excess plan and fund expenses and that the 5 percent most expensive plans forced participants to bear a whopping 1.12 percent in excess fees. Participants cannot avoid excess fees if the cheapest fund in the plan's menu has an annual expense ratio of say, 1.5 percent. A central claim of the book is that fiduciaries may also bear responsibility for some of the allocation errors that participants have some ability to avoid, but can be attributed to imprudent menu design. Fiduciaries, by designing the plan elements, choosing whether there is a default, and what the default fund is can powerfully influence the prevalence of fee, diversification, and exposure errors. Indeed, the increasing prevalence of target date fund as plan defaults (what ERISA calls qualified default investment alternatives, or QDIAs) has led to dramatic reductions in diversification and exposure errors for new participants who disproportionately stick with the default. However, the advent of target date QDIAs also shows how the fiduciary decisions about their plan's "choice architecture" can also induce allocation errors – as made evident by the prevalence of plans with target date defaults charging excessive fees (exceeding 70 basis points).

Substantial progress has been made in the struggle to improve participant allocations. The unavoidable fees and expenses have fallen over the past twenty years. As previously mentioned, plans have also gone beyond just giving participants *the option* to diversify by choosing wisely to offering well-diversified and well-exposed investments by default. This is all for the good. But much remains to be done:

- Many plans still include what we call "dominated" funds. These are funds with high fees that are dominated by a similar, lower-fee fund included in the plan's menu;
- Many plans still include brokerage windows with excess fees and transaction costs, and allow participants to sacrifice diversification by investing all of their retirement savings in meme stocks and even crypto-currency funds (a favorite among millennials!);
- Many plans include sector and region funds, and some even offer company stock options that allow investors to sacrifice diversification by investing all of their retirement investments in narrow asset classes;

- Many plans allow participants, including participants in their twenties, to invest all of their retirement savings in money market accounts paying zero interest – the ERISA equivalent of putting savings under one's mattress.

ERISA allocations have now evolved to a point where avoidable errors are more important than unavoidable errors. The bad old days of plans with across-the-board high fees and missing asset-class investment options are not completely gone. But the most grievous allocation errors today are ones that participants could avoid by making different menu choices.

These errors are not beyond the influence of fiduciaries. On the contrary, many of these errors are a direct and intended byproduct of design decisions of the plan advisor industry. Almost all fiduciaries hire plan advisors to design and administer the ERISA plan. Advisors are hurt when fee mistakes are reduced because it is the advisor who reaps the benefits of excessive fees. Indeed, we've estimated that reducing excessive fees by just 10 basis points would save participants more than $6.9 billion annually, and most of these savings would come out of advisors' pockets. So advisors naturally resist efforts to reduce fees. One might think advisors would not be as resistant to changing the design of plans in ways that would predictably reduce diversification and exposure mistakes. The proliferation of high-cost target date defaults in fact shows that advisors can help reduce these mistakes while still making supra-competitive fees. However, we show that advisors often have a strong economic interest in adding high-fee, undiversified options to plans that are especially attractive to participants who misguidedly believe they can beat the market by concentrating their savings in a narrow set of securities.[4]

In this book, we present a case study of how participants in the University of Virginia retirement plan allocated their 403(b) savings.[5] As of January

---

[4] Our view on this issue has evolved. We previously concluded that "the advisor community was able to cooperate with the diversification project without sacrificing revenues," Ayres & Curtis, *supra* note 2, at 1533. Now we see that eliminating or limiting participant holdings in poorly diversified investment can at times cause advisors to sacrifice revenue.

[5] A 403(b) account is similar to a 401(k), but at a non-profit institution. As a state university, the University of Virginia is not subject to ERISA, but its plan operates like a typical ERISA plan in most respects, and it provides an ideal environment in which to observe the impact of different design choices. In addition, UVA undertook a major improvement of the plan menu during the period covered by our dataset, removing the gold fund and improving the menu in other ways. We use these changes to investigate the impact of menu enhancements on investor welfare.

2018, this plan had 11,765 participants consisting of both current and past employees of the university with more than $673 million invested. We do not use this plan because it is an egregious example of subpar fiduciary behavior. On the contrary. It is generally a well-run plan and we are happy (past and current employees) to both be participants in it. We analyze this particular plan because it provides powerful evidence of how even well-educated employees in a university setting may still fall prey to substantial allocation errors. A minor claim of this book might be called the "cowboy" hypothesis. A subset of participants who are disproportionately male and higher earners are disproportionately likely – because of unjustified over-confidence – to make substantial diversification, fee, and exposure errors in their benighted efforts to beat the market. In designing their plans, fidu-ciaries shouldn't just worry about their poorer and less educated partici-pants, but also about their overconfident cowboys.

For example, let's consider how participants use the Virginia plan's gold fund. Gold coins as an investment are hawked on late-night TV com-mercials and seem to be particularly attractive to doomsday preppers who are "stocking up on canned beans and ammo as [they] wait for the apoca-lypse."[6] In a *New York Times* column, Greg Mankiw asked: "Should gold be a part of [a retirement] portfolio?"[7] He viscerally recoiled at the idea of joining the ranks of "goldbugs" by investing in the precious metal.[8] But when he looked into this asset class, he found there is a reasonable case for a limited investment. Gold historically has been a risky investment – with "the volatility of gold's return, as measured by standard deviation … about 50 percent greater than the volatility of stocks."[9] However, gold's return is "largely uncorrelated with stocks and bonds" which means that adding a little to a portfolio can help diversify risk. In the end, Mankiw concluded that holding "a small sliver, such as the 2 percent weight in the world market portfolio, now makes sense to me as part of a long-term investment strategy."[10]

So how were UVA participants using the gold option? The good news is that of the handful of participants holding the gold fund, many held

---

[6] N. Gregory Mankiw, *Budging (Just a Little) on Investing in Gold*, THE NEW YORK TIMES (July 27, 2013), www.nytimes.com/2013/07/28/business/budging-just-a-little-on-investing-in-gold.html.

[7] *Id.*

[8] This sobriquet refers to people who are "a person who invests in or hoards gold." *Goldbug*, *Merriam-Webster* (2019), www.merriam-webster.com/dictionary/goldbug.

[9] Mankiw, *supra* note 3.

[10] *Id.*

reasonable allocations. In 2016, when the UVA plan was offering the Fidelity Select Gold Fund, a quarter of the participants who were invested in the fund had less than 1.1 percent of their portfolio invested in it, and half of the participants who were invested in this fund had invested less than 4.8 percent of their portfolio.[11] Five percent is a lot of gold, two and a half times the size of the small sliver settled on by Mankiw. But these allocations to our minds are at least close to the range that reasonable investors might adopt.[12]

The bad news is that many of the gold fund investors were unreasonably overinvested in this narrow asset class. In 2016, 13 percent of the participants invested in the fund had more than 70 percent of their portfolio invested therein; and 11 percent had all their plan savings invested in gold.[13] Holding such high proportions in a gold fund is not reasonable. Why did the Virginia plan include a gold fund? Probably, part of the reason was to satisfy the demand of goldbugs, who had strong preferences to put all their eggs in this precious metal. Perhaps they were joined by more sophisticated investors who wanted to hold a Mankivian sliver to better diversify their portfolio. On the other hand, the plan's advisor, Fidelity, had a strong financial interest in including the fund in the plan's menu, because the fund's annual fees were an outrageous 93 basis points.[14]

Our study of the UVA plan reveals that this diversification failure by overweighting narrow investments was not limited to a few zealous goldbugs. We also see that 13 percent of the people investing in Fidelity's Biotech fund had more than 40 percent of their UVA portfolio in this particular fund.[15] More generally, we show that, in 2016, 21.6 percent of participants that held any domestic equity sector funds held more than half their portfolio in domestic equity narrow-sector funds.[16]

These types of allocation mistakes are incredibly common – and costly. The problem is that the legal regime, at least superficially, appears to shield fiduciaries from concerns about how investors use menus. The ERISA § 404(c) safe harbor protects plan sponsors from liability for participant

---

[11] *See infra* Appendix Figure 1.
[12] *See* Mankiw, *supra* note 3 (a precise recommended percentage is elusive "because optimal portfolios are so sensitive to expected returns on alternative assets, and expected returns are hard to measure precisely, even with a century or two of data").
[13] *See infra* Figure 1.
[14] Charging such high fees for a gold fund is particularly outrageous because there is no credible need for active management.
[15] *Id.*
[16] *See infra* Appendix Figure 2.

choices so long as the menu is prudently constructed. As a result, when investment committees meet, they routinely consider the performance of individual funds offered in their menu relative to other funds in the same asset class. But they do not consider the extent to which individual participants are making diversification, fee, or exposure errors.

Our first contribution is to argue that the ERISA fiduciary duty of prudence requires the consideration of menu misuse. An analogy to product liability supports this normative claim. A manufacturer who has ready access to information of injurious customers misuse of their product, and ready means of reducing the probability of harm would have a legal duty to act. Plan administrators who have taken on the higher duty of a fiduciary should have an analogous duty to learn and act. Fiduciaries' appeal to the 404(c) safe harbor as ground for ignoring participant choice is misguided, because the safe harbor applies only to menus that are prudently constructed, and therefore cannot be used to establish prudence in the first instance. We show that becoming better informed can naturally lead to substantive menu redesign.

This book's second contribution is to present an analysis of UVA participants as proof of concept, demonstrating two straightforward calculations that fiduciaries should undertake on an ongoing basis to better assess the likelihood and extent to which participants are misusing their plan's menu. We will refer to these two calculations as *over-weighting analysis* and *portfolio performance analysis*. First, to undertake an overweighting analysis, fiduciaries should calculate the proportion of participants that have disproportionate investments in narrow sector or regional funds, as well as the proportion of participants who have disproportionate investments in various asset and fee classes. Even cursory investigation of individual menu allocations is likely to uncover substantial menu misuse, as we find at UVA and other scholars have found with regard to other plans.[17]

To accomplish a portfolio performance analysis, fiduciaries should calculate the historic return and risk of each participant's portfolio. We will show how risk/returns estimates can help substantiate evidence of menu misuse. We will also present examples of how such calculations can be arrayed in powerful scatterplot diagrams. The overweighting and performance analysis are powerfully complementary in that fiduciaries can test

---

[17] See *infra* Part II.B; *see also* Donald B. Keim & Olivia S. Mitchell, *Simplifying Choices in Defined Contribution Retirement Plan Design: A Case Study*, 17 J. PENSION ECON. FINANC. 363 (2018).

whether participants who have made presumptive menu mistakes experience inferior portfolio risk and return outcomes relative to other plan
participants.[18]

Our third contribution is to argue that corrective action for these issues
is both feasible and productive. If fiduciaries find that substantial numbers
of participants have made problematic portfolio allocations, they should
consider two types of corrective actions: *streamlining the fund menu* and
imposing allocation guardrails. The streamlining strategy is already part of
the fiduciary toolkit. Its potential utility is vividly illustrated by our earlier
gold fund example. Learning that 10 percent of gold fund investors hold
more than 75 percent of their portfolio in that fund might suggest simply
dropping the gold fund from the menu of offered funds. This "streamlining" redesign strategy has been embraced in recent years by a number
of large plans, including both of our home institutions.[19] For example, in
2016, UVA streamlined its menu of fund offerings, moving from offering
241 funds to just 39 funds.[20] Under ERISA rules, a plan that decides to
discontinue investments in a preexisting fund must notify plan participants invested in that fund that their investment will be "remapped" into
another fund in the future unless the participant affirmatively chooses
another menu option.[21] The UVA streamlining eliminated all 43 of its
preexisting narrow sector fund offerings – including its gold fund – and
remapped balances in these funds to the plan's target date funds or to
broad-based equity indexes. We show that streamlining substantially
improved the diversification of participant plan balances.

Instead of the all-or-nothing choice of streamlining, fiduciaries who
learn that participants are misusing their menu options should also consider imposing various forms of allocation *guardrails* – that is, limitations

---

[18] Part II. A responds to two arguments claiming that it is not feasible for the foregoing
calculations to reliably identify whether or not particular participants are making menu
mistakes. For example, we show that it is implausible that many of the Goldbugs had sufficient outside assets to offset their plan holdings of the precious metal. Moreover, we argue
that the possible intent of participants to "beat the market" by concentrating their non-
diversified investments should not prevent fiduciaries from inferring likely error.

[19] In 2019, Yale University streamlined its menu of fund offers moving from more than 100
funds to 11 funds. However, the streamlined menu gave participants the ability to invest
at higher cost in a brokerage window. *See* Janet Linder, *Upcoming Changes to Your Yale
Retirement Savings Program*, YALE UNIVERSITY (2018), www.tiaa.org/public/pdf/Yale_
Lindner_Letter.pdf; *infra* Part II.E (discussing brokerage windows).

[20] *See infra* Figure 17. These counts include only funds that were both offered to and held by
individuals in our analysis.

[21] Keim & Mitchell, *supra* note 17.

on allocations to specific investments or classes of investments. For example, instead of eliminating the Fidelity gold fund, the UVA plan might have capped the percentage of new contributions that could be allocated to gold to say 10 percent. Guardrail interventions represent a kind of "asymmetric paternalism" in that they can help "individuals who are prone to making irrational decisions without harming those making informed, deliberate decisions."[22] A guardrail capping gold fund contributions at 10 percent asymmetrically binds – protecting those who would have unwisely over-weighted gold risk in their portfolio while allowing other, more prudent investors to continue making moderate investments in this precious metal fund. Caps can assure that participants do not invest too much in narrow-gauged sector funds, while guardrail floors can assure that participant portfolios maintain some exposure to certain asset classes, such as international equities and real estate.

For readers who initially balk at the idea that ERISA plans could offer but limit the proportion of funds that can be invested in a particular investment option, we're happy to report that such percentage caps already exist in a number of plans with regard to participants' ability to invest in one specific investment: company stock. Roughly two-thirds of plans that offer company stock often limit participant contributions to no more than 20 percent, and these limits are consistent with existing regulations. Chapter 6 details the myriad ways in which these guardrail caps are imposed. And Chapter 8 describes their impact, but spoiler alert: these company-stock guardrails have been highly effective at improving participant diversification! Vanguard reports that in 2005, 14 percent of Vanguard-advised participants had company stock portfolio concentrations greater than 20 percent, but by 2020 this proportion was only 4 percent.[23]

A second kind of ERISA guardrail is far more ubiquitous. Virtually all ERISA plans restrict participant choice by placing guardrails on the kinds of passwords that participants can choose to access their retirement

---

[22] George Loewenstein, Troyen Brennan & Kevin G. Volpp, *Asymmetric Paternalism to Improve Health Behaviors*, 298 JAMA 2416 (2007); Colin Camerer, Samuel Issacharoff, George Loewenstein, Ted O'Donoghue & Matthew Rabin, *Regulation for Conservatives: Behavioral Economics and the Case for Asymmetric Paternalism*, 153 U. PA. L. REV. 1211 (2003); Richard H. Thaler & Cass R. Sunstein, *Libertarian Paternalism*, 93 AM. ECON. REV. 175 (2003). *See also* Cass R. Sunstein & Richard H. Thaler, *Libertarian Paternalism Is Not an Oxymoron*, 70 U. CHI. L. REV. 1159 (2003).

[23] *Id.* at 5. *See also* Olivia S. Mitchell & Stephen P. Utkus, *The Role of Company Stock in Defined Contribution Plans*, NBER WORKING PAPER 9250 (2002) ("Today an estimated 11 million participants have concentrated stock positions exceeding 20% of account assets.").

account. For example, the University of Virginia plan which is advised/
managed by Fidelity requires that passwords be at least six characters and
prohibits sequences (e.g., 12345 or 11111), personal info (SSN, phone #,
and DOB), or previously used passwords.[24] Such restrictions on personal choice can be justified by a mixture of paternalism and externality
concerns. Fiduciaries are right to prohibit plan participants from choosing "11111" as their password to access their retirement savings. What is
bizarre is that similar logic does not currently apply to limit a participant's choice to allocate all their plan contributions to a gold fund or
to company stock. A participant's retirement nest egg can be devastated
by misuse of allocation choice just as much as by misuse of password
choice. Both password guardrails and allocation guardrails help protect
participant savings from the risk of loss: password guardrails help protect
against loss from theft, while allocation guardrails help protect against
loss from idiosyncratic risk.

In addition to these "hard" allocation guardrails, Chapter 6 describes a
range of softer allocation protections that include varying warnings and
altering rules that modify the steps that participants would need to take
in order to select a potentially problematic allocation. Just as websites at
times give warnings about the weakness of proposed user passwords and
provide advice on strengthening protection, fiduciaries might also deploy
a mixture of warnings and prophylactic procedures to help assure that
proposed participant allocations are not erroneous. In addition to the
hard guardrail restriction on password choice, Fidelity offers advice on
the attributes of a strong password.[25] Something as simple as asking participants "Are you sure you really want this allocation, because it seems to
sacrifice substantial diversification benefits" might go a long way towards
preventing menu misuse. For those who can't imagine the law requiring
such warnings, we'll discuss how the law already does require this kind of
warning with regard to overinvestment in company stock.[26]

Our fourth contribution is to examine how fiduciaries should weigh
the trade-offs entailed when fiduciaries or regulations intervene to restrict
participants' allocative choice. Hard guardrails and menu streamlining are not unalloyed goods. In the case of streamlining, remember that

---

[24] *Create a Strong Password*, FIDELITY (2019), www.fidelity.com/security/create-a-strong-
password.
[25] *Id.* ("The strongest passwords are long and employ a mix of numbers, upper and lower case
letters, and special characters.").
[26] See *infra* Chapter 6.

roughly half the investors in the pre-existing gold fund were making presumptively reasonable "small sliver" allocations of less than 5 percent of their plan savings. Removing the gold fund option from the menu arguably hurts these participants by taking away their option to diversify risk. Hard guardrails present similar issues. The UVA experience suggests that streamlining and guardrails will rarely represent a Pareto improvement.

Chapter 8, however, argues that fiduciaries should not be bound by the Paretian principle.[27] Instead, we argue that ERISA fiduciaries should be guided by an enhanced Kaldor-Hicks standard. To wit, fiduciaries should embrace any change that they expect will increase the overall welfare of plan beneficiaries so long as the change does not substantially impair the welfare of any substantial subgroup of beneficiaries. This welfare standard fulfills the fiduciary's duty of impartiality among plan participants. We will show how UVA's decision to remove the gold fund from its menu lineup likely satisfies this enhanced Kaldor-Hicks requirement. The removal caused substantial improvements in the diversification of the overweighted participants while in expectation producing relatively small diversification costs for the more reasonably invested participants. Chapter 8 shows that streamlining more generally succeeded in reducing idiosyncratic risk and fund expenses. Our simulation of guardrailing shows even greater promise of satisfying the enhanced Kaldor-Hicks standard. Imposing three guardrails – related to diversification, fees, and exposure mistakes – not only would improve average portfolio performance, but we also predict that the class of guardrailed losers would be relatively small and this class would experience relatively mild losses.

The remainder of this book is divided into 12 chapters. Chapter 1 develops our argument that plan fiduciaries should structure plan menus to proactively promote investor welfare, not just by giving suitable choices, but by actively monitoring selections over the menu, and – where appropriate – adopting soft or hard constraints on participant choice. Chapters 2–4 focus on the historic problem of high fees and the limited ability of litigation to respond to excess fees. We document the problem of high costs in retirement plans, the non-problem of sufficient choices in plan menus, and discuss the progress that has been made in improving plan quality. Chapter 3 examines interventions with potential impact on plan quality, including a study of lawsuits targeting plans for excessive fees, which have played an important role in recent improvements to plan quality. Chapter 3

---

[27] *See* Guido Calabresi, *The Pointlessness of Pareto*, 100 YALE L. J. 1211 (1990).

also describes the results of a controversial randomized letter experiment we conducted where one of us had the temerity to send letters (from Ian's letterhead) to a randomized subset of high-fee plans.

Chapters 5–9 lay out the details of our enhanced fiduciary duty proposal. Chapters 5 and 9 describe two types of participant portfolio-level analysis – weighting and performance analysis – that plan fiduciaries should undertake to assess whether there is substantial menu misuse. These chapters show how these analyses can be implemented using our Virginia plan data, where we find substantial evidence of allocation mistakes.

Chapters 6–8 then discuss how fiduciaries should respond to findings of menu misuse. Chapter 6 first describes the multitude of ways in which streamlining and guardrailing can be (and have been) implemented. Chapter 7 then considers under what circumstances these interventions might be justified and argues that fiduciaries should adopt an enhanced Kaldor-Hicks standard in deciding whether to restrict participant freedom. Under this standard, restrictions can be justified if they increase the expected average performance of participants without imposing substantial losses on identifiable subgroups. Using Virginia's own experience with streamlining, combined with our counterfactual simulations of guardrail allocations, Chapter 8 concludes that guardrailing is likely not only Kaldor-Hicks superior to streamlining and also likely meets the enhanced Kaldor-Hicks standard. Our use of UVA data shows how our enhanced fiduciary proposal can be implemented – both with regard to the enhanced duty to become informed of participant allocation errors and with regard to adopting and assessing the success of efforts (soft or hard guardrails or streamlining) to mitigate these errors.

Chapter 9 applies this book's ideas to the brokerage windows (aka self-directed brokerage accounts or SDBAs). Brokerage windows are features of some plans that allow participants to transfer some or all of their plan balances to brokerage accounts where they can invest in a wider universe of funds and ETFs and, in some plans, individual securities. Brokerage windows are shrouded in mystery. Fiduciaries know next to nothing about how participants use these plan features. Chapter 9 provides evidence that some windows cause investors to mistakenly invest savings in money markets that pay zero interest, and allow other participants to invest in individual securities. Crypto currency funds and meme stocks are increasingly popular, and it is only a matter of time before NFT funds and other exotics become available. We suggest that fiduciaries become better informed about how their participants are using brokerage windows and, where appropriate, impose allocation limitations. We take on and reject the "squeaky wheel" argument that brokerage windows allow fiduciaries to satisfy the intense allocation preferences of a subset of participants without degrading the quality of the core menu.

We conclude this book by looking beyond the question of appropriate portfolio allocation to take on two other retirement savings problems. We examine whether participants succeed in having appropriate inflows and outflows from their plan account. The inflow problems include whether people have plans offered at their places of employment, whether they participate in such plans, and whether they make sufficient contributions to their plan. The outflow problems include whether interim balances "leak" out through early withdrawals or loans while participants are employed, whether balances are withdrawn or rolled over to inefficient IRAs when participants change jobs, and whether balances are not sufficiently annuitized when participants ultimately retire. For readers who make it to the conclusion, we will also briefly discuss a bonus proposal that will make progress on these inflow and outflow problems. To wit, we'll suggest giving Americans the public option of purchasing supplemental social security benefits – a program we call "Social Security Plus."[28] Under this program employers would be required to establish "Social Security Plus" as their plan's EQDIA with an opt-out default contribution of 6.2 percent invested in supplemental social security annuity benefits. We close with this bonus proposal in part to signal that the struggle to improve retirement protections for Americans is far from over, and this book is not the final word on policies that might aid in this struggle.

---

[28] *See* Ian Ayres & Jacob Hacker, *Social Security Plus*, 26 ELDER LAW J. 261 (2019); *see also* Ganesh Sitaraman & Anne L. Alstott, *The Public Option: How to Expand Freedom, Increase Opportunity, and Promote Equality* (2019).

1

The Case for Proactive Fiduciaries

For most of us, our employers play an important role in our retirement savings. There is the salary of course, and – for some of us – matching contributions or other benefits. For a dwindling minority there may be an employer-based pension. But most of us rely on our employers for more than just the dollars that go into our retirement accounts. For most of us, our employer also administers our retirement plan. Employers, in concert with an array of service providers they retain, choose the terms of the plan, select the investment options, and forward contributions to custodians. Workers rely on their employers to build a retirement plan conducive to their success, and plan sponsors have a legal obligation to their employees.

Employers offer these plans because employees expect them to. Many middle-class workers would look askance at an employer that failed to offer any kind of tax-preferred savings program. At the same time, it is hard to imagine that the *quality* of the plan administration (as opposed to the generosity of a match or other direct financial support)[1] is a dispositive factor in most employees' decisions to accept a job. As a result, for most employees, a substantial ingredient in their retirement savings success is the diligence and good faith of their employer in designing and overseeing the plan. Fortunately, plan sponsors are held to stringent fiduciary duties in administering plans, but such duties go only so far, and it is fair to ask how much employee welfare is being left on the table by our current system.

The central argument of this book is that employers can and should do more to ensure the success of their employees through the design of their retirement accounts. In this chapter, we consider the legal duties of plan sponsors, and make the case that sponsors, acting as fiduciaries for plan participants, ought to proactively structure plans to increase the likelihood of participant success, including monitoring participant choices and taking steps to make deleterious choices less likely. Merely providing

---

[1] *See* Ryan Bubb & Patrick L. Warren, *An Equilibrium Theory of Retirement Plan Design*, 12 Am. Econ. J. Econ. Policy 22–45 (2020) (developing a theory of plan design in equilibrium).

a list of individually defensible choices and leaving employees to their own devices is not enough. Future chapters will more fully develop what, specifically, sponsors should do. This chapter outlines the duties of plan sponsors in law, and argues that these duties create an obligation for plan sponsors to be proactive in promoting the welfare of plan participants when constructing and monitoring menus.

1.1 The Duties of Plan Sponsors

The defining characteristic of participant-directed retirement plans is that plan investors control how their assets are allocated over a menu of investment options. This is in contrast with conventional, defined-benefit pension plans in which plan assets are managed on behalf of employees collectively by a portfolio manager. Since defined-contribution plans make no promises as to the value of assets at retirement, plan investors bear the burden of managing their investment decisions.

Under ERISA, plan sponsors have a fiduciary duty to operate the plan with care and prudence.[2] ERISA 404(c)[3] provides a safe harbor, shielding plan sponsors from liability for participant investment choices over a sponsor-provided menu so long as investors are permitted to direct their investments in choosing among a diverse set of options. In particular, the 404(c) safe harbor eliminates a fiduciary's liability for "any loss, or by reason of any breach, which results from [a] participant's or beneficiary's exercise of control."[4] In order to qualify for this safe harbor, DOL regulations state that the plan sponsor must, among other requirements, "provide[] an opportunity for a participant … to choose, from a broad range of investment alternatives the manner in which some or all of the assets in his account are invested."[5] In particular, a plan seeking the safe harbor must offer no fewer than three investment alternatives, "each of which is diversified."[6]

---

[2] 29 U.S.C. § 1104(a)(1)(B).
[3] 29 U.S.C. § 1104(c).
[4] 29 U.S.C. § 1104(c)(1)(A)(ii).
[5] 29 C.F.R. § 2550.404c–1(b)(1)(ii).
[6] 29 C.F.R. § 2550.404c–1(b)(3)(i)(B)(1) (this does not impose a duty that *all* investment alternatives offered by the plan must be diversified); *Tatum v. RJR Pension Inv. Comm.*, 761 F.3d 346, 356 (4th Cir. 2014) ("[L]egislative history and federal regulations clarify that the diversification and prudence duties do not prohibit a plan trustee from holding single-stock investments as an option in a plan that includes a portfolio of diversified funds"); *Harmon v. FMC Corporation*, No. 16-cv-6073, 2018 WL 1366621 at 4 (E.D. Pa. Mar. 16, 2018) ("[Section] 404(c) and the corresponding regulations allow plans to include undiversified investment options as long as the plans are diversified as a whole").

While a plan complying with 404(c) must offer some diversified choices, neither 404(c) nor its attendant regulations require that all choices be diversified,[7] nor do they require that investors' individual portfolios be diversified.[8] Indeed, there is evidence that Congress's intent in adopting the safe harbor was to shield fiduciaries from liability for investor allocation mistakes. The conference report on the provision, which several courts have discussed, states:

> [I]f the participant instructs the plan trustee to invest the full balance of his account in, e.g., a single stock, the trustee is not to be liable for any loss because of a failure to diversify or because the investment does not meet the prudent man standards ...[9]

On this view, even an extreme and obvious allocation mistake (such as investing one's entire retirement portfolio in a single stock) is not per se liability-creating for the plan sponsor.

The 404(c) safe harbor could conceivably be read as essentially eliminating fiduciary liability in defined contribution plans that offer diversified menus, but the regulatory picture is more complicated. The DOL has argued that the safe harbor does not protect decisions related to the construction of the menu itself, which remains a fiduciary responsibility of the plan sponsor. The DOL initially took this position in the preamble to the 1992 rule outlining requirements to qualify for the safe harbor. The DOL said in a footnote that "the act of limiting or designating investment options which are intended to constitute all or part of the investment universe of an ERISA 404(c) plan is a fiduciary function which ... is not a direct or necessary result of any participant direction of such plan."[10] The DOL reiterated this position more explicitly in a 2010 rulemaking.[11]

The Supreme Court has twice characterized the duties of plan sponsors. In *Tibble v. Edison*,[12] the Court considered whether the fiduciary duty of plan sponsors was a continuing one. That is, can a plan sponsor breach a duty only when a change to the menu is made, such that the statute of

---

[7] *Harmon v. FMC Corporation*, No. 16-cv-6073, 2018 WL 1366621 at 4 (E.D. Pa. Mar. 16, 2018) ("[Section] 404(c) and the corresponding regulations allow plans to include undiversified investment options as long as the plans are diversified as a whole").

[8] *See* 29 C.F.R. § 2550.404c–1(f)(5) (providing an example of a plan participant "invest[ing] 100% of his account balance in a single stock" and noting that the plan fiduciary "will not be liable for any losses that necessarily result").

[9] *Id.*

[10] 57 Fed. Reg. 46906–01, 46,924 n.27 (Oct. 13, 1992).

[11] 29 C.F.R. § 2550.404c–1 (Dec. 20, 2010).

[12] 575 U.S. 523 (2015).

limitations will eventually shield the sponsor for including the choice, or must a plan sponsor continually monitor the options in the plan menu? The Court unanimously held that the duty to ensure menu quality is a continuing one, writing that "a fiduciary normally has a continuing duty of some kind to monitor investments and remove imprudent ones. A plaintiff may allege that a fiduciary breached the duty of prudence by failing to properly monitor investments and remove imprudent ones."[13]

The second case, *Hughes v. Northwestern University*, directly presented the question of whether merely including high-cost funds among a menu of other options could constitute a fiduciary breach. In that case, the Court – once again unanimous – held that *Tibble* settled the issue: "A fiduciary normally has a continuing duty of some kind to monitor investments and remove imprudent ones. A plaintiff may allege that a fiduciary breached the duty of prudence by failing to properly monitor investments and remove imprudent ones."[14] The Court also put to bed the notion that merely providing some good options should insulate plan sponsors from liability for including bad ones, writing: "The [court below] erred in relying on the participants' ultimate choice over their investments to excuse allegedly imprudent decisions by respondents."[15]

Together, *Tibble* and *Hughes* establish that plan sponsors have an ongoing duty to monitor the quality of all menu options and eliminate imprudent ones. The notion that merely including some good options suffices can be dispensed with. But while *Tibble* and *Hughes* provide some clarity as to the scope of the ERISA fiduciary duty for plan sponsors, they provide little guidance as to exactly what plan sponsors are required to do to monitor their menus. While the case law in lower courts, reviewed in more detail later, provides more robust guidance, the fiduciary duties of plan sponsors are remarkably thinly characterized, a situation which this book – in part – seeks to remedy.

1.2 The Importance of Menu Effects

The defining characteristic of participant-directed retirement plans is that ultimate responsibility for choosing particular investments falls on the plan investors. Conversely, responsibility for setting up the plan, negotiating the fees of the plan, and establishing the menu falls on the employer

---

[13] *Id.* at 530.
[14] *Hughes* slip op at 6.
[15] *Id.*

as a plan fiduciary. The plan sponsor has a fiduciary duty of prudence in menu construction and maintenance, but the consequences of choices over the menu fall on the plan participants.

While superficially tidy, this division of labor relies on a clean distinction between menu construction and participant choice that is undermined by economic reality: A large body of economic research demonstrates that – both inside and outside of retirement plans – *menus matter*.[16] There seems to be an inherent tension between the position that menu construction is a fiduciary function and the 404(c) safe harbor's immunity for participant choices. An investment option imprudently included in a plan menu harms participants only if some of them choose to invest in it. On the other hand, the inclusion of certain options – such as a retail class mutual fund when the plan would qualify for lower-cost institutional shares – would seem to contravene the duty to prudently construct a menu. This tension is exacerbated by a vast literature in behavioral economics establishing that menu design can have significant effects on participant choices.[17] Indeed, some of the highest-profile work in behavioral economics has specifically addressed retirement plan design.

Benartzi and Thaler[18] found that plan participants engage in a type of naïve diversification, holding funds in rough proportion to their representation in the menu. Choi, Laibson, and Madrian[19] found that this effect extends even to index funds with different fees tracking the same index. These and other studies demonstrate, beyond any doubt, that the construction of retirement plan menus predictably impacts participant choice, even when changes to the menu don't structurally constrain participant choice. What Sunstein and Thaler[20] dub *choice architecture* has been demonstrated to play an important role in retirement savings decisions, and a substantial literature in economics documents these effects. How choices are presented and framed will affect the decisions that employees make. Given more choices of a particular asset class, participants will hold more

---

[16] *See* Richard H. Thaler & Cass R. Sunstein, NUDGE: IMPROVING DECISIONS ABOUT HEALTH, WEALTH, AND HAPPINESS 103–17 (2008) (proposing various menu constructions that would increase personal savings rates); Ian Ayres, *Menus Matter*, 73 U. CHI. L. REV. 3 (2006) among many other works.

[17] *Id.*

[18] Shlomo Benartzi & Richard H. Thaler, *Naive Diversification Strategies in Defined Contribution Saving Plans*, 91 AM. ECON. REV. 79 (2001).

[19] James J. Choi, David Laibson & Brigitte C. Madrian, *Why Does the Law of One Price Fail? An Experiment on Index Mutual Funds*, 23 REV. FIN. STUDS. 1405, 1407 (2010).

[20] Richard H. Thaler & Cass R. Sunstein, NUDGE: IMPROVING DECISIONS ABOUT HEALTH, WEALTH, AND HAPPINESS (2008).

of that asset class. Given default options, participants will hold more of the default. Given too many choices, participants may be overcome by the scope of options and save less.[21]

This central insight of behavioral economics – that menus matter even when choice is not constrained – has an important legal corollary: If menu construction is causally related to participant choice, then a prudent fiduciary should take account of that reality. It is now clearly established that the 404(c) safe harbor, which insulates employees from responsibility for menu decisions, does not forestall employer liability for imprudent menu design. It is similarly well established, following *Hughes*, that including high-fee options in a plan menu can be the basis for fiduciary liability, even if other, better options are included.

But the idea that fiduciaries should evaluate and exclude imprudent options from plan menus is only the beginning of the menu design inquiry, not its end. What does it mean for a choice to be imprudent? When do the benefits of including certain options outweigh the costs? What does it mean to have a fiduciary duty to act in the interest of plan participants when designing a menu? Most importantly, how can we take the lessons of behavioral economics, and the concept of choice architecture, seriously when conceiving the fiduciary obligations of plan sponsors? Despite the extensive litigation surrounding retirement plans, these questions remain largely unaddressed.

1.2.1 *The Legal Case for a Duty to Monitor Menu Misuse*

What does a duty of prudence in menu construction mean if the menu is causally connected to participant choice? We argue that a fiduciary, in fulfilling their duty of prudence, should take into account the connection between menu design and participant choice. This entails understanding the choices that plan participants are actually making and seeking to design a menu that actively promotes their welfare.

Our argument is simple: A fiduciary does not serve the interest of plan participants by creating pitfalls that must be avoided. While a prudent menu need not be robust against every conceivable mistake, it should – to the extent possible – avoid options that are undesirable for

---

[21] Julie R. Agnew & Lisa R. Szykman, *Asset Allocation and Information Overload: The Influence of Information Display, Asset Choice, and Investor Experience*, 6 J. BEHAV. FIN. 57 (2005); Sheena Sethi-Iyengar, Gur Huberman & Wei Jiang, How Much Choice Is Too Much? Contributions to 401(k) Retirement Plans, *in* PENSION DESIGN AND STRUCTURE 83, 88–91 (Olivia S. Mitchell & Stephen P. Utkus eds., 2004).

most participants or prone to egregious misuse. Can this obligation be squared with the 404(c) safe harbor, which attempts to isolate menu construction from participant decision-making as a legal matter? For balance of this section, we argue that while a fiduciary is not liable for every decision made over the plan menu, prudence does require that a fiduciary inform themselves as to the way the plan menu is actually used and proactively shape the menu to improve participant outcomes. In particular, fiduciaries for retirement plans ought to be attuned to the possibility that options in the plan menu are being misused by plan participants. That is, sponsors ought to evaluate whether plan options that might have some legitimate role in a retirement portfolio are being misused in ways likely to reduce participants' retirement assets.

The starting point for this argument is the *Tibble* and *Hughes* cases discussed above that have signaled individual imprudent funds can constitute a fiduciary breach. What is wrong with including, for example, a high-cost option in a 401(k) plan when a lower-cost equivalent was available? Presumably, the issue is that the inclusion of a high-cost option creates a pitfall for plan investors. Even when presented alongside a diversified menu of prudent options, a fund with imprudently high costs will be predictably held by some investors, and the plan fiduciary – in assembling the menu – should anticipate this fact. The purpose of having plan sponsors provide employees with a curated menu is that the plan sponsor will exercise judgment to increase the likelihood of participant success. A fiduciary that includes an imprudent option fails to realize that policy goal and reduces the likelihood that investors will succeed.

This argument is simple enough and has been broadly accepted by courts, but it incorporates the ingredients of a broader claim. If liability for including a high-fee fund arises because it creates the menu equivalent of an attractive nuisance, then it is not clear why fees should be the only basis for regarding an option as imprudent to include. Plan fiduciaries should take a broad view in menu construction and avoid any fund whose inclusion is likely to harm plan participants.

Can this be squared with 404(c)? Consider the explicit delineation of the safe harbor provided in *Howell v. Motorola*:

> If an individual account is self-directed, then it would make no sense to blame the fiduciary for the participant's decision to invest 40% of her assets in Fund A and 60% in Fund B, rather than splitting assets somehow among four different funds, emphasizing A rather than B, or taking any other decision.[22]

---

[22] 633 F.3d 552, 567 (7th Cir. 2011).

This seems clear enough. If it is prudent to include both Fund A and Fund B in a menu, then the fiduciary can't be liable for the decision made by a participant to choose a particular allocation over Fund A and Fund B, even if some other allocation might have been a better decision. Plan participants could allege that Fund B was imprudently included, perhaps because a lower fee version was available, but so long as the inclusion was prudent, the fiduciary's obligation is fulfilled.

Let's now complicate the picture. Suppose that Fund B tracks a high-risk sector of the market and that, on conventional measures of portfolio optimization, Fund B should make up only about 5 percent of a typical portfolio and never more than 10 percent. Suppose further that year after year more than half of the plan participants hold 60 percent or more of their portfolio in Fund B. Can it still be said that a prudent fiduciary should include Fund B in the menu? Are the interests of plan participants served by including Fund B, even if a majority of participants seem to be misusing it? If it is reasonably foreseeable, or even observable in practice, that plan participants will misuse a menu option in ways that are harmful to their overall financial welfare, then a prudent plan sponsor should decline to include it, or – as we argue later – limit allocations to mitigate the harm.

Here, an analogy to product liability can be developed. Product manufacturers are held to an ordinary duty of care, rather than a fiduciary duty. Nevertheless, a manufacturer may be liable for the foreseeable misuse of their product, even when that misuse is a result of choices made by product purchasers rather than by the manufacturer.[23] As we will show below, a plan fiduciary needn't guess about how their menu is being used. Every plan fiduciary has access to real-time data about plan holdings. All that is required to identify problems is the sort of straightforward analysis we demonstrate in Section II, *infra*. The higher duty of plan sponsors, coupled with the ease of executing that duty (since plan sponsors have access to real-time holdings data), suggests that fiduciaries should be engaged in this sort of analysis as a matter of prudent menu design.

A plan sponsor confronted with such an argument might look to the 404(c) safe harbor to claim that they are not liable for participant choices over a prudently constructed menu. This argument begs the question.

---

[23] A manufacturer may face liability for foreseeable consumer misuse of a product. See RESTATEMENT (THIRD) OF TORTS: PRODUCTS LIABILITY § 2 cmt. M. In instances where misuse is foreseeable, a manufacturer may be liable if a reasonable alternative design was available that might have avoided the harm. RESTATEMENT (THIRD) OF TORTS: PRODUCTS LIABILITY § 3 cmt. P.

The majority rule, following the DOL, is that the safe harbor does not protect imprudent menu design. A plan sponsor therefore can't appeal to the safe harbor to establish that they have complied with their duty of prudence. It is, of course, true that Fund B harms only investors who choose to overallocate to it, but high-cost funds harm only those investors who choose to hold them, and courts have been willing to permit suits based on the inclusion of individual high-cost funds. Once one rejects the "large menu defense" – the idea that merely giving employees sufficiently many good options among a list of potentially bad ones insulates the employer from liability – it is incumbent on fiduciaries to consider how the inclusion of options in the menus will affect participant welfare.

What of the view in *Howell* that participant choices are beyond the control of the plan sponsor? This argument falls flat for two reasons. First, as *Howell* notes,[24] the menu is in the control of the plan sponsor and so is the choice of whether to include Fund B. Second, part of menu design is not just whether or not to include a fund, but whether to allow unlimited investments in that fund. We know this because many menus include company stock but simultaneously cap the amount participants can invest in this option. If the sponsor is aware, or should be aware, that Fund B is inducing widespread menu misuse, then the decision to continue offering the fund (or the decision to allow unlimited allocations to that fund) is certainly a choice that is within the sponsor's control. Second, behavioral economics teaches us that menu design impacts participant decisions.[25] Indeed, the widespread practice of dividing plan menus into tiered options can be understood as exploiting menu design to improve participant decisions. The sharp distinction between menu design and participant choice is a judicial attempt to find a distinction that extensive empirical work suggests is illusory. While a fiduciary cannot literally control the choices of plan participants, the fiduciary's choices in designing the menu predictably affect those choices, and a prudent fiduciary should consider those effects.

Note that our argument does not write the safe harbor out of existence. Plan sponsors would still be protected from liability for choices over menu items that are prudently included with full consideration of potential misuse. For example, if a plan includes a prudently chosen, low-cost target date fund with a date of 2025, and a 25-year-old employee whose target

---

[24] 633 F.3d at 567 (7th Cir. 2011).

[25] Ian Ayres & Quinn Curtis, *Beyond Diversification: The Pervasive Problem of Excessive Fees and Dominated Funds in 401(k) Plans*, 124 YALE L.J 1346, 1391–95 (2015).

retirement date is 2065 decides to hold it, 404(c) would protect the plan
from liability for that mistake. The requirement is that fiduciaries act prudently in the interest of plan investors to balance the potential misuse of
a menu option against the benefit of its legitimate use. While a target date
fund can be misused by inappropriately aged investors, that risk is likely
outweighed by the benefit to other investors of including it.[26]

Nor would this approach require clairvoyance on the part of plan sponsors. ERISA requires prudence, not infallibility, in menu design. Courts
emphasize the importance of a thorough process in deciding which
options to include in the menu[27] and carefully avoid hindsight bias related
to investment performance. The same requirements would apply here. If
a plan can demonstrate that they made a prudent effort to understand
potential misuse, weighed those risks against the merits of including the
option in the plan and came to a considered, defensible conclusion that
the option was worth including, then the plan would be entitled to safe
harbor protection even if there are participant mistakes. On the other
hand, if a plan fiduciary simply closes its eyes to repeated and egregious
menu misuse, then it is not acting prudently and should not be entitled to
the safe harbor protection.

1.3   An Ideal Fiduciary

Questions about the scope of fiduciary duties are inevitably freighted with
the risk of litigation and the specter of financial damages. Let's set aside
these concerns for a moment and focus on the simpler question what a
plan sponsor, in constructing a menu, could do to increase the chances
that plan participants will be able to retire successfully and on schedule.

To make it concrete, suppose (somewhat fancifully) that the likelihood
of a large public company making its quarterly earnings target depended
not just on its product sales, but on how well the investors in its 401(k)
plan were doing. For example, we might imagine a world where the success of a plan advisor, such as Fidelity, in marketing its advising services
was tied to the success of its own employees' portfolio in a plan utilizing those services. That is, suppose that the interests of the plan sponsor
and plan participants were truly aligned. What would the plan look like?
We submit that if the business success of the plan sponsor were directly

---

[26] As described below, however, we needn't rest there; plan sponsors could adopt guardrails
to discourage this sort of age-inappropriate allocation.
[27] Thaler & Sunstein, *supra* note 20.

affected by how well the portfolios of its retirement investors were per-
forming, plans would look quite a bit different. We doubt that employers
would present participants with a menu of dozens of options and leave
then to make choices unattended, especially if the surplus choices include
risky options likely to lead to allocation problems or high-cost options
that were likely to underperform. A plan sponsor with incentives to
ensure employee success would craft a menu carefully and closely monitor its use, keeping an eye out for problems and adjusting the menu in
light of actual employee choices. To the extent permissible, the employer
might even prevent employees from making choices particularly likely to
end badly. In short, our hypothetical employer would likely be far more
proactive in ensuring that employees make informed, optimal decisions
in their retirement savings.

Our thesis is that fiduciaries of retirement plans should act more like
the employer in the thought experiment above. While extensive litigation has encouraged fiduciaries to internalize the interests of plan participants to avoid clearly bad options in the plan menu, there is much
more that plan sponsors can and should do to ensure participant success. In succeeding chapters, we will describe tools that fiduciaries
should be using to proactively promote positive outcomes for retirement plan savers.

Our first prescription is that plan sponsors should adopt a more
aggressive approach to streamlining plan menus to eliminate questionable choices. Not all mutual funds are reasonable choices for inclusion
in an employer retirement plan. A normative premise of our system of
employer-managed plans is that the interposition of a plan fiduciary with
incentives and resources to screen options can leave employees better
off. It is inconsistent with this premise (as well as positive law) to include
options that are presumptively poor choices.

Our second prescription, going beyond the mere screening of individually bad option, is that plans should be carefully monitoring employee
choices for consistency with generally accepted investing best practices.
While it is not possible to prevent every mistake, and employers don't
have insight into every plan participant's household portfolio, there is
nevertheless concrete, actionable information that plan fiduciaries can
learn from carefully monitoring investor selections. Are some investors
overallocating to niche sectors or commodity funds? Are some investors
holding portfolios that are clearly too conservative for their age? Do some
funds in the plan menu seem particularly prone to strange allocations?
All plan sponsors have the needed information to answer such questions.

Finally, we suggest a new mechanism for improving investor welfare: guardrails. By guardrails, we mean any mechanism that erects a barrier, either an outright prohibition or simply a warning, associated with choices in a retirement plan that fall outside of certain parameters and are therefore particularly likely to be mistakes. A simple example of a guardrail already used by some companies is a prohibition on holding more than 10 percent of one's retirement portfolio in company stock. Because investing in the stock of one's own employer presents an obvious diversification problem, the inclusion of company stock as an option in 401(k) plans has become less popular over time. While we regard this as a positive development, employers remain attracted to the idea of having employee-investors share in the fortunes of the company, and some employees want that option in their retirement plan.

For those readers who would appreciate a more explicit foreshadowing of the book's argument, we briefly list here our six central proposals:

1. The Enhanced Default Proposal – The DOL should require that all plans offer low-cost target-date or balance funds as their default investments. Currently, plans *can* adopt defaults but are *not required* to do so, and there is no limitation on the expenses charged by this default fund. Any fund that would currently qualify as a QDIA would qualify as an Enhanced QDIA (or EQDIA) if its annual expenses were less than 50 basis points. Given the "iron law" of default inertia, requiring EQDIAs would reduce the prevalence of all three allocation errors.

2. Dominated Fund Proposal – The DOL should prohibit plans from including dominated fund options in their menu. Dominated funds are definitionally investment options that rational investors should not take, given the other funds offered by the plan. We show in this chapter that these funds are offered in many plans and that substantial participant assets mistakenly languish in these dominated investments. Prohibiting dominated funds would reduce fee errors.

3. High-Cost Plan Proposal – The DOL should designate any plan in which the average annual expenses are more than 150 basis points as a "high-cost" plan, and mandate that participants in such plans be allowed "in-service" rollovers to IRAs offering EQDIA investments. Facilitating the rolling over of such high-cost portfolios would reduce fee errors.

4. DOL Portfolio Guardrail Proposal – The DOL should impose guardrails that limit participants' ability to create portfolios that overinvest in individual securities or asset classes, or that have high expenses or

imprudent market exposures. Regulatory guardrails with appropriately wide tolerances can maintain substantial participant autonomy while reducing the most egregious allocation errors.

5. Altering Rule Proposal – The DOL should require plans with fund options that would not qualify as EQDIAs to warn participants about the additional risks of portfolios with poor diversification, fees, or exposure. These plans should allow participants to choose allocations that violate the DOL guardrails only if the participant passes a sophistication test which establishes some understanding of these risks. These warnings and sophistication tests would predictably reduce all three types of allocation errors.

6. Enhance Fiduciary Duty Proposal – Courts (supported by the DOL) should require fiduciaries to assess and remedy allocation errors.

While the book makes an argument for the enhance fiduciary duty proposal, most of our proposals rely on *ex ante* DOL rules rather than on *ex post* equitable standards. Chapters 2 and 3 show that using private litigation as an instrument to change fiduciary behavior is a substantially limited approach. For example, Chapter 3 details how funds with less than $100,000,000 in assets under management are de facto immune from such litigation – even though we find that such plans are particularly likely to have supra-competitive plan and fund expenses.

Our proposals, previewed in this chapter and developed in detail in Chapters 4 through 8, are a mixture of default, altering and mandatory rules which unabashedly are attempts to use the law to improve how people invest for retirement. These interventions are in part justified by the external effects of those private actions. The tax code's subsidy of defined-contribution plans represents an annual tax expenditure on the order of $64 billion.[28] It is one thing for a person to sacrifice diversification and speculate to try to beat the market with their private brokerage accounts (or these days, say, on their Robinhood app). It is quite another to claim a right to speculate while simultaneously claiming the tax subsidy provided by fellow Americans – especially because if their investments go south, there will be pressure to bail them out (as we saw in the aftermath of the housing crisis).

---

[28] Ryan Bubb & Richard H. Pildes, *How Behavioral Economics Trims Its Sails and Why*, 127 HARV. L. REV. 1631 (2014). *See also* Office of Management and Budget, *Analytical Perspectives: Budget of the U.S. Government*, Executive Office of the President of the U.S., at 254, 257 (2013), www.govinfo.gov/content/pkg/BUDGET-2014-PER/pdf/BUDGET-2014-PER.pdf.

The more mandatory limitations are also justified in part by libertarian paternalism. Even people who are committed to maintaining freedom of choice to preserve personal autonomy or to enhance welfare can support interventions which help "influence choices in a way that will make choosers better off, as judged by themselves."[29] We will argue that if participants were better educated about the expected risks and returns, many would not regret being forced to comply with guardrailed portfolios that are well diversified, low cost, and reasonably exposed.

Finally, it is important to reiterate how much our proposals preserve allocation autonomy. Participants in defined-benefit plans (and in the Social Security system) have no allocative choice. Their retirement security is tied to the allocative choices of their fiduciaries. Allocative guardrails also preserve more autonomy than streamlining. Deleting a fund from a plan menu is effectively capping contributions at 0 percent and hence is more restrictive than a guardrail that caps contributions at 10 percent.

While we are skeptical that any allocation to company stock outside of its inclusion in an index fund is a good idea for a retirement saver, *all* can agree that allocating a very large percentage of one's portfolio to company stock is courting disaster. The 10 percent guardrail provides a middle ground between exclusion of the option from the plan and allowing employees to make potentially devastating diversification mistakes.

---

[29] Thaler & Sunstein, *supra* note 16, at 1162.

2

Fees and Dominated Funds

In 2007, Wal-Mart sat atop the Fortune 500 as America's largest company by revenue, taking in more than a third of a trillion dollars.[1] It was also America's largest private employer with 1,900,000 employees in its ranks.[2] Unsurprisingly, Wal-Mart's 401(k) plan was also enormous, with over a million participants and a staggering $10,000,000,000 in assets.[3] Managing these assets was among the most sought-after contracts in plan administration, and Merrill Lynch acted as the plan's trustee.[4]

As a retailer, Wal-Mart famously wields its buying power to extract the lowest possible prices from its suppliers. Wal-Mart executives are well known for pressuring suppliers to cut marketing and other costs and keep prices as low as possible. But when it came to its employees' 401(k) dollars, Wal-Mart's cost-cutting philosophy was nowhere to be found. Wal-Mart's plan offered a spare menu of ten mutual funds. Remarkably, despite the enormous buying power of the billions in retirements assets, the plan offered only retail share classes of those mutual funds – the same that you or I could select for a small online account. Famous for extracting every penny of savings from its supply chain, Wal-Mart was almost shockingly indifferent to the price paid by its employees for managing their retirement assets.

In 2008, plaintiffs' attorneys filed a class action lawsuit against Wal-Mart on behalf of employees, arguing that they had paid more than $60,000,000 in excessive fees, pointing to lower-cost options that might have been included in the plan, and seeking damages.[5] The lawsuit alleged that Wal-Mart had – in effect – been asleep at the switch while Merrill

---

[1] Fortune 50 2007, FORTUNE, https://fortune.com/fortune500/2007/.
[2] *Id.*
[3] *Braden v. Wal-Mart Stores, Inc.*, 590 F. Supp.2d 1159 (W.D. Mo. 2008).
[4] *Id.*
[5] *Id.*

Lynch suggested in-house funds for the plan that routed some of their fee revenue back to the trustee. The case was initially dismissed, but on appeal, the 8th Circuit delivered an opinion that not only revived the case but opened the door for many more 401(k) fee suits. The case against Wal-Mart ultimately settled for more than $13,000,000.

Wal-Mart was hardly unique in being a large corporation running a huge retirement plan and offering a menu of high-cost funds. The problem of inattention to costs in retirement plans is long standing. And smaller plans, lacking economies of scale, tend to be even more expensive.

But the problem of costs is not as straightforward as a simple price tag attached to each plan. The costs of investing depend on choices that investors make over differently priced options in the plan menu, and so costs and menu design interact. One of our central claims is that the design of plan menus has predictable effects on investor welfare. Well-designed menus can induce good choices, and poorly designed menus create pitfalls that leave investors vulnerable. A core aspect of menu design is the cost structure, and, as we show below, well-designed menus can lower the cost to participants, while poorly designed menus can increase them.

This section gives an overview of our prior empirical work on the problem of high fees and what we term "dominated funds" in the 401(k) plan menu using a large, proprietary dataset of data for more than 3,500 retirement plans as of 2010. We demonstrate an effect of the structure of the plan menus on the total cost of the plan: menus with more pitfalls tend to induce investors to pay higher fees relative to the optimal port-folio. These results highlight the importance of sound menu design to investor success at the plan level. In later chapters, we will offer a consid-erably higher-resolution view of this effect using participant-level data. We also demonstrate that plan size strongly affects total plan cost (which is not surprising) and that menu quality is lower at smaller plans (a more novel finding).

We document the widespread phenomenon of excessively expen-sive funds. Additionally, we show that many plans include "dominated funds," with cost and risk characteristics that should deter any reasonable investor from committing assets. Our key finding is that the average plan in our dataset caused investors to incur a cost of 78 basis points in excess of a well-diversified menu of low-cost index funds. These problems are worse in smaller plans in our data, and the very smallest plans are not part of our dataset.

We conclude by discussing developments in plan costs over the last decade.

2.1   The Cost of Retirement Plans[6]

The impact of fees has long been an issue for retirement plan policy. Plans, of course, cost money to run: The tasks of collecting and tracking contributions, tracking the holdings of investors, and producing documentation and records all cost money, and plan sponsors are permitted to use plan assets to fund reasonable expenses.[7] But fees are also a drag on returns, and because fees are often charged as a percentage of assets under management, they compound and can have a major impact on investor welfare. The Department of Labor points out that a 0.5 percent reduction in return due to fees can lead to a 28 percent reduction in retirement assets over the course of a 35-year career.[8]

There are two main classes of expenses in operating a retirement plan. The first component is fees that are charged directly against plan assets and are typically associated with the costs of operating the plan. These include record-keeping fees that cover the costs of tracking plan accounts, and other administrative expenses. ERISA fiduciaries are entitled to charge reasonable fees against plan assets, and these fees are disclosed to employees and reported publicly on Form 5500, filed with the Department of Labor. For most plans, these plan-level fees are the smaller component of costs.

The most substantial share of plan costs are the fees associated with the investments themselves. The menu of options in typical retirement plans consists of mutual funds or similar pooled investment vehicles. These funds charge fees as a percentage of assets invested. For mutual funds, the fees will be the costs associated with the particular share class of the fund offered. For other types of pooled investments, such as collective trusts used by large plans, the fees might be negotiated with the plan sponsor. In either case, the costs of different investment options will vary, and – as a result – the total costs paid by each participant in the plan will depend on the selections they make over the plan menu.

---

[6] This section and Section 2.2 are adapted from Ian Ayres & Quinn Curtis, *Beyond Diversification: The Pervasive Problem of Excessive Fees and Dominated Funds in 401(k) Plans*, 124 YALE L.J. 1346 (2015).

[7] 29 U.S.C. § 1104(a)(1)(A)(ii).

[8] U.S. DEPT. OF LABOR, A LOOK AT PLAN FEES www.dol.gov/sites/dolgov/files/ebsa/about-ebsa/our-activities/resource-center/publications/a-look-at-401k-plan-fees.pdf.

While the costs of asset-based fees for individual investment options are disclosed to plan participants, those costs are not disclosed on Form 5500. It can be difficult to gauge from the outside whether plans are good deals, and employees themselves may not have the skills or context to evaluate the costs of plan options. The issue of cost opacity is exacerbated, because in many cases, the aggregate costs of operating the plan are also covered by the asset-based fees through a practice known as revenue sharing, meaning that the costs of operating the plan are rolled into the investment fees.

An additional concern is that the construction of plan menus is subject to conflicts of interest that might mean that menus are not optimally designed for participant welfare. Employers rely on the advice of financial professionals in assembling plan menus, especially smaller employers who lack in-house expertise. These service providers are generally not fiduciaries, and – because of revenue sharing – often have an interest in their own funds appearing in the plan menu, especially if those funds are high-cost, high-margin options.[9] Empirical evidence has shown that plan service providers' own funds are more likely to stay in the plan menu after a period of poor performance.[10]

Since the bulk of retirement plan fees are incurred at the level of individual investments and these investments vary in cost, the individual costs of investing in a retirement plan depend on the selected portfolio. An investor who allocates everything to low-cost index funds will pay less than one who choose actively managed or specialty fund options. When these differences in costs arise out of supracompetitive fees on some of the investment options, then the investors who hold those funds pay more than necessary, to their detriment and potentially to the benefit of the service providers involved in constructing the plan menu.

The inclusion of high-cost, low-performance options in plan menus is the most frequently discussed and widely litigated problem in retirement plan design. Allegations that plans imprudently include high-cost funds is the driving factor behind more than one hundred lawsuits against plan sponsors, many of which have results in large settlements. Of course, merely including a high-cost, underperforming option in a plan menu is insufficient to harm investors: only if investors choose the fund will they

[9] Sheldon M. Geller, *401(k) Revenue Sharing Creates Employer Liability*, CPA J., Dec. 2015, at 3.
[10] Veronika K. Pool, Clemens Sialm & Irina Stefanescu, *It Pays to Set the Menu: Mutual Fund Investment Options in 401(k) Plans*, 71 J. FIN. 1779 (2016).

pay the fees and bear the opportunity cost of lower performance. But, as the evidence below demonstrates, investors will hold high-cost funds if such funds are offered.

Plan service providers understand this. Indeed, they often count on it as part of their revenue model. Including a high-cost option is likely to generate revenue, even if investors are free to choose other, low-cost substitutes, and one of the reasons high-cost funds end up in plan menus is that their fee income can offset some of the cost of running the plan. Indeed, a plan fiduciary who attempts to remove a high-cost option from the menu may be advised that plan-level fees would increase to offset the lost revenue. In effect, the faulty choices of some plan investors subsidize the cost of operating the plan.

The basic issue of excessive plan fees reduces to a simple agency problem: Plan sponsors have a fiduciary duty in menu construction, but do not directly bear the costs of plan options, and often rely on the advice of plan service providers who have incentives to include high-cost options in plan menus. Sophisticated investors can often sidestep these costly options, so long as some lower-cost options are available, and so have little incentive to agitate for a more efficient menu. In fact, fee-sensitive investors may be subsidized by the choices of less sophisticated participants. The result, in many cases, is that there is no plan stakeholder with the knowledge and incentive to remove poor options from plan menus.

2.2   Empirical Evidence on Plan Fees: Data and Methodology

To study the impact of plan fees, we used data from an industry data provider derived from Form 5500 which we pair with data from the CRSP Mutual Fund Database. For each plan, we observe the list of options in the plan menu including expenses, the plan-level expenses, plan size, and basic information about the plan sponsor. While the proprietary data includes expense information for more than 10,000 plans, we focus on the subsample of plans where we can independently verify the investment expenses.

For 3,519 plans, the investment menu includes only public mutual funds whose expenses are disclosed in their prospectuses. We analyze data for this subsample of plans. This subsample omits some of the largest plans (which tend to use proprietary investment products without public prospectuses) and also omits some of the smallest plans (which are not required to file a list of investment options on Form 5500). Nevertheless, the sample of more than 3,500 plans remains the most comprehensive academic study of costs in participant-directed retirement plans.

The restriction of investors in retirement plans to a designated menu of investment options could affect investor welfare in several ways. First, the restricted list of funds might limit investors' ability to fully diversify. If the menu doesn't offer a fund with, for example, international equities, then the investor will be unable to gain that exposure within the plan. Second, investors' returns are affected by the fees associated with the investment options in the plan menu. A rational, informed investor will optimize a risk-adjusted performance net of fees, but if – for example – every fund in the plan charges more than 1 percent in fees, then being restricted to those funds will reduce performance relative to an investor making an unrestricted choice.

These dimensions interact. Consider two stylized 401(k) plans: The first plan's menu consists of only a money market fund and a large-cap mutual fund with fees of 1.5 percent (150 basis points). The second plan's menu offers the same options but adds a large-cap index fund with fees of just 12 basis points. While the total fees paid for participants in both plans are a function of the portfolio held, investors in the second plan have the opportunity to get exposure to large-cap stocks at either a low or a high cost, while participants in the first plan can only hold the high-cost fund or forego the exposure altogether. In the first plan, costs are mostly a function of the plan menu, while in the second they are mostly a function of investors' choice of how to gain exposure to large-cap equities.

By dividing the total costs of 401(k) investing into those that would be incurred by a fee-optimizing investor attempting simply to obtain optimal factor exposure, and those that are attributable to investor decision making, we are able to shed light on the degree to which plan menus curtail investor choice. In the stylized example above, an investor might opt for the actively managed fund in hopes that it will outperform the market and therefore recover the additional cost. But in the first plan, even an investor with a strong preference for index funds would be forced to incur the high costs of active management to the extent the investor desires equity exposure.

The third dimension of plan costs results from the fact that investors do not always choose a portfolio that optimally diversifies risk. An additional source of loss to investors is making suboptimal diversification choices from the plan menu. If, for example, a plan offers two large-cap equity funds at widely divergent fees, allocating to both may increase expenses without improving diversification.

To measure these dimensions of loss, we first divide costs into two categories: costs imposed as a result of the structure of the plan that cannot be avoided by optimal participant choice, and costs that are the result of participant choices over the menu. By loss, we mean both the direct effect of fees and the cost of diversification as a result of being restricted to a limited menu of investment options. As described below, we use a risk-return model from the literature to render both types of costs as a reduction in returns. We then measure impact of fees on each of these cost categories as described below.

For each fund in the menu, we use historical returns data to estimate a factor model for the fund in question and compute an optimal portfolio over the plan menu as follows. We begin by implementing a factor model that can be used to estimate the moments of return for each fund. Since 401(k) plans include funds other than domestic equity funds, we use a model that includes factors reflecting systematic risks in non-equity markets.[11] The model is as follows:

$$R_{it} - r_f = \beta_i^1 * \left(r_{mkt,t} - r_f\right) + \beta_i^2 * \left(r_{bond,t} - r_f\right) + \beta_i^3 * \left(r_{intl,t} - r_f\right) + \varepsilon$$

Here R_{it} is the return of ith mutual fund for the month t. In the model, r_{mkt} is the return on the Russell 3000, r_{bond} is the return on the Barclay's US Aggregate Bond index, and r_{intl} is the return on the MSCI EAFE international equity index. We estimate the model for all mutual funds using monthly data between January 2002 and December 2009.[12] If mutual funds are missing more than 3 years of data during this period, those funds, and their associated plans, are excluded from the sample.

The model provides estimated betas for every fund in each plan, $\widehat{\beta_i^1}, \widehat{\beta_i^2}, \widehat{\beta_i^3}$. The model also provides a variance–covariance matrix of idiosyncratic risk, $\widehat{\Sigma}_{idio}$ computed as the variance–covariance matrix of the residuals. For each plan we define, $\widehat{\beta} = \begin{bmatrix} \widehat{b}_i \\ \dots \\ \widehat{b}_i \end{bmatrix}$ where i indexes funds in the plan and $\widehat{b}_i = \left(\widehat{\beta_i^1}, \widehat{\beta_i^2}, \widehat{\beta_i^3}\right)$. Let ϕ_i be the management fee for each fund in the plan as of 2009. We compute three sets of expected returns. The vector of pre-fee expected excess returns on each fund in the plan is

$$\widehat{\mu}_p = \widehat{\beta}\,\widehat{\mu}$$

The vector of after-fee expected excess returns is computed as

---

[11] Our methodology is similar to Ning Tang et al., *The Efficiency of Sponsor and Participant Portfolio Choices in 401(k) Plans*, 94 J. Pub. Econ. 1073 (2010), but includes the effect of fees.
[12] The risk free rate, r_f is taken from 3-month treasuries.

$$\hat{\mu}'_p = \hat{\beta}\hat{\mu} - \hat{\phi}$$

where $\hat{\phi}$ is the vector of fees for the funds in the plan menu.[13] Expected returns after fund-level fees and plan-level expenses is

$$\hat{\mu}'_p = \hat{\beta}\hat{\mu} - \hat{\phi} - \rho\hat{1}$$

where ρ is the scalar value of plan-level expenses and $\hat{1}$ is a vector of ones. Since the fund and plan management fees are constant, they do not affect the variance–covariance matrix, given by

$$\hat{\Sigma}_p = \hat{\beta}\hat{\Sigma}\hat{\beta}' + \hat{\Sigma}_{idio}$$

where $\hat{\Sigma}_{idio}$ is the matrix of idiosyncratic variances of funds in the plan menu. For a given portfolio over plan options, w, we are now equipped to compute the Sharpe ratio of the plan portfolio:

$$\widehat{SR}(w) = \frac{\hat{\mu}_p}{\sqrt{w'\hat{\Sigma}_p w}}$$

The post-fee and post-fee expense Sharpe ratios are computed using the equivalent methodology.

To compute the optimal pre-fee portfolio, w_p, for each plan, we use an optimization package to find the no-short-sale portfolio that maximizes

$$\frac{\hat{\mu}_p}{\sqrt{w'\hat{\Sigma}_p w}} .$$

Similarly, to find the post-fee portfolio, w_f, we solve the same maximization problem using post-fee returns. Finally, the actual expected Sharpe ratio is computed using the observed balances for each fund in the plan, w_a

Using this procedure, we compute the Sharpe ratios for the following portfolios: global optimum formed directly on the factors, pre-fee optimum, post-fee optimum, post-fee and expense optimum, and the actual plan portfolio. Figure 2.1 illustrates the mean-variance spaces of the portfolios. The upper curve is the mean-variance frontier of portfolios formed directly on the three factors. The tangency line to this frontier gives the Sharpe ratio of the globally optimum portfolio. The second curve is the pre-fee mean-variance frontier for portfolios formed over a given plan

---

[13] While 401(k) plan menus sometimes include shares that carry loads, these loads are generally waived, and so we exclude them from the calculation.

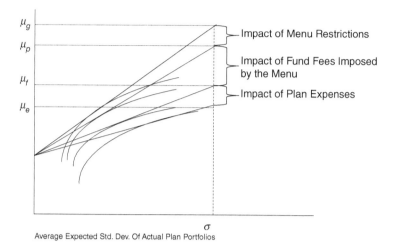

Figure 2.1   Disaggregation of plan losses

with the associated tangency line. The lower curve is the mean-variance frontier of the post-fee portfolios. Below the post-fee mean-variance frontier is the point corresponding to the mean and variance of the observed portfolio.

Using these optimum portfolios, we disaggregate losses into four components:

- "Menu Limitation Cost" is the expected reduction in returns associated with the difference between the globally optimal pre-fee portfolio and the optimal pre-fee portfolio for the plan. This is essentially the reduction in utility associated with the diversification-limiting effect of a restricted menu conditional on making the optimal choice over that menu on a pre-fee basis.
- "Plan Asset-Based Fees" measures the plan-level administrative fees that are charged independently of any particular choice over the plan menu. We assess this relative to a minimal benchmark fee of 8 basis points, which is in line with the lowest observed costs in our sample.
- "Menu Fund Fees" are the mutual fund fees associated with the optimal post-fee portfolio. That is, if an investor is optimizing the risk-return tradeoff net of fees, how much in fees would the investor end up paying? "Menu" in the name indicates that these are fees associated with the structure of the menu, and not suboptimal choices over that menu. We assess this relative to a benchmark fee of 22 basis points, which (at the time) reflected the costs associated with typical retail index funds.

- "Investor Choice Additional Fund Fees" are the costs investors actually incur in excess of the optimum. Since these are deviations from the optimal risk-return portfolio, these are fees that investors could have avoided without reducing the expected return on their portfolio or taking increased risk.

2.3   Empirical Evidence on Plan Fees: Results

The average of each type of loss for the 3,534 plans in our sample is presented in Table 2.1.

Several things are notable. First, diversification isn't much of an issue. Only 6 percent of the total loss investors incur relative to choosing over an unrestrained menu comes from the inability to diversify. Evidently, menus give investors plenty of exposure to different asset classes.[14] The largest individual component of cost is the Plan Menu Additional Fund Fees, which are costs in excess of retail index fund fees that even an investor making optimal choices over the menu would be unable to avoid. The second largest component are Investor Choice Additional Fund Fees. Between the two excess fee components, investors are paying nearly 60 basis points more than the typical costs of retail index funds, or about triple the cost of many retail index funds.

Looking at plans cross-sectionally in Table 2.2, which presents regressions of components of plan costs on size, we find that the value of total assets under management is a major factor in determining costs. This is not surprising, since retirement plans produce considerable economics of scale, but Table 2.2 nevertheless contains some interesting results. First, as plans get larger, menu quality seems to increase: there are lower unavoidable fees, more index fund options, and lower total fees. But, as the unavoidable costs in the plan go down (presumably due to more low-cost options in the menu), the investor choice cost goes up (presumably because investors can make larger fee mistakes when the optimal fee is very low). Nevertheless, the total cost of large plans is substantially lower.

The key finding here is that cost isn't a simple function of plan size. First, while costs increase in smaller plans, some of that increase is a function of menu quality and not just cost. Small menus offer fewer index funds, not just more expensive index funds. Second, while costs decrease as plans grow, investors do not fully benefit from the availability of low-cost

---

[14]   This finding is consistent with Ning Tang et al., *The Efficiency of Sponsor and Participant Portfolio Choices in 401(k) Plans*, 94 J. PUB. ECON. 1073 (2010).

Table 2.1 *Summary of menu costs*

		% of total	Mean	Std. dev.	Min	5th percentile	95th percentile	Max
Investment constraints	Menu limitation cost	6.20%	0.0006	0.0010	0.0000	0.0000	0.0022	0.0303
Plan asset-based fees	Plan fees benchmark	8.03%	0.0008					
	Plan additional fees	5.21%	0.0005	0.0023	−0.0008	−0.0008	0.0048	0.0315
Plan costs	Retail index benchmark fees	22.07%	0.0022					
Fund fees	Plan menu additional fund fees	38.23%	0.0038	0.0035	−0.0017	−0.0005	0.0101	0.0189
Investor choice costs	Investor-choice additional fund fees	20.26%	0.0020	0.0023	−0.0065	−0.0017	0.0056	0.0238
	Total fees	93.80%	0.0093					
	Total cost	100.00%	0.0100	0.0062	0.0001	0.0054	0.0251	0.0720

Table 2.2 *Plan size and plan costs*

The regressions in this table investigate the relationship between plan size, plan balances, and cost variables of interest. Total Plan Excess Expense is the sum of Plan Excess Fees and Plan Menu Excess Fund Fees. Total Excess Fees is the sum of total Plan Excess Expense and Total Excess Fees. Employee contribution share is the proportion of total contributions to the plan made by the employer.

	(1) Menu limitation cost	(2) Percent of index funds	(3) Total plan excess expense	(4) Investor-choice excess fees	(5) Total excess fees
Log(total net assets)	-0.000229***	0.0153***	-0.00239***	0.000179***	-0.00221***
	(-10.44)	(9.38)	(-21.51)	(3.70)	(-20.45)
Empl. contribution share	-0.000172	0.0249***	0.000102	-0.000373*	-0.000271
	(-1.63)	(2.81)	(0.29)	(-1.73)	(-0.81)
Log(plan participants)	0.0000868***	-0.00707***	0.000883***	0.0000676	0.000951***
	(4.34)	(-4.48)	(9.65)	(1.46)	(10.91)
Constant	0.000757***	0.0759***	0.00544***	0.00124***	0.00668***
	(7.05)	(9.61)	(15.09)	(5.50)	(19.65)
Observations	3519	3519	3519	3519	3519
R^2	0.046	0.033	0.292	0.012	0.289

t statistics in parentheses; * $p < 0.10$, ** $p < 0.01$, *** $p < 0.001$.

options, because they incur additional fees based on the sub-optimal
menu choices they make. If menus were designed to induce better choices,
investors might better enjoy the benefits of plan scale.

How does the structure of the plan menu affect choice? We will have
much more to say about this when we analyze the individual participant choices of the UVA plan, but it is possible to shed some light on this
question using plan level data. Table 2.3 presents the results of regressing our disaggregated cost components on measures of menu quality.

Table 2.3 *Investor excess fees and menu quality*
Regressions in this table measure the effect of menu design on investor excess
fees. Models 1 and 2 examine the effect of the percentage of index funds in men.
Models 3 and 4 examine the distance in portfolio space between the optimal
portfolio and the 1/N equal-weighted portfolio. The regressions include a
dummy variable indicating whether the plan is missing an index fund option.
Employee contribution share is the proportion of total contributions to the plan
made by the employer. Models 1 through 3 include the entire sample, while
models 3 and 4 include the subsample of plans that could be successfully
coded for industry.

	(1) Investor-choice excess fees	(3) Investor-choice excess fees
Percent of index funds	−0.00147** (−3.14)	
Optimal portfolio to 1/N portfolio distance		0.00489*** (14.28)
Number of investment options	0.0000423*** (9.25)	0.0000431*** (9.91)
No index funds indicator	−0.00285*** (−28.56)	−0.00243*** (−28.27)
Log(total net assets)	−0.000142*** (−3.46)	−0.0000964* (−2.41)
Empl. contribution share	−0.0000469 (−0.25)	−0.00000695 (−0.04)
Log(plan participants)	0.000111** (2.79)	0.0000935* (2.42)
Constant	0.00151*** (6.42)	−0.00187*** (−6.07)
Observations	3519	3519
R^2	0.273	0.311

t statistics in parentheses; * $p < 0.05$, ** $p < 0.01$, *** $p < 0.001$.

The literature suggests that offering more funds of a particular type or menus that are robust to naïve diversification should improve outcomes.

Our results support this hypothesis. We find that menus with more index funds have lower investor choice excess fees, suggesting that simply adding more low-cost options to the menu leads to investors incurring lower costs (even controlling for the presence of at least one index fund in the menu). Similarly, the second regression in the table shows that menus where simply allocating an equal amount to each fund was closer (in Euclidean distance) to the optimal portfolio had lower investor excess choice fees as well. In both specifications, investor-incurred fees increased when the number of investment options in the menu increased. Since diversification is largely a non-problem, this result suggests that relatively succinct menus with fewer choices are likely desirable, so long as they include low-cost choices, because they tend to prevent participants from investing in funds with excess fees.

2.4 The Problem of Dominated Funds

To further focus on the problem of menu pitfalls, we also explored the presence in menus of what we term "dominated funds," whose fee, performance, and diversification characteristics suggest that no reasonable investor would hold them. Dominated funds are thus options that prudent investors would not choose. They are funds to be avoided. We define dominated funds as follows:

- A fund is dominated if:
  - there is another fund of the same investing style offered in the same plan menu as the candidate fund with fees at least fifty basis points lower;
  - the candidate fund has fees twenty-five basis points higher than the mean fees of funds with the same investing style in our sample of 401(k) plans; and
  - the candidate fund receives less than 1 percent weight in our computation of the optimal portfolio for the plan.
- Alternatively, a fund is dominated if:
  - there is no other fund in the plan menu with the same style;
  - the candidate fund has fees that are fifty basis points higher[15] than the mean fees of funds with the same investing style in our sample of 401(k) plans; and

---

[15] Fifty basis points is about two standard deviations in fees. Thus, the fund would be roughly two standard deviations above mean fees.

 ○ the candidate fund receives less than 1 percent weight in our computation of the optimal portfolio for the plan.

Unsurprisingly, dominated funds perform poorly, with the typical dominated fund in our sample posting returns 60 basis points below average in
the three years between 2010 and 2013.

Despite relatively stringent criteria for being classified as a dominated
fund, such funds are common. A majority of the plans in our sample, 52
percent, contained at least one dominated fund. And while prudent investors would never invest (or invest almost nothing) in these funds, we find
that when offered, a substantial proportion of dollars make their way to
these inferior options. In plans with at least one dominated fund, 11.5 percent of plan assets were typically held in the fund. Notably, dominated
funds are more common in small plans: 52 percent of plans with dominated funds hold only 22.6 percent of all assets, and while 8.9 percent of
funds are dominated, they hold only 3.4 percent of all plan assets.

The prevalence of dominated funds reflects the perils of poor menu
construction. In principle, investors could simply avoid these funds. The
requirement that dominated funds get less than 1 percent weight in the
optimal portfolio means that these funds don't provide essential diversification benefits that offset their considerable fees. The data demonstrates,
consistent with other work on retirement plans, that if the menu gives
investors an option, investors are likely to allocate to it. This is the ERISA
analog to the *Field of Dreams* motto, "If you build it, they will come." If
you offer it, they will invest in it – no matter how poor an option it is.

An important conclusion from this data is that investor mistakes are a
significant contributor to high plan costs. While expensive funds in plan
menus are a problem, the most important component of plan costs is not
high-cost funds that are unavoidable, but high-cost funds that investors
choose over lower-cost options. This phenomenon has both legal and
policy consequences. From a legal point of view, and as will be discussed
at length in later chapters, some courts have previously construed the
fiduciary duties of retirement plan sponsors to limit liability when a plan
offers at least some good options alongside bad ones. Our results suggest
that this approach is likely to insufficiently protect investors.

These results reinforce the importance of requiring well-designed
menus. Investors do not always avoid pitfalls, and including options in
a fund menu that are inappropriate for most investors is likely to lead to
worse performance for the typical investor in the plan. Our central claim is
that a prudent fiduciary should be aware of this phenomenon and design
a menu that is sensitive to the likely choices investors will actually make.

While these results illustrate the impact of menu design on investor outcomes, two limitations are notable. First, the data used in this study is now more than a decade old. Industry-wide, fees in retirement plans have declined in the time elapsed since our data was collected. Driven partly by the success of lawsuits challenging high fees, as well as a move to low-cost index strategies across the asset management industry, fees have declined since our dataset was complied. This is a positive development, but, as we will see, fee lawsuits target only the largest of plans, and the evidence suggests that small plans have lagged larger plans in progress on costs. The problem of excessively expensive small plans lingers.

Second, while our dataset included a large number of plans, it consists of only plan-level data and, as such, we can observe only plan-level allocations. While we can examine the general effect of the menu on fees incurred at the plan level, we are unable, in this study, to observe the choices of individual investors. In subsequent chapters, we will present results using individual portfolios from the University of Virginia plan that provide additional insight into how investor choices are affected by the options in the menu.

2.5 Progress in Retirement Plan Design

Whether because of fear of litigation, increased competition, or simply a growing sensitivity to fees among investors, total plan costs have declined. By how much? According to a 2020 report from the Investment Company Institute and Brightscope, fees in the average plan fell from about 1.02 percent to 0.92 percent between 2009 and 2017.[16] While still quite high in our view, this is a positive trend. More encouragingly, when plan costs are scaled by number of plan participants, the average investor across all plans pays 0.58 percent.[17]

A more ambiguous development is that the number of offerings in plan menus has modestly increased, even when adjusting for the inclusion of target date funds, which offer different options an array of target dates and so increase menu size when present.[18] Our results suggest that menu size is not generally associated with better outcomes. On the other hand,

---

[16] BrightScope & Inv. Co. Inst., THE BRIGHTSCOPE/ICI DEFINED CONTRIBUTION PLAN PROFILE: A CLOSE LOOK AT 401(K) PLANS, 2017, at 9, 56 (Aug. 2020), www.ici.org/system/files/attachments/20_ppr_dcplan_profile_401k.pdf.
[17] Id.
[18] Id. at 36.

the growth in menu size has been fairly modest, increasing by just a single fund on average between 2006 and 2019, though the smallest plans have added three funds on average. If more streamlined menus are better, there may still be progress to be made, but – as discussed below – plan administrators may be reluctant to remove options on account of blowback from plan participants.

The bottom line is that, in a world where many index options for large plans cost just a few basis points, plans remain an expensive proposition for many investors. While the overall downward trend in fees is a positive development, the results of our analysis point to a lingering issue. As more good options become available, the component of excess costs induced by investor mistakes will loom larger. Table 2.2 shows that investor fee losses actually increase as lower-cost options are added to the menu, as some investors don't avail themselves of these better options. While reducing overall costs and adding low-cost index options to menus should tend to leave investors better off, to the extent more expensive options linger, at least some investors are likely to choose them and have worse outcomes as a result. The frontier of plan fiduciary duties is not simply offering desirable options, but to monitor their uptake, being aware of presumptively problematic choices, and using the tools of behavioral economics to encourage choices likely to lead to good outcomes.

3

Of Lawsuits and Letters

This chapter empirically explores the impact of two different interventions on improving the quality of plan design. First, we present a study of recent lawsuits challenging 401(k) fees. Then, we present the results of a randomized field experiment where one of us sent 6,000 letters to the sponsors of plans with above-average fees. While these legal and scholarly interventions may have produced modest benefits, the larger lesson across these studies is intransigence. The results underscore the difficulty of taking on a well-organized advisor industry that has so much to lose if fees become more competitive.

3.1 401(K) Fee Lawsuits and Their Limits

In September of 2006, attorneys from a small plaintiffs' law firm in St. Louis, founded by Jerry Schlichter, filed class action lawsuits against 12 of America's largest companies.[1] The list of defendants was a rundown of America's industrial giants, among them Boeing, Caterpillar, United Technologies, and CSX. Their retirement plans were among the largest in the country. The lawsuits alleged that these companies had breached their fiduciary duty under ERISA by offering excessively costly investment options and paying excessive recordkeeping fees to administer their plans. As a result, employees – these suits alleged – experienced a drag on their retirement savings that could have been avoided by more careful oversight.

In pressing these suits, Schlicter faced an uphill climb. While ERISA had been on the books since 1974, no one – no employee, no plaintiffs' firm, and not the Department of Labor – had ever pressed the claim that an overly expensive plan might breach the fiduciary duties at the heart of ERISA. That the new wave of lawsuits represented a new theory of liability was not lost on the defendant companies, or their insurers, who fought the cases

---

[1] Portions of this chapter are based on an interview with Schlichter, Bogard, and Denton managing director Jerome Schlichter.

vigorously. The lawsuits were not just a threat to the 12 defendant companies, who faced tens of millions of dollars in liability; they represented a
threat of liability to hundreds more companies who had been lackadaisical
in running their plans. The lawsuits also struck at the foundations of the
retirement plan industry, which was ultimately on the receiving end of any
imprudently paid fees. In taking on retirement plan costs, the lawyers of
this small firm were staring down defendants with hundreds of billions in
market cap, and financial giants with trillions under management.

It is no exaggeration to say that these fee lawsuits, and dozens more like
them that followed, have reshaped the retirement landscape in the US.
The lawsuits, which now number more than 100 from several firms, have
enjoyed considerable success, resulting in settlements totaling hundreds of
millions of dollars. More importantly, the lawsuits have focused the minds
of the plan industry on costs. It is now clearly established that imprudently
high costs in plan offerings can be a basis for liability, and the strong private
liability regime in ERISA means that plans must tread carefully.

In this section, we review the history and law of retirement plan fee
litigation to understand their origins, and the courts' construction of plan
fiduciary duties. We then examine the pattern of fee suits empirically to
answer a critical question: Do fee lawsuits target problematic plans or
simply chase deep pockets? Given the importance of fee lawsuits in driving plan design, the question of whether such suits are meritorious in their
targeting is critical, but as yet unanswered.

We draw several conclusions. First, the law of fiduciary liability for
excessive fees has evolved, albeit slowly, in a productive direction. The
current state of play in ERISA creates incentives to at least ensure that
each individual menu inclusion is defensible. We also show empirically
that fee lawsuits seem to target plans that are considerably more expensive
than their similarly sized peers, suggesting that the mechanism of private
enforcement, on average, provides incentives to keep costs low. Finally,
we note that, as effective as fee litigation has been, it targets only a small
slice of the industry – plans with hundreds of millions of dollars in assets
under management. The vast majority of smaller plans, including plans
that are likely far more expensive than the giant plans targeted by fee lawsuits, are functionally immune from suits.

3.1.1   A Brief History of Retirement Plan Fee Litigation

The initial, 2006 wave of fee suits brought by Schlichter's firm alleged that
the defendant companies had breached their fiduciary duty under ERISA to

operate plans with "care, skill, prudence, and diligence,"[2] and to incur only reasonable fees.[3] The specific allegations varied across the suits, but included the failure of plans in the use of public mutual funds when lower-cost collective investments would have been available, the use of revenue sharing that concealed the total costs of operating the plan, and generally high costs.

At the time the suits were filed, there was no developed body of law regarding how fiduciary duties applied in the context of investment fees. Indeed, in the case against Boeing, Boeing disputed its status as a fiduciary for plan participants, given that plan participants controlled the allocation of funds in their accounts.[4] The court sided with the plaintiffs on that issue, but that this issue was even disputed suggests the degree to which the law in the area was unsettled during this initial stage of litigation.

Fee lawsuits did not meet with early success. Insurers with industry-wide exposure to this potential new form of liability were reluctant to settle cases, even when they survived motions to dismiss and class certification. Schlichter relates that he was told the insurers for the defendants had agreed not to settle in hopes of putting his small firm out of business. This was hardly an idle threat: The suits were brought on contingency and were complex litigation against huge plaintiffs with deep pockets. Even if the suits were successful, any payment would be years away. Indeed, the Boeing and Lockheed cases didn't reach settlement for more than a decade. In the meantime, while the senior partners at Schlichter, Bogard, and Denton worked for a payday far in the future, the salaries of junior attorneys, paralegals, office assistants, and all the expenses of running a firm had to be paid. To bridge the gap, the partners took out a line of credit secured by, among other things, their own homes.

The first of the initial fee lawsuits to come to trial was *Tussey vs ABB*. The case included allegations that plan had paid excessive recordkeeping fees via revenue sharing and that plan had mapped plan participants from an eliminated fund into a new fund that had a business relationship with a plan service provider. The trial was conducted, more than five years after the initial claim was filed.[5] To that point, fee litigation had met with a few successes but remained a tenuous enterprise. The outcome of the trial would determine the fate of a fiduciary claim worth tens of millions

---

[2] 29 U.S.C. § 1104(a)(1)(B).
[3] 29 U.S.C. § 1104(a)(1)(A)(ii).
[4] Spano v. Boeing Co., No. 06-CV-743-DRH, 2007 WL 1149192, at *3 (S.D. Ill. Apr. 18, 2007) ("As Defendants point out, an employer does not automatically become a fiduciary merely because it establishes a benefits plan for its employees").
[5] *See Tussey v. ABB.*, 06-CV-04305-NKL (W.D. Mo. Aug. 16, 2019).

of dollars and, quite possibly, the fate of fee litigation generally. At the trial, defendant ABB was represented by two national law firms, and co-defendant Fidelity had retained three more high-profile firms. Between the two defendants, eleven lawyers sat at the defendants table and nine more sat in the gallery. ERISA contains a discretionary fee-shifting provision that can apply to either party. According to Schlichter, the defendants had incurred more than $43 million in defense costs by the time the 16-day trial ended.

In March 2012, in what proved a watershed moment for fee litigation, the trial court in *Tussey v. ABB* found for the plaintiffs and awarded damages of $36.9 million. While the verdict was appealed and remanded multiple times, the suit was ultimately settled in 2019 for $55 million,[6] the verdict – and the substantial damages – both proved the viability of fee litigation through trial and exposed the risk of the "never settle" strategy pushed by some insurers. A wave of copycat lawsuits followed in a surge of litigation that is ongoing to the present day.

In 2016, Schlichter, Bogard, and Denton expanded the targets of fee suits to include the retirement plans at major private universities. These suits were novel because universities, as nonprofits, operate plans under 403(b) rather than 401(k). Nevertheless, 403(b) plan operators are, in many cases, including the defendant universities, subject to the same ERISA duties as 401(k) plans. Despite their functional similarity to 401(k) plans, university 403(b) plans showed evidence of significant path dependence, as such plans historically only offered annuities, and then attempted to escape fiduciary status by foregoing curated menus in favor of lists of sometimes hundreds of funds. The result at many universities was lengthy menus with little oversight that were a sharp contrast to private-employer menus, which already showed the impact of fee litigation in pressing fiduciaries to increase oversight.

The university 403(b) suits produced numerous settlements and resulted in many universities reforming plans to better align with the practices of private employers by streamlining menus. It was this wave of suits that produced the 2022 Supreme Court victory for Schlichter's firm in *Northwestern v. Hughes*, which we discussed in Chapter 1. It was also in the shadow of this fee litigation that the University of Virginia reformed its own menu. While, as a state school, Virginia faced no risk of private litigation, UVA nevertheless responded to changing practices among university plans to make investing easier for its employees. We study these reforms in detail in Chapters 4 through 8.

---

[6] www.plansponsor.com/12-years-litigation-deliver-final-settlement-tussey-vs-abb/.

3.1.2   The Law of Fee Litigation

While the original twelve fee suits crawled through the litigation process alongside fee suits from other firms, the law of fee litigation began to take shape. Courts initially were conflicted about how to approach fiduciary duties in the menu construction process. A modest circuit split evolved that was not resolved until the recent *Northwestern v. Hughes* case.

ERISA 404(c)[7] provides a safe harbor, shielding plan sponsors from liability for participant investment choices over a sponsor-provided menu so long as investors are permitted to direct their investments by choosing among a diverse set of options. In particular, the 404(c) safe harbor eliminates a fiduciary's liability for "any loss, or by reason of any breach, which results from [a] participant's or beneficiary's exercise of control."[8] In order to qualify for this safe harbor, DOL regulations state that the plan sponsor must, among other requirements, "provide[] an opportunity for a participant ... to choose, from a broad range of investment the manner in which some or all of the assets in his account are invested."[9] In particular, a plan seeking the safe harbor must offer no fewer than three investment alternatives, "each of which is diversified."[10]

While a plan complying with 404(c) must offer some diversified choices, neither 404(c) nor its attendant regulations require that all choices be diversified,[11] nor do they require that investors' individual portfolios be diversified.[12] Indeed, there is evidence that Congress's intent in adopting the safe harbor was to shield fiduciaries from liability for investor allocation mistakes. The conference report on the provision, which several courts have discussed, states:

---

[7] 29 U.S.C. § 1104(c).

[8] 29 U.S.C. § 1104(c)(1)(A)(ii).

[9] 29 C.F.R. § 2550.404c–1(b)(1)(ii).

[10] 29 C.F.R. § 2550.404c–1(b)(3)(i)(B)(1) (This does not impose a duty that *all* investment alternatives offered by the plan must be diversified); *Tatum v. RJR Pension Inv. Comm.*, 761 F.3d 346, 356 (4th Cir. 2014) ("[L]egislative history and federal regulations clarify that the diversification and prudence duties do not prohibit a plan trustee from holding single-stock investments as an option in a plan that includes a portfolio of diversified funds"); *Harmon v. FMC Corporation*, No. 16-cv-6073, 2018 WL 1366621 at 4 (E.D. Pa. Mar. 16, 2018) ("[Section] 404(c) and the corresponding regulations allow plans to include undiversified investment options as long as the plans are diversified as a whole").

[11] *Harmon v. FMC Corporation*, No. 16-cv-6073, 2018 WL 1366621 at 4 (E.D. Pa. Mar. 16, 2018) ("[Section] 404(c) and the corresponding regulations allow plans to include undiversified investment options as long as the plans are diversified as a whole").

[12] *See* 29 C.F.R. § 2550.404c–1(f)(5) (providing an example of a plan participant "invest[ing] 100 % of his account balance in a single stock" and noting that the plan fiduciary "will not be liable for any losses that necessarily result").

> if the participant instructs the plan trustee to invest the full balance of his account in, e.g., a single stock, the trustee is not to be liable for any loss because of a failure to diversify or because the investment does not meet the prudent man standards...[13]

On this view, even an extreme and obvious allocation mistake (like investing one's entire retirement portfolio in a single stock) is not *per se* liability-creating for the plan sponsor.

The 404(c) safe harbor could conceivably be read as essentially eliminating fiduciary liability in defined contribution plans that offer diversified menus, but the regulatory picture is more complicated. The DOL has argued that the safe harbor does not protect decisions related to the construction of the menu itself, which remains a fiduciary responsibility of the plan sponsor. The DOL initially took this position in the preamble to the 1992 rule outlining requirements to qualify for the safe harbor. The DOL said in a footnote that "the act of limiting or designating investment options which are intended to constitute all or part of the investment universe of an ERISA 404(c) plan is a fiduciary function which ... is not a direct or necessary result of any participant direction of such plan."[14] The DOL reiterated this position more explicitly in a 2010 rulemaking.[15]

In one of the earliest suits to characterize the safe harbor, *Hecker vs. Deere*,[16] plaintiffs challenged a menu of mutual funds in the 401(k) plan of Deere & Co. The menu included a number of high-cost options that the plaintiffs alleged were imprudently offered and were included only because the funds shared revenue with plan trustee Fidelity. The plan also included a brokerage option through which plan participants could access thousands of other options. By modern standards, the menu of the Deere & Co. plan was certainly lacking, but the court didn't focus on the more egregious options that Fidelity and Deere included, but instead on the choices that plan participants *could* have made if they used the other options and the brokerage window effectively.

Largely discounting the DOL's argument that menu design is within scope of the sponsors' fiduciary duty, the 7th Circuit argued that so long as investors were given " the ability materially to affect potential return and degree of risk in the investor's portfolio; a choice from at least three investment alternatives each of which is diversified and has materially different

---

[13] *Id.*

[14] 57 Fed. Reg. 46906–01, 46,924 n.27 (Oct. 13, 1992).

[15] 29 C.F.R. § 2550.404c–1 (Dec. 20, 2010).

[16] *Hecker v. Deere & Co.*, 569 F.3d 708, 709–11, 47 Employee Benefits Cas. (BNA) 1097 (7th Cir. 2009).

risk and return characteristics; and the ability to diversify sufficiently so as to minimize the risk of large losses,"[17] then the plan would not be liable. Similarly, the 5th Circuit decision *Langbecker v. Elec. Data Sys. Corp.*, held that the DOL position that menu design decisions were not protected by 404(c) was inconsistent with the statutory language.[18]

In contrast to these decisions, in *Braden v. Wal-mart Stores*,[19] an 8th Circuit case decided around the same time as *Hecker*, a claim for imprudent menu construction was allowed to proceed against the Wal-Mart plan. While the 404(c) issue was not explicitly settled, the case provided some support for the view that liability could attach to menu construction if the *entire* menu was imprudent. The key allegation in the case was that the Wal-Mart plan, despite being among the largest in existence at the time, used only retail classes of mutual fund shares and that seven of the ten funds in the plan charged 12b-1 fees. Like the *Hecker* plan, Wal-Mart's plan was egregious by modern standards (and likely by contemporary standards as well), but where Deere's plan offered at least some good options, the Wal-Mart plan menu was a more comprehensive failure. Unlike *Hecker*, it was not clear that even a hypothetical optimal investor in the Wal-Mart plan could have successfully navigated such a treacherous menu.

In 2010, the DOL updated its regulations to more forcefully assert that imprudent menu construction decisions would not receive the protection of 404(c), stating explicitly in the rule (rather than a footnote) that the safe harbor "does not serve to relieve a fiduciary from its duty to prudently select and monitor any ... designated investment alternative offered under the plan."[20] Since 2010, most courts to address the issue have accepted the DOL position that the construction of the menu is a fiduciary function and that breaches of duty in menu construction are not insulated by 404(c).[21] *Howell v. Motorola*, a 7th Circuit case rejecting the circuit's earlier approach in *Hecker*, characterized the dichotomy as follows:

---

[17]   Citing 29 C.F.R. § 2550.404c1(b)(3)(i)(A)-(C).

[18]   *Langbecker v. Electronic Data Systems Corp.*, 476 F.3d 299, 39 Employee Benefits Cas. (BNA) 2352 (5th Cir. 2007).

[19]   *Braden v. Wal-Mart Stores, Inc.*, 588 F.3d 585, 48 Employee Benefits Cas. (BNA) 1097 (8th Cir. 2009).

[20]   See 29 C.F.R. § 2550.404c-1(d)(2)(iv), amended by 75 Red. Reg. 64910, 64946, October 20, 2010, effective for plan years beginning on or after November 1, 2011.

[21]   *See e.g., Tibble v. Edison Intern.*, 729 F.3d 1110 (9th Cir. 2013); *Pfeil v. State St. Bank & Tr. Co.*, 671 F.3d 585, 599–600 (6th Cir. 2012); *DiFelice v. U.S. Airways, Inc.*, 497 F.3d 410, 418 n. 3 (4th Cir. 2007).

> The purpose of section 404(c) is to relieve the fiduciary of responsibility for
> choices made by someone beyond its control.… If an individual account
> is self-directed, then it would make no sense to blame the fiduciary for the
> participant's decision to invest 40% of her assets in Fund A and 60% in
> Fund B, rather than splitting assets somehow among four different funds,
> emphasizing A rather than B, or taking any other decision. In short, the
> statute ensures that the fiduciary will not be held responsible for decisions
> over which it had no control.…The choice of which investments will be
> presented in the menu that the plan sponsor adopts is not within the par-
> ticipant's power. It is instead a core decision relating to the administration
> of the plan and the benefits that will be offered to participants.[22]

This hypothetical example characterizes the sort of participant decision that
would not create liability for the sponsor, but it leaves many questions open,
including what sort of menu construction choice *would* create liability.

For example, would including a single high-cost option in an otherwise
acceptable menu be exempt from the safe harbor as an imprudent menu
construction decision, or insulated from liability since a participant could
only be harmed if they decided to hold the imprudently chosen fund?
Here, helpful guidance can be taken from so-called "stock-drop" litigation
in which a breach is alleged when a company includes its own stock as an
investment option, which then falls in value.[23] In *Pfeil v. State Street Bank
and Trust*, the 6th Circuit explicitly rejected broad application of the safe
harbor:

> A fiduciary cannot avoid liability for offering imprudent investments merely
> by including them alongside a larger menu of prudent investment options.
> Much as one bad apple spoils the bunch, the fiduciary's designation of a
> single imprudent investment offered as part of an otherwise prudent menu
> of investment choices amounts to a breach of fiduciary duty.…[24]

This is a clear rejection of the view, hinted at in *Hecker*, that a fiduciary can
claim safe harbor simply because a participant's loss wasn't an inevitable
result of the menu.

In rejecting *Hecker's* broad reading of the safe harbor, courts have
invited the question of what it means for an investment choice to be

---

[22] 633 F.3d 552, 567 (7th Cir. 2011).

[23] George S. Mellman & Geoffrey T. Sanzenbacher, 401(K) LAWSUITS: WHAT ARE THE
CAUSES AND CONSEQUENCES?, CENTER FOR RETIREMENT RESEARCH BOSTON
COLLEGE 3 (May 2018), https://crr.bc.edu/wp-content/uploads/2018/04/IB_18-8.pdf.

[24] *Pfeil v. State St. Bank & Tr. Co.*, 671 F.3d 585, 597 (6th Cir. 2012). But see Langbecker *v.
Electronic Data Systems*, 476 F.3d 299, 310–12 ("A plan fiduciary may have violated the
duties of selection and monitoring of a plan investment, but § 404(c) recognizes that participants are not helpless victims of every error.").

imprudent within a larger menu of prudent options. Lawsuits alleging fiduciary breaches in 401(k) plan administration[25] have given rise to some viable theories. One basis for liability is the imprudent inclusion of a fund that persistently underperforms its benchmarks.[26] In *Troudt v. Oracle Corp.*,[27] plaintiffs survived summary judgment on the issue of whether Oracle had acted prudently in including an allegedly persistent poor performer in the plan menu. The aforementioned stock-drop cases similarly implicate the prudence of including company stock in the plan.[28]

In addition to considering performance, plaintiffs have charged plans with a failure to consider the related issue of fees. While courts have not required plans to focus only (or even sufficiently[29]) on cost,[30] plans that offer higher-cost versions of funds when identical lower-cost versions of funds are available, risk liability, regardless of other options in the menu.[31] One lawyer advising plans called retail share-class funds "a neon light flashing on the plaintiff's radar screen,"[32] and a consultant noted that using the cheapest available share class of mutual funds is "the most important fiduciary compliance item."[33] For a plan to include an investment option with pre-fee performance identical to a lower-cost option available to the plan seems unquestionably imprudent as a matter of menu construction. Choosing the lower-cost option can only leave investors better off. Indeed, one plan advisor noted that plans failing on this basic aspect of plan design "look like fat targets right off the bat."[34]

3.1.3   Do the Merits Matter in Retirement Plan Fee Litigation?

Retirement plan fee suits have had a significant effect on the industry. Plans, particularly large ones, are now run in the shadow of potential

---

[25] Mellman & Sanzenbacher, *supra* note 50.

[26] *Id.* at 2.

[27] 2019 WL 1006019 (Dist. Col., Mar. 1, 2019).

[28] Mellman and Sanzenbacher *supra* note 42 at 2.

[29] *See generally* Ayres & Curtis, *supra* note 1.

[30] *See Brotherston v. Putnam Investments*, 907 F.3d 17 (2018). *Tibble v. Edison Intl.*, 729 F.3d 1110 (2013).

[31] *Feinberg v. T. Rowe Price*, 2018 WL 3970470 (Aug. 20, 2018).

[32] *Id.*

[33] Robert C. Lawton, *Most Important 401k Improvements For 2020*, LRPC's PAN SPONSOR INSIGHT (Nov. 28, 2019), https://lawtonrpc.com/401k-improvements/.

[34] Robert Steyer, *Sponsors take steps to reduce company-stock litigation risk*, PENSIONS & INVESTMENTS, Nov. 25, 2019. *See also* Robert Steyer, *401(k) suits point to need for litigation risk prevention*, PENSIONS & INVESTMENTS, Dec. 24, 2018.

liability. Unlike fee suits against mutual funds under 36(b),[35] which have mostly served as a nuisance to the fund industry, fee suits against retirement plans have enjoyed considerable success. The question naturally arises whether these suits are targeting plans that actually have serious fee problems. One needn't dive deeply into the data to notice that retirement plan fee suits are targeting huge employers: Boeing, Caterpillar, and a number of large universities have all faced suits. These plans each manage billions of dollars for many thousands of employees.

Targeting large plans is not problematic per se. While large plans tend to cost less than smaller plans because of their economies of scale, excessive fees in larger plans will impact more employees, and lawsuits that address those fees could produce larger aggregate savings than those pursuing small plans with arguably more egregious fees. Moreover, if large plans enjoy economies of scale as a general matter, then large plans that fail to take advantage of those economies of scale may present a particular problem.

To better understand the phenomenon of fee litigation, this section analyzes a sample of fee lawsuits to evaluate the quality of targeted plan menus. We begin by compiling a list of fee lawsuits that contain allegations of excessive investment fund fees or recordkeeping fees. We draw lawsuits from an academic report of retirement plan fee litigation,[36] a since-discontinued litigation aggregator by BNA, as well as Westlaw searches. Using these sources as a starting point we were able to identify 122 lawsuits for which complaints could be matched with specific plans in the Form 5500 litigation database maintained by the Department of Labor. These lawsuits run back to 2010 (corresponding to the beginning of detailed Form 5500 data, and the most recent lawsuits in our dataset were filed in 2018). Some fee lawsuit complaints did not include sufficient detail to identify a unique form 5500, and these are excluded from the sample.

This simple crosswalk between fee lawsuits and Form 5500 is sufficient to compare targeted plans with the general population of plans in assets under management. Figure 3.1 compares the distributions of sued and unsued plans with respect to the log of plan size, demonstrating that typical sued plans are orders of magnitude larger than typical plans. Figure 4.1 and Table 4.2 are histograms of the sued plans by percentile of

---

[35] For an overview of 36(b) litigation, see Quinn Curtis and John Morley, *The Flawed Mechanics of Mutual Fund Fee Litigation*, 32 YALE. J. REG. 1 (2015).

[36] 401(k) Lawsuits: What Are the Causes and Consequences? | Center for Retirement Research, https://crr.bc.edu/briefs/401k-lawsuits-what-are-the-causes-and-consequences/.

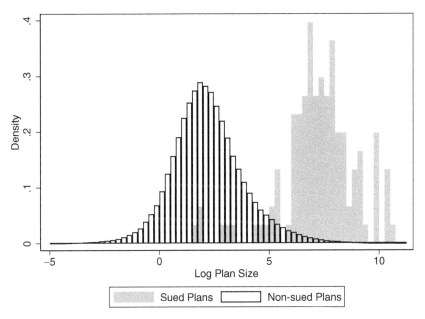

Figure 3.1   Density histograms of log (assets under management) for sued and non-sued plans

assets under management relative to the population of plans in the Form 5500 database. Figure 3.2 shows that the vast majority of sued plans, more than 80 percent, are in the top 5 percent by assets under management. The modal sued plan is in the 99th percentile of size. Sued plans are vastly larger than ordinary plans.

This is not a surprising outcome. Fee suits are brought by plaintiff's attorneys on contingency. The total fees for these plans, even expensive ones, are less than 2 percent of plan assets, and the maximum conceivable recovery in litigation is the portion of those fees that are found to be excessive. Fee lawsuits involve complex litigation against deep-pocketed defendants, with a substantial probability of no recovery. With the high-fixed costs of bringing these types of cases, such litigation only makes sense in plans that put millions in fees at issue, and those plans will have hundreds of millions under management.

The Department of Labor form 5500 dataset includes basic cost information for expenses that are charged against plan assets, as opposed to investment fund expenses or expenses funded through revenue sharing. Many, indeed most large plans do not record any expenses on Form 5500. Only 22 of the sued plans recorded any expense on Form 5500.

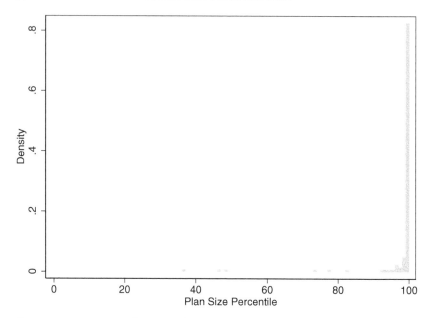

Figure 3.2 Histogram of assets under management percentile of sued plans

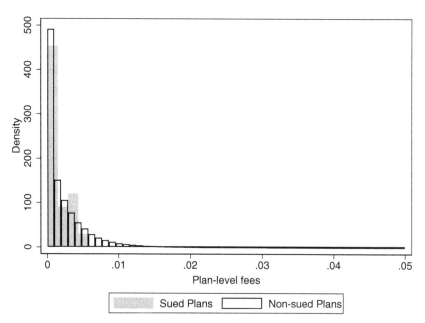

Figure 3.3 Density histograms of plan-level expenses (as fraction of assets under management) for sued and non-sued plans

Table 4.3 compares the reported fees as a percentage of assets under management of sued plans reporting non-zero with the larger sample of plans. There is no significant difference in the plan-level fees of sued and unsued plans: At the Form 5500 level, size is the key driver.

But the expense data disclosed on the Form 5500 excludes the largest component of fees, the fees associated with specific investment options. To measure these costs, it is necessary to have data on the plan menu. Data on the composition of plan menus are not available for the universe of retirement plans. Instead, such data must be collected by hand from Form 5500 filed annually by each plan. Even then, expense data is not directly disclosed. Rather, menu data from Form 5500 must be matched, often imperfectly, with mutual fund fee data to get a picture of expenses.

Despite these difficulties in measuring expenses, the key question regarding fee litigation remains whether lawsuit targeting correlates with the real costs of investing through the plan. Indeed, that it is difficult to discern fees associated with a plan from the outside makes measuring the correlation of fees with litigation targeting more pressing, because such difficulties apply to plaintiffs' attorneys as well.

In order to determine the costs of sued plans relative to plans not targeted by lawsuits, we adopt a matching strategy. Because size is the key driver of litigation, we pair each sued plan with the unsued plan closest in size (by assets under management) as of the last Form 5500 filed prior to the filing of the lawsuit. For each plan, we collect Form 5500 and attempt to recover menu data. Some plans, like those operated pursuant to a master trust agreement, do not disclose menu details. Other plans might disclose only proprietary investment products that cannot be reconciled with the CRSP Survivor-Bias-Free Mutual Fund Database. These plans are dropped from the sample.

The pairing process itself provided some indication of how size-driven retirement plan fee litigation is. In our initial sample of sued plans, there were multiple instances in which the closest plan in size to the sued plan was also sued in the same year despite the Form 5500 database containing hundreds of thousands of plans. When these collisions occurred, we proceeded to the next closest size match that had not been targeted by a lawsuit.

We identified 83 instances of retirement plans targeted by lawsuits with sufficient data to analyze plan fees among 93 plans with at least some menu data available. For these plans, we examine four proxies for menu quality: First, we compute the average fees of options in the plan menu. Not all plans disclose which share class of mutual funds they offer, and different share classes have different fees. We take a conservative approach and assume that all funds not indicating a share class are offered using the lowest-fee share class available. Fund expenses are equally weighted across menu options. Second, for plans that do indicate share class, we calculate the percentage of plan offerings that are the cheapest share class of the fund in question. Many suits include allegations that a plan failed to secure the lowest-cost available options, and this is a measure of the degree to which the plan is seeking out the best possible prices. Third, we look at the percentage of funds in a plan menu that are index funds. As outlined in Chapter 2, the presence of index funds in a menu is correlated with lower overall costs. Finally, we look at the total number of funds. While total fund count is not a direct measure of quality, given the trend toward shorter menus, an excessively long menu may indicate less aggressive fiduciary oversight of the plan.

Table 3.1 compares sued and unsued plans based on these measures.

Our results suggest that sued plans tend to be considerably more expensive than unsued plans, with sued plans offering investment options that are about 33 percent more expensive than the paired sample of plans. There is essentially no difference in the propensity of sued or unsued plans to offer index funds, and the difference in offering the lowest-cost share class is small as well.

Aside from fund expenses, sued plans tend to offer menus that are much larger than other plans. This is in part driven by the lawsuits against university plans, which had very long menus in many cases. As noted, long menus, particularly with higher-priced options, raise a question as to whether plans are monitoring their menus and removing imprudent options, as the Supreme Court has required in *Hughes* and *Tibble*.

Examining menu changes *after* lawsuits were filed proved challenging because many plans moved to master trust arrangements that concealed their menu offerings and some plans were discontinued and merged into other plans. Nevertheless, we were able to identify 68 plans with menu data and 60 with fee data three years after the initial observation to explore whether the fact of being sued may have impacted menu choice. Table 3.2 presents before and after comparisons for the sued plans. These plans are somewhat less costly (with borderline significance), more likely to offer the cheapest share class, and have dramatically shorter menus. While our methodology is at best impressionistic causal evidence,[37] all of these post-litigation changes are consistent with improved menu quality.

---

[37] One might have looked to see what changes occurred during the same period with the paired unsued plans to find some additional causal evidence on whether these plan improvements were a result of litigation or whether were part of more general industry improvements in plan quality.

Table 3.1 t-*Tests of menu quality measures for sued and unsued plans*

	Mean sued plans	Mean paired plans	t-Test on diff (p-value)
Mean menu expense ratio	0.45%	0.36%	2.99***
Pct. cheapest share class	66.4%	69.1%	0.66
Pct. index fund	21.4%	21.4%	0.013
Count funds in menu	121.1	48.5	3.188***

t statistics in parentheses; * $p < 0.05$, ** $p < 0.01$, *** $p < 0.001$.

Table 3.2 t-*Tests of menu quality measures pre- and three years post-suit*

	Mean pre-suit	Mean post-suit	t-Test on diff (p-value)
Mean menu expense ratio	0.46%	0.42%	1.60
Pct. cheapest share class	66.2%	58.1%	1.72*
Pct. index fund	22.8%	22.4%	0.15
Count funds in menu	98.3	41.7	5.44***

t statistics in parentheses; * $p < 0.05$, ** $p < 0.01$, *** $p < 0.001$.

* * *

These results provide evidence that sued plans are not simply deep pockets but have fee problems relative to plans that would enjoy similar economies of scale (and present similarly tempting targets for litigation). Nevertheless, the size issue is inescapable. We observe only seven lawsuits against plans with less than $100,000,000 under management, and the median targeted plan in our data has over $1,000,000,000 under management. Given that fee problems concentrate in smaller plans, policy solutions beyond litigation are critical to ensuring investor welfare.

3.2 Can Nudges Prompt Fiduciary Action?
Evidence from a Field Experiment

The evidence in the section suggests that litigation targets high-cost plans and that the menus of sued plans may improve. The consensus in the plan industry is that litigation has led to lower costs, and the evidence supports this consensus, but it is clear that only the largest plans need fear litigation. Industry best practices may well trickle down to smaller plans, but the recent evidence on fees discussed in Chapter 2 points to continued excessively high costs in small plans. These plans offer fewer economies of scale, but also often lack the in-house expertise to select fee-efficient options and depend on often-conflicted service providers to structure plan menus. Think, for example, of a physicians' group that wants to do right by its employees by offering a 401(k) plan, but never learned in medical school how many basis points are reasonable to charge for plan record keeping.

If fees are high in some plans simply because plan sponsors don't appreciate the importance of keeping costs down and rely on conflicted advice, then perhaps informing sponsors that their current advisors/ menu providers are charging them suspiciously high fees (and that they have a fiduciary obligation to run the plan with prudence in the interests of plan participants) could cause them to change to lower-cost advisors or negotiate for better terms. This chapter discusses a field experiment in which we tested this hypothesis. In 2013, Ian sent 6,000 letters to sponsors of plans with above-average fees. Some plans simply received a letter notifying them of the fee study outlined in Chapter 2, while others received a letter stating that their fees were higher than average and listing specific funds that were high-cost.

Far less notable than any effect in the different letter treatments was the conflagration the letters caused in the plan industry. The letters immediately became front-page news in the trade press and eventually were covered by the Wall Street Journal as well. Ian was bombarded with phone calls and emails, not from the letter recipients themselves, but from their plan advisors, whose cost-efficiency had been called into question by a third party.

This chapter reviews the letter ordeal and provides some limited empirical examination of whether the letters had any effect.

There were six different letters, each randomly assigned to plans with above-average total costs in 2010 as measured by the data from the Chapter 2 fee study. The letters were sent from Ian on the Yale Law School letterhead and were addressed to the plan fiduciary (who is usually an employee of the sponsoring employer) listed on the plan's Form 5500. We focus on two of the treatments in this chapter.[38] The first was a control letter, which simply pointed to our study of plan fees as

---

[38] Due to data collection limitations, we focus on the control and one treatment. The text of the other treatments is available in the online appendix.

something the plan sponsor might be interested to look at. The control letter told the fiduciary:

> My name is Ian Ayres, and I am the William K. Townsend Professor at Yale Law School. I am currently engaged in a study of the financial impact of investment and administrative fees in retirement plans. I recently conducted an empirical research study with Prof. Quinn Curtis, Associate Professor of Law at University of Virginia School of Law, which aimed to measure the relative costs to 401(k) plan participants of menu limitations, excess fees, and investor allocation mistakes. Our results are available online at http://islandia.law.yale.edu/ayres/CurtisAyres.pdf.

The treatment letter we analyze below began with the same text as the control letter, but went on to notify the plan sponsor that the plan "may be high cost," and included a list of three mutual funds in the plan menu with the highest fees. The additional text of this treatment said:

> As a reminder, fiduciary duties are the most stringent imposed by the law, and require administrators to act solely in the interests of participants. We recommend the following steps:
>
> - As of 2009, your plan included [number] investment options with fees in excess of one percent. Research in fund performance shows that funds with high costs are unlikely to outperform low-cost funds. You should consider low-cost alternatives to these options. Below are the three highest-cost funds in your plan as of 2009:
>   [List of three most expensive funds]
> - Index funds often outperform funds with higher fees. You should ensure that there are low-cost index options available to participants.
> - Consider contracting separately for plan administration services. Although we understand that fund providers sometimes offer low/no-cost administrative and bookkeeping services in exchange for plans accepting a suite of funds, our results indicated that plans which pay for services separately often have lower total costs. Several companies now offer low-cost administrative services.

3.2.1   Blowback

As soon as the letters arrived, Ian began to get calls and emails. Some simply acknowledged receipt of a letter, but many of the calls were from industry professionals whose client had received the letters and asked about their costs. The severity of the industry blowback was unexpected. Ian failed to anticipate that these individual fiduciaries would turn around and contact their advisors. While Ian only mailed one letter to each plan, the plan advisors who were charging high fees were suddenly receiving dozens of calls from their clients. The Wall Street Journal reported that "Companies have lighted up the phone lines of 401(k) consultants, administrators and trade groups in their search to figure out if they are doing something wrong."[39]

The good news is that these reactions of plan fiduciaries are consistent with the hypothesis that providing information could move them to action. It's pretty clear that the letters caused many fiduciaries to at least call their advisor. The bad news is that the publicity that ensued undermined the acoustic separation between the various treatments. The advisor industry did not let the letters go unnoticed. More than a dozen articles in trade and popular press disseminated the advisor spin. They argued that the study was based on old data, and that it didn't control for fund performance and services (For example, "the professors' study didn't take into account the services – participant education, advice, and automatically enrolling workers – which typically come at a cost but also can improve retirement investors' returns, industry experts said.").

Some of the articles were particularly concerned about the treatment letter (which was sent to one-sixth of our recipients) which mentioned that we planned to make the results of the study available to "newspapers (including the New York Times and Wall Street Journal), as well as disseminate the results via Twitter with a separate hashtag for your company." One industry participant described the letter, which had been approved by Yale's Human Subjects committee, as "Unsolicited and unwanted advice … with a hint of menace."[40] Others heard implied threats in the letters more generally. In response to the suggestion in other letters that fiduciaries add lower-fee options, one commentator wrote, "Or else? Ayres doesn't have a history of filing lawsuits, but the tone rings ominously for 401(k) plan sponsors, who have faced 30 lawsuits for having overly high fees over the past several years."[41] An article colorfully characterized the letters as threatening: "That's a nice 401(k) plan you've got there … it'd be a shame if something happened to it."[42] The industry

---

[39] Kelly Green, *Letters about 401(k) Plan Costs Stir Tempest*, WALL ST. J. (July 24, 2013).

[40] Green, supra note 39. In response to push back on the "threat" of publicity, Ayres released a statement saying in part that "no company-specific data will be published that is based on 2009 data." Id.

[41] www.morningstar.com/articles/603555/article.

[42] *Id.*

news site 401kwire.com was particularly pointed, posting headlines referring to "Yale bully Ian Ayres" and "Yale threat letters."

We were surprised by what seemed like a coordinated industry response. In addition to the avalanche of articles, Ian's Yale colleague, the Nobel-prize-winning economist, Robert Shiller, forwarded a voicemail left by an industry participant who refused to take part in a study because of Shiller's association with Yale and thereby with Ayres.

The peak of publicity happened a couple of days after the Wall Street Journal article when the study was featured in a 3-minute segment on the CBS morning news.[43] As a researcher, the problem with this unexpected press deluge is that it makes it harder to identify causal impacts of different treatments. Even recipients of the innocuous control letter, which did not identify the recipient's plan as potentially high cost, might have been moved to action after hearing about the publicity and realizing that they too had received a letter from a Yale professor.

Somewhat to our surprise, none of the publicity mentioned the possibility that the letters were part of a randomized experiment. This represents a failure of imagination. Journalists did review our resumes. One asked Ian whether the letters were some kind of school project with their children.[44] But none of the reporters asked why there were different kinds of letters. And industry participants, at least in their quotations, couldn't conceive that the letters were partly motivated by public spirit – trying to make the world a better place by alerting plan sponsors that they might be paying too much to their advisors.

3.2.2   Results

Without access to the full set of plan data post-treatment, we nevertheless endeavored to determine if the letters had any measurable effects by manually collecting a subsample of data on our own. We randomly selected 300 plans from the treatment and control groups and hand-collected plan menus and pulled the Form 5500 data for those plans. There was significant and asymmetric attrition of the random sample in terms of menu availability, as documented in Table 3.3.

---

[43] www.cbsnews.com/news/decoding-401k-fees-what-you-need-to-know-to-make-great-decisions/.

[44] See, e.g., Ian Ayres & Antonia Rose Ayres-Brown, *Unhappy Meals: Sex Discrimination in Toy Choice at Mcdonald's*, 21 WM. & MARY J. WOMEN & L. 237 (2015); Ian Ayres, Antonia Ayres-Brown & Henry Ayres-Brown, *Seeing Significance: Is the 95% Probability Range Easier to Perceive?*, 20 CHANCE 11 (Winter 2007).

Table 3.3 *Sample attrition for treated and control group*

	Control		Treated	
Number of plans processed	300		300	
Has pre-period Form 5500 menu	216		148	
Pct. of total		72.0%		49.3%
Has post-period Form 5500 menu	133		91	
Pct. of total		44.3%		30.3%
Pct. of pre-		61.6%		61.5%
Form 5500 pre- and post-period	130		88	
Pct. of total		43.3%		29.3%
CRSP fund data for some funds in the pre-period	188		133	
Pct. of total		62.7%		44.3%
Pct of plans with menu data		87.0%		89.9%
CRSP fund data for some funds in the pre-period post-period	115		67	
Pct. of total		38.3%		22.3%
Pct of plans with menu data		86.5%		73.6%
CRSP fund data for some funds in both pre- and post-period	105		63	
Pct. of total		34.0%		21.0%
Pct of plans with menu data		80.8%		71.6%

Table 3.3 shows that most of the treated funds do not have menu information available for the year preceding receipt of a letter, while substantially more in the control group do. This obviously can't be ascribed to any treatment effects. There is some possibility that this reflects non-random selection, as the letters' recipients were higher-cost plans, and perhaps these plans were more likely to merge, be discontinued, or adopt a master trust arrangement that concealed menu data. In any case, the effect of this attrition is that there are fewer menus available for treated funds than for other funds.

Below, we present results of comparisons between the treatment and control groups of letter recipients. Clearly, the limited dataset reduces the power to identify any causal changes, but we see no evidence of a significant effect on plan behavior among the treated plans.

Table 3.4 presents summary statistics on the treatment and control groups pre- and post-treatment. For each group, we report the mean

Table 3.4 *Summary statistics pre-treatment*

	(1) Treatment		(2) Control		(3) Difference	
	Mean	SD	Mean	SD	(1)–(2)	t
Exp. ratio	0.008	0.003	0.008	0.003	0.001	(1.148)
Lowest cost	0.122	0.251	0.128	0.240	−0.013	(−0.346)
Pct. index funds	0.123	0.211	0.147	0.258	−0.016	(−0.419)
Pct. with 12b-1	0.544	0.369	0.542	0.400	0.056	(0.915)
					−0.035	(−0.683)
Observations		133		188		168

t statistics in parentheses * $p < 0.1$, ** $p < 0.05$, *** $p < 0.01$.

investment fund expense ratio, the percentage of funds that are the lowest-cost share class, the percentage of funds that are index funds, and the percentage of funds that carry 12b-1 charges. The 12b-1 fees are sales charges associated with some funds that cover marketing expenses for the fund. They are associated with load funds (though loads in retirement plans are typically waived) and reflect costs to the plan not directly related to money management. There are no statistically significant differences in the pre-treatment variables, conditional on having post-treatment data available. This gives some comfort that the differential attrition in the post-treatment period is random.

To measure potential treatment effects within the random subsample, Tables 3.5 and 3.6 present regressions of the main measures of cost on a treatment dummy (in 3.8) and a treatment dummy with a size control (in 3.9). None of the results suggest that the letter treatment is associated with lower costs. The only (borderline) significant change is an *increase* in funds with 12b-1 expenses among treated plans. Subject to the significant caveat of reduced power resulting from our limited sample, we conclude that the letter had no measurable effects.

The letter also included a list of three of the most expensive funds in the plan menu. In Table 3.7, we examine whether these funds (or any others) were less likely to be retained in the menu from the pre-period to the post-period. The regressions in 3.10 take each fund observed in the pre-period as a unit of observation and asks whether that fund is retained

Table 3.5 *Treatment effects estimates*

	(1) Change in expense ratio	(2) Change in lowest cost	(3) Change in index funds	(4) Pct. with 12b-1
Treated (Ind.)	0.057	−0.040	−0.032	0.079*
	(1.63)	(−1.58)	(−0.85)	(1.70)
Constant	−0.116***	0.025	0.116***	−0.071**
	(−5.55)	(1.30)	(4.73)	(−2.47)
Observations	168	168	168	168
R^2	0.016	0.012	0.004	0.017

t statistics in parentheses * $p < 0.1$, ** $p < 0.05$, *** $p < 0.01$.

Table 3.6 *Treatment effects estimates (size controls)*

	(1) Change in expense ratio	(2) Change in lowest cost	(3) Change in index funds	(4) Pct with 12b-1
Treated (Ind.)	0.057	−0.039	−0.029	0.083*
	(1.62)	(−1.55)	(−0.78)	(1.78)
Assets under management	−0.000	−0.000	−0.000*	−0.000
	(−0.14)	(−0.64)	(−1.97)	(−1.50)
Constant	−0.114***	0.030	0.133***	−0.046
	(−4.97)	(1.40)	(4.73)	(−1.50)
Observations	168	168	168	168
R^2	0.016	0.014	0.015	0.034

t statistics in parentheses * $p < 0.1$, ** $p < 0.05$, *** $p < 0.01$.

in the menu in the post-period. Standard errors are clustered at the plan level. We find no significant treatment effect either on its own or interacting with fund properties. In fact, funds in treated plans seem more likely to be retained in general. Even the high-cost funds explicitly listed in the letter are retained at about the same rate.

Table 3.7 *Predictors of fund retention (linear probability model)*

	(1) Retained	(2) Retained	(3) Retained	(4) Retained	(5) Retained
Treated	0.081				
	(1.49)				
Treated X index fund		0.052 (0.55)			
Treated X lowest-cost fund			0.063 (0.56)		
Treated X expense ratio as of fiscal year-end				−5.023 (−0.92)	
Treated X most expensive 3 in plan					−0.033 (−0.26)
Constant	0.591***	0.645***	0.632***	0.716***	0.644***
	(16.12)	(16.86)	(16.33)	(16.88)	(17.28)
Observations	5450	2132	2132	1889	2139
R^2	0.007	0.001	0.003	0.005	0.001

t statistics in parentheses * $p < 0.1$, ** $p < 0.05$, *** $p < 0.01$.

* * *

Given the limited ability to collect follow-up data, we are reluctant to draw any strong conclusions from the empirics, which we present mostly for completeness. What was telling, though, was the response of the plan industry to an attempt to sensitize their customers to high costs. Even modest attempts to induce greater cost sensitivity met with significant pushback.

4

What More Fiduciaries Should Learn

Assessing the Prevalence of Allocation Errors

The next two chapters operationalize our argument that prudent fiduciaries ought to guard against menu misuse. Our goal here is to show that credible assessments of likely allocation errors in participants' plan choices are feasible using analysis techniques that are well within the abilities of plan administrators. We illustrate the feasibility of such analysis by undertaking it ourselves using data on the retirement plan savings allocation of University of Virginia employees.

This chapter shows how fiduciaries can undertake "weighting" analysis to assess the prevalence of menu misuse. We will show that it is straightforward to assess the extent to which participant allocations are subject to three different menu mistakes. More specifically, this chapter shows how fiduciaries can learn whether participants are making: diversification mistakes (with portfolios that are overinvested or underinvested in particular asset classes), exposure mistakes (with portfolios with too little or too much market risk), and fee mistakes (with portfolios with funds that are too expensive).[1]

Before proceeding to our core analysis providing actual examples of the kind of analysis of what fiduciaries should learn, we take on two preliminary matters. First, we respond to two possible objections to our claim that it is feasible to assess these allocation errors. Second, we summarize the existing literature showing the substantial allocation errors in 401(k) plans and other tax-deferred investments.

4.1 Responding to Alpha and Outside-Asset Criticisms

Some might argue that it is impossible ex ante to assess whether any allocation is mistaken because a seeming mistake might be justified by

---

[1] The possibility of these three allocation mistakes is also discussed in Ian Ayres & Edward Fox, *Alpha Duties: The Search for Excess Returns and Appropriate Fiduciary Responsibilities*, 97 TEXAS L. REV. 445 (2019).

a participant's belief that their particular allocation will beat the market. A seeming diversification mistake, for example, may be justified if the participant believes that particular funds will produce above-average risk-adjusted returns. "Seeking alpha" is a general term for investment strategies that seek greater returns than well-diversified, low-cost market portfolios. Seeking alpha necessitates sacrificing diversification because one cannot simultaneously hold the market and beat the market. Any participant with a portfolio allocation that facially seems to have committed a diversification error might respond that they are doing so advisedly because their undiversified investments are market beaters.[2]

While such "market-beating" investment opportunities might arise, fiduciaries should be aware that it is unlikely that many retail investors have sufficient information to justify taking on the high costs of failing to diversify. The more a particular sector is overweighted or the more an asset class is underweighted, the higher the expected alpha that is required to justify the allocation. For example, Ayres and Fox have shown that in order to justify investing half your savings in gold, one would need to believe that the return on gold would exceed that of stocks by more than 5 percentage points.[3] Fiduciaries have good reason to be suspicious that many participants have insufficient warrant for making investments that sacrifice diversification or expose the participant to high expense ratios or non-standard exposure to stock market risk.[4]

This is not to deny that some investors may have sufficient acumen to consistently beat the risk-adjusted returns of diversified portfolios. But for every Warren Buffet or David Swensen, there are tens of thousands of retail traders who cannot plausibly make informed "alpha" investment. One heuristic lens through which to evaluate the propriety of an individual portfolio allocation is to imagine how courts would react if such an allocation had been utilized by the fiduciary of a defined benefit plan. If it would be imprudent for a defined benefit's fiduciary to invest a substantial proportion of the firm's assets in biotech stocks, then it should be

---

[2] Analogously with regard to a potential exposure mistake, a critic might argue that a 25-year-old who ignores the consensus advice of investing a substantial proportion of one's portfolio in diversified equities and instead invests all of their savings in money markets might be justified, if the participant reasonably believes that the stock market will soon crash.

[3] Ayres & Fox, *supra* note 1, at 482 (Figure 4). The figure shows that for an investment like gold (which in standard deviation terms has a 30 percent risk) expecting a 5.5 percent excess return would justify allocating 49 percent of savings to the alpha opportunity.

[4] *Id.* at 463 (discussing alpha necessary to justify what would otherwise be fee or exposure mistakes).

concerning for a fiduciary to learn that a substantial number of its participants made such allocations.

Second, we reject the nihilistic idea that fiduciaries cannot ever be sure
that an allocation represents a diversification mistake because the fiduciaries are not privy to the possibility of outside investments.[5] It is not necessary for fiduciaries to identify mistakes by specific individuals to have
confidence that there likely are diversification mistakes in a class of overweighted investors. For example, suppose that a plan fiduciary learns that
a substantial number of the participants have over 90 percent of their plan
assets in a biotech fund. It is hard to imagine that those participants own
counterbalancing, diversifying portfolios of all other assets except biotech
stock in the non-plan investments. We provide examples below showing
that the amount of non-plan savings necessary to implement this counterbalancing strategy would far outstrip the plausible savings of participants
with known salaries. Moreover, there is no economic reason why a participant would need to hold specialized portfolios inside the plan, rather
than make adjustments to their non-plan holdings. It is not unreasonable
for the law to implicitly require a few participants to adjust their outside
portfolio instead of allowing many more to be harmed by massively undiversified retirement investments.

For the vast majority of investors, their investment commitments within
the plan are reflective of their overall investment profile. Evidence from
the Survey of Consumer Finances "indicates that asset allocations are quite
similar inside and outside" of tax-deferred accounts.[6] An article uncovering

---

[5] Outside investments might more easily justify seeming exposure mistakes. We might imagine situations where a participant inherited a substantial quantity of bonds, say, from a
deceased parent and was reluctant to sell them after some period of time because of capital
gain tax consequences. That participant might choose to hold fewer bonds and more equities in her plan allocation to achieve the desired exposure. *See also* Kenneth Anderson &
Daniel Murphy, *Stocks and Bonds: What to Put in and What to Leave Out of Individual
Retirement Accounts and Qualified Plans*, 68 J. FIN. SERVICE PROF. 39 (2014) (arguing
that tax deferred status of ERISA balances provides a reason for holding more income-
producing assets inside a plan). Accordingly, a fiduciary might be less likely to characterize
a participant's low equity exposure as an exposure error if the participant was likely to have
large non-plan equity holdings.

[6] Ning Tang, Olivia S. Mitchell, Gary R. Mottola & Stephen P. Utkus, *The Efficiency of Sponsor
and Participant Portfolio Choices in 401(k) Plans*, 94 J. PUB. ECON. 1084 (2010). *See also* Daniel
Bergstresser & James Poterba, *Asset Allocation and Asset Location: Household Evidence from
the Survey of Consumer Finances*, 88 J. PUB. ECON. 1893 (2004) (concluding "[a]sset allocation inside and outside tax-deferred accounts is quite similar, with about 70 percent of
assets in each location invested in equity securities"); Zvi Bodie & Dwight B. Crane, *Personal
Investing: Advice, Theory, and Evidence*, 53 FIN. ANALYSTS J. (1997) (finding investors
choose similar asset allocations in their taxable and tax-deferred accounts).

substantial portfolio inefficiencies summarized the relative unimportance of outside assets in assessing the reasonableness of participant allocations:

> Asset allocations outside the 401(k) plans will probably not mitigate these efficiency results, because retirement plan assets represent "all or almost all" of the households' total retirement savings. Furthermore, evidence from the SCF suggests that allocations in tax-deferred and taxable accounts at the aggregate level are similar, providing some limited indication that households may not be adjusting assets outside the tax-deferred accounts.[7]

For all these reasons, fiduciaries should analyze plan portfolios *as if* they represent the bulk of participant's retirement savings, not only because this will often be the case, but also because participants with significant outside assets tend to invest them in similar ways or can rebalance their outside investments to achieve diversification inside and out. Just as we don't worry whether participants have sufficient assets to offset non-diversified plan holdings of company stock, fiduciaries have good reason to discount the possibility of offsetting outside investments when they learn of overweighting of narrow-gauged sector funds.

4.2 Evidence of Substantial Allocation Errors in Tax-Deferred Accounts

Another objection to our claim could be that the likelihood of finding substantial allocation errors is so small that requiring fiduciaries to expend the effort to self-educate themselves on this issue is unlikely to be worth the candle. We respond to this concern in this section by showing that substantial allocation errors have already been shown to be prevalent for a substantial proportion of participants across a large swath of tax-deferred plans.

Consider the 2010 study of Ning Tang and co-authors analyzing the efficiency of more than a million participant portfolios in more than a thousand 401(k) plans managed by Vanguard.[8] The authors found that average monthly shortfall in return relative to what could be achieved in a diversified portfolio of equivalent risk was "approximately 11 basis points."[9] The authors explained the long-term impact of such a shortfall:

---

[7] Ning Tang et al., *supra* note 6 at 1081.
[8] Ning Tang et al., *supra* note 6.
[9] The achievable benchmark returns were derived from the fund returns of three market indices: the Russel 3000 index (for the broad domestic equity market), Lehman Aggregate index (for the investment grade bond market) and the MSCI EAFE index (for the international equity market).

> To put these results in context, if one expected a diversified 401(k) port-
> folio to generate an annual real return of 5% after expenses, the typical
> participant would be predicted to forfeit 23% of their expected retirement
> wealth over a 35-year work life by having a less-than-adequate plan invest-
> ment menu and by failing to diversify adequately.[10]

The failure to adequately diversify could thus substantially reduce the
final retirement nest egg of participants. But a subset of participants fared
much worse. The authors found that the "top 5% of participants has an
idiosyncratic risk share of more than 0.77, meaning that 77% of the portfolio variance is not rewarded by higher expected return."[11] And the worst
1 percent of participant portfolio allocations had "a total return loss of
over 0.4% or 40 basis points per month."[12] Such losses would cause these
participants to sacrifice more than half of the terminal retirement wealth
they might have achieved with an equally risky portfolio that had been
more efficiently diversified.

AON Hewitt's analysis of more than 3 million employees/participants
across 144 defined contribution plans finds similar substantial "suboptimal diversification:"

> [Self-directed participants], on average, had significantly less diversified
> portfolios than those using the professionally designed target date fund.
> This case study ... shows that suboptimal diversification costs 30 basis
> points in annual performance for more than 50% of participants. Carried
> over a participant's career, an annual return shortfall of 30 basis points
> amounts to 0.8 times final pay—a substantial sum.[13]

These results, buttressed by our own analysis of 2010 data from more than
3,500 401(k) plans with more than $120 billion in assets, are described in
Chapter 2.[14] With plan-level information on the total amounts invested
in particular funds, we were able to estimate lower bounds on the return-
equivalent losses from failing to fully diversify. We also estimated the
excess expenses incurred by participants.

---

[10] Ning Tang et al., *supra* note 6 at 1079 (citations omitted).
[11] *Id.* at 1081.
[12] *Id.* at 1079.
[13] Aon Hewitt, *Customize DC Investments for Participant Success: How Custom Investment
Options Improve Participant Outcomes* (2015), www.aon.com/attachments/human-
capital-consulting/custom-dc-investments-for-participant-success-wp-july2015.pdf; Aon
Hewitt, *2014 Universe Benchmarks: Measuring Employee Savings and Investing Behavior
in Defined Contribution Plans* (2014), https://docplayer.net/6669086-2014-universe-
benchmarks-highlights-measuring-employee-savings-and-investing-behavior-in-
defined-contribution-plans.html.
[14] This is the same dataset discuss above in Chapter 1.

The average annual diversification loss in these plans was 71 basis points – with 6 basis points of loss stemming from menu limitations and 65 basis points of loss stemming from participant choices. The worst 5 percent of plans had annual diversification losses of more than 134 basis points. What's worse is that these estimates are lower-bound estimates because the plan-level data on which they are based aggregates the holdings of the individual plan participants in which unbalanced individual portfolios undoubtedly counterbalance each other.

Across multiple studies, there is substantial evidence of diversification and fee mistakes. We know that some participants fail to diversify by allocating too much of their portfolio to own-company stock or individual equities, and that they exhibit home-country bias.[15] The failure to diversify has been tied to "familiarity bias," the reluctance to invest in assets with which one is less familiar.[16] And the failure to appreciate the value of diversification is particularly understandable for 55 percent of Americans who cannot correctly answer the financial literacy question: "True or false: buying a single company's stock usually provides a safer return than a stock mutual fund."[17] Many participants are not sensitive to mutual fund fees and exacerbate the problem of excess expenses by choosing high-fee funds from their plan menu.[18]

There is also consensus that it is an exposure mistake for participants to invest too little or too much in equity, given their age. Exposing one's portfolio to "the wrong amount of market risk is a mistake because

---

[15] Stephen G. Dimmock et al., *Ambiguity Aversion and Household Portfolio Choice Puzzles: Empirical Evidence*, 119 J. FIN. ECON. 559, 564 (2016) ("Seventeen percent of the sample owns individual shares. Conditional on nonzero equity ownership, the average fraction allocated to individual stocks is 42%.... Consistent with other studies of household portfolios, we find that, conditional on owning individual stocks, the median number of individual companies held is two, which suggests that individual stock ownership is a reasonable proxy for under-diversification.").

[16] *Id.* at 561.

[17] This result is taken from the 2019 Survey of Household Economics and Decision making (SHED) which survey more than 12,000 U.S. adults. Report on the Economic Well-Being of U.S. Households in 2019, Featuring Supplemental Data from April 2020, 52 (May 2020) www.federalreserve.gov/publications/files/2019-report-economic-well-being-us-households-202005.pdf.

[18] For example, in an experiment, 730 Harvard employees were given prospectuses for four S&P index funds and were asked to allocate $10,000 among these funds and subjects were rewarded by the amount of the chosen portfolio's subsequent return. The subjects overwhelmingly failed to minimize fees, the major determinant of their reward. Instead, subjects place "high weight on normatively irrelevant historical returns." James J. Choi, David Laibson & Brigitte C. Madrian, *Why Does the Law of One Price Fail? An Experiment on Index Mutual Funds*, 23 REV. FIN. STUD. 1405, 1432 (2010).

investors who take on too much or too little stock market risk fail to optimally trade off risk and return."[19] Investors can make exposure mistakes by exposing their portfolio to either too much or too little stock market risk given their personal risk tolerance and the number of years until retirement. It should raise fiduciary concern to see 20-somethings investing little or nothing in stocks, both because of the risk-premium in expected returns that stocks tend to pay relative to bonds, and because investments in stocks can help diversify idiosyncratic risk. So too, most participants (who are relying on their 401(k) savings to pay for their retirement) should lower the proportion of their portfolio in stocks as they approach the date of their retirement. Lifecycle funds do just that – automatically adjusting stock exposure as participants approach their retirement target date.[20] There is quantitative evidence that a substantial number of participants make exposure mistakes. For example, AON Hewitt's analysis of 144 defined contribution plans found marked evidence of inappropriate equity exposure:

> Participants often do not take the most appropriate level of risk for their time horizons. We found that approximately 60% of participants who do not seek professional help had inappropriate risk levels. Approximately two-thirds of those were taking on too much risk—such as a 65-year-old with 100% equity. Approximately one-third were taking on too little risk—such as a 25-year-old with 100% cash.[21]

An analysis of 2007 participant allocations uncovered analogous evidence of exposure mistakes with roughly half of participants in their 20s having no exposure to equity, and with more than a fifth of older 401(k) participants (ages 56–65) holding more than 90 percent of their portfolio in equities.[22] Fidelity's 2021 analysis of its 401(k) plans found smaller, but still concerning proportions of participants with too little or too much stock exposure: 9 percent of participants held 100 percent or 0 percent in equity, and 25 percent had had "higher than suggested" stock allocations.[23] The Fidelity report emphasized the dangers of excessive

---

[19] Ian Ayres & Edward Fox, *supra* note 1. Exposure mistakes are also referred to as "beta" mistakes because "in the Capital Asset Pricing Model (CAPM), beta is a numeric measure of how exposed a portfolio is to market risk." *Id.* at 455.

[20] *See* Ian Ayres & Barry Nalebuff, *Diversification across Time*, 39 J. PORT. MGT. 73 (2013).

[21] Aon Hewitt, *supra* note 86.

[22] Jack VanDerhei, *What Will Happen to Retirement Income for 401(k) Participants After the Market Decline?* 22 J. AGING & SOC. POL'Y. 129, 134–35 (2010).

[23] Fidelity Investment, *Building Financial Futures* (1st Quarter 2021) at 10, https://sponsor .fidelity.com/bin-public/06_PSW_Website/documents/Building_Financial_Futures.pdf.

equity exposure for older workers, concluding that "[b]aby boomers are most likely to be too aggressive potentially putting them at risk so close to retirement."[24]

Stepping back, we can see that in some plans, a majority of participants are making substantial diversification and fee mistakes in ways that will erode a large proportion of their final retirement savings.[25] But to be clear, fiduciaries should consider taking action even if they can just identify a substantial minority of participants who are making a particular mistake. For example, later, in Chapter 9, we will learn that investing in Bitcoin funds is one of the most popular 401(k) brokerage window investments for Millennial participants. If a fiduciary learned that participants investing in Bitcoin or Gamestop or AMC stock were investing unreasonable proportions of their retirement portfolios in these hyper-speculative investments, fiduciaries should consider removing (streamlining) or limiting (guardrailing) these investment options – even if these participants represented only a discrete minority of plan participants.

4.3   How Fiduciaries Can Identify Potential Diversification Mistakes

The last section presents evidence that there are credible reasons to believe that in many plans a *substantial* number of participants are making *substantial* allocation errors. Here we show how fiduciaries can become better informed about whether this is happening in their own plans. To illustrate how an evaluation of menu misuse can be practically accomplished, this section undertakes an allocation "weighting" analysis using participant-level allocation data from the University of Virginia's 403(b)

---

[24] *Id.* at 10.

[25] While this book is focused on allocation mistakes, employees can also err by not becoming participants or by not saving a sufficient amount. In particular, a substantial number of employees err by not taking sufficient advantage of employers' matching contribution. For example, an analysis of more than 5,000 participants in plans with employer matching found that "36% of match-eligible employees over age 59½ forgo arbitrage profits that average 1.6% of their annual pay, or $507." James J. Choi, David Laibson & Brigitte C. Madrian, *$100 Bills on the Sidewalk: Suboptimal Investment in 401(k) Plans*, 93 (3) REV. ECON. STAT. 761 (2011). These employees could costlessly increase their take home pay by contributing and simultaneously withdrawing the larger matched amount. But we do not believe that employers have a fiduciary obligation to make employees participants or to increase their savings, and laws that did so might reduce employers' willingness to match retirement contributions. Ryan Bubb & Patrick L. Warren, *An Equilibrium Theorem of Retirement Plan Design*, 12 AM. ECON. J.: ECON. POL'Y. 22, 45 (2020).

plan merged with its Optional Retirement Plan (the default plan for faculty contributions).[26] The data in this section focuses on the allocations of plan participants who were invested in the plan on two discrete dates: January 31, 2016, and January 31, 2017.[27] In 2016, the plan offered participants a menu that included 303 investment options and the default investment funds in the plan were Fidelity target-date funds (TDFs).[28] Chapter 8 will later analyze the impact of UVA's subsequent substantial streamlining of its plan menu, but our goal here is to assess the likelihood of allocation errors in the original plan.

To that end, we begin with a straightforward analysis of allocations that potentially sacrificed diversification by overweighting narrow-sector and regional funds. Fiduciaries should be concerned about the problem of overweighting of any fund that could not qualify as a QDIA. It is impossible to overweight target date or balance funds because those funds are constructed to provide substantial diversification with exposure to major asset classes. Of the 280 funds we analyze, overweighting is a possibility with regard to the 101 sector, region, real estate and bond funds, and to a lesser extent with regard to the 82 broad domestic equity funds.[29] By reporting the share of participants who have substantial portions of their plan portfolio in a few individual sector funds, Table 4.1 identifies participants who are likely to sacrifice diversification.

---

[26] The University provided us with deidentified holdings data for the period of 2012–2018. The data provides a snapshot of the value of each plan participant's holdings for each fund held, along with demographic data including gender, marital status and current salary on an annual basis. UVA offers a number of different retirement plans for faculty, staff, and hospital staff. Our data is based on the primary plan used by faculty as a default option (the "ORP plan") and the plan used as the primary plan for staff and for additional contributions by faculty (the "403(b) plan"). We do not have data for the default plan used by hospital staff, and so drop from our sample employees whose main employment is listed as the medical center. Due to data limitations, matching between the plans is based on demographic data not available for all employees and so is subject to some noise and omits a number of investors with incomplete demographic information in the plan data, leaving 7,707 participants for analysis. Our online appendix, which can be found at www.ianayres.com, shows that the results for the 403(b) plan data are quite similar to the results of the combined ORP/403(b) plan data providing additional support for the idea that people tend to invest in similar kinds of investment in different portions of their savings.

[27] Our analytic sample also filters to investors that hold funds for which returns data is available for 2016–2018.

[28] Our analyses exclude fixed income funds, money market funds, and funds for which insufficient returns data is available, leaving 280 funds held by plan investors.

[29] The 8 money market funds can be overweighted in the sense of an exposure mistake, but these funds don't expose participants to substantial non-systemic risk.

Table 4.1 *Overweighting analysis*

Fund	N	Share of investors with over 50% of assets in fund	Share of investors with over 70% of assets in fund	Share of investors with over 90% of assets in fund
Fidelity Select Gold Fund	28	35.7%	25.0%	17.9%
Fidelity Pacific Basin Fund	20	20.0%	10.0%	10.0%
Fidelity Select Biotech	124	11.3%	5.6%	3.2%
Fidelity Select Chemicals	32	9.4%	3.1%	0.0%
Fidelity Select Natural Gas	13	7.7%	7.7%	7.7%
Fidelity China Region Fund	45	6.7%	4.4%	2.2%
Fidelity Select Retail	30	6.7%	3.3%	3.3%
Fidelity Select Healthcare	57	5.3%	0.0%	0.0%
Fidelity Select Healthcare	43	4.7%	0.0%	0.0%
Fidelity Global Commodity Stock Fund	47	4.3%	2.1%	2.1%

Note: Share of investors that own a given fund and hold over x% of assets in fund (pre-reform).

The table shows that UVA has 28 investors with holdings in the Fidelity Select Gold fund and that more than a third of these participants (35.7 percent) had over half their plan savings invested in the gold fund with more than 17 percent of the fund investors investing more than 90 percent of their plan assets in the fund. While the gold fund was only used by 0.4 percent of plan investors, what should be relevant for fiduciaries in deciding whether to eliminate or guardrail a particular fund is the *rate* of misuse among those opting to use the menu item. If anything, the low number of investors choosing to allocate any assets to the funds mitigates in favor of its elimination. Investing over half of your retirement investments in gold is highly imprudent. Any fiduciary of a defined benefits plan who invested plan assets on such an undiversified basis would be liable for breaching their prudential duty. A prudent fiduciary should consider whether offering a gold fund is doing more harm than good to plan participants when designing the menu, and consider exercising their discretion to eliminate the option, as the University of Virginia did in January 2017.

The table shows that the overweighting of narrow-gauged sector funds is not limited to a few goldbug investors. A substantial proportion of investors in several other sector funds hold analogously disproportionate allocations.

For example, 11 percent of the 124 participants invested in Fidelity Select Biotech fund have more than half of their plan balances in that one fund. Substantial failures to diversify also attend a substantial proportion of investors in telecommunications and consumer staple funds. Overall, we find that 3.5 percent of plan participants held more than 10 percent of their plan balance in a single-sector fund and 1.1 percent of plan participants held more than 50 percent of their portfolio in single-sector funds.

While we do not observe the size of outside savings that these participants hold, the UVA data does tell us the age and salary of current employees. If we assume, conservatively, that employees have saved 10 percent of their current salary since they were 22 years old and earned 5 percent annually on those savings, we can speculate on the plausibility that non-plan savings might offset seemingly undiversified fund holdings within the plan.[30] These assumptions produce estimates of external savings that are on average more than five times that of plan holdings for people who invested excessively in individual sector funds. If Greg Mankiw's suggestion that a gold portfolio share of 2 percent is reasonable,[31] plan investors with gold fund holdings would need total savings 50 times larger than their gold holdings to produce optimal diversification. Unsurprisingly, we find that a large share (38 percent) of the participants invested in the plan's gold fund have estimated savings that fall short, and those that fall short do so by over $1.1 million on average.[32] Applying a similar analysis to investors with salary and age information who have invested more than 10 percent in a narrow-gauged sector fund, we estimate that more than 47 percent would not have the requisite outside assets to offset the undiversified positions in their plan holdings.[33]

Failing to diversify by overweighting sector funds predictably causes participants to bear uncompensated idiosyncratic risk. Chapter 5 will describe the details of factor regressions, which can be used to produce the expected risk and return of each participant's portfolio.

---

[30] These assumptions are generous because most adults have not averaged savings of 10 percent of their current pretax income (and many do not average a 5 percent annual real return on their investment). Shlomo Benartzi & Richard H. Thaler, *Behavioral Economics and the Retirement Savings Crisis*, 339 SCIENCE 1152, 1153 (2013); John Watson & Mark McNaughton, *Gender Differences in Risk Aversion and Expected Retirement Benefits*, 63 FIN. ANALYSTS J. 59 (2007). We also generously assume 100 percent employer matching for all contributions in the UVA plan.

[31] Mankiw, *supra* note 7.

[32] Salary data is only available for current employees, which limits this analysis to the 24 that hold the gold fund and have available salary data.

[33] Our analysis is restricted to individuals for which salary data is available.

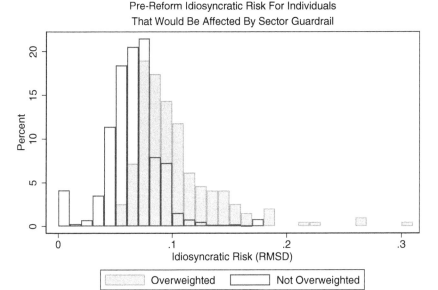

Figure 4.1 Estimates of idiosyncratic risk of portfolios that are overweighted and those that are not overweighted

Note: For this analysis, we classify a portfolio as overweighted if it holds more than 10 percent of its balance in a sector fund.

These regressions also produce estimates of the idiosyncratic risk of each participant's portfolio.[34] These estimates are a powerful measure of the degree of non-diversification. Idiosyncratic risk is an undesirable feature of overweighting because it increases the risk of a portfolio without increasing the expected return. Figure 4.1 shows a histogram comparing the idiosyncratic risks of participant portfolios that are overweighted in sector funds and would be affected by a potential allocation guardrail to the risk of portfolios that are not so overweighted.

The figure illustrates the costs in terms of added risk of failing to diversify. The portfolios that are overweighted in sector funds display dramatically higher estimates of uncompensated, idiosyncratic risk than those portfolios that are not overweighted. The average risk of the overweighted portfolios is 4.6 basis points higher than the portfolios that are not overweighted (11.0 vs. 6.4 percent).

---

[34] The standard deviation of the factor regression residuals is a standard measure of idiosyncratic risk. *See e.g.*, Keim & Mitchell, *supra* note 15, at 378.

Table 4.2 *Analysis of international share of equity holdings*

Share of investors with less than 10% of equities in international equities	Share of investors with less than 20% of equities in international equities	Share of investors with less than 30% of equities in international equities	Share of investors with less than 40% of equities in international equities	Share of investors with less than 50% of equities in international equities
0.40	0.67	0.81	0.91	0.96

In addition to this overweighting of sector funds, participants can sacrifice diversification by underweighting major asset classes. For example, as mentioned above, it is well understood that individuals often exhibit a "home-country bias" in allocating investments among equity funds.[35] This bias leads to a systematic underweighting of international equities. While there are several theories of how to optimally allocate among different asset classes,[36] there is a consensus that, for prudent investors, 30 percent to 50 percent of equities should be international stock. At the time of our analysis, the Vanguard and the Fidelity target date funds fell within this range: 40 percent of Vanguard and 44 percent of Fidelity target date fund equities were international, respectively.[37]

Self-directed investors who affirmatively choose funds from plan menus are much less likely to possess sufficient international holdings. Table 4.2 provides information on the international share of equity holdings of those UVA participants who were not fully invested in the plan's target date funds.[38]

---

[35] Kenneth R. French & James M. Poterba, *Investor Diversification and International Equity Markets*, 81 AM. ECON REV. 222 (1991).

[36] Heiko Jacobs, Sebastian Miller & Martin Weber, *How Should Individual Investors Diversify? An Empirical Evaluation of Alternative Asset Allocation Policies*, 19 J. FIN. MARKETS 62 (2014) (assessing performance of 11 optimization allocations – including Sharpe ratio maximization and variance minimization approaches – as well as 6 heuristic approaches – including market-weighted and GDP-weighted approaches).

[37] Prior to 2016, the international share of equities for Vanguard lifecycle funds was still within the range but was only 30 percent. Vanguard, *Vanguard Bringing Lower Costs to Target Retirement Fund Investors*, PR NEWSWIRE (Feb. 26, 2015), www.prnewswire .com/news-releases/vanguard-bringing-lower-costs-to-target-retirement-fund-investors-300042024.html.

[38] The figure excludes investors that held no equities in their portfolio – i.e., were 100 percent in fixed-income or money-market funds.

The table shows that 81 percent of the self-directed participants held less than 30 percent of their stock portfolios in international equities, and that 40 percent had less than 10 percent of their stock in international equities.

Fiduciaries would also be prudent to consider whether their participants were adequately exposed to real estate investments. Existing research indicates that underweighting this asset class can impair the risk/return efficiency of retirement portfolios.[39] Commentators suggest that between 10 percent and 30 percent of the non-fixed asset portion of retirement portfolios should be allocated to diversified real estate investment vehicles, such as REITs.[40] However, there is less consensus about the appropriate portion to invest in this asset class, because real estate funds often charge substantially higher expenses. For example, across the six real estate funds offered by the UVA plan in 2016, the average expense ratio was 43 basis points and the highest had annual expenses of 71 basis points. By any measure, a majority of UVA participants invested paltry amounts in real estate. The Fidelity Freedom TDFs allocated nothing to real estate holdings – by our reckoning less than 1.5 percent of the portfolio for any target date. In comparison, other target date funds in 2019 allocated between 6 and 19 percent of their assets in real estate for their youngest participants.[41] And UVA's addition of six real estate funds to its menu did little to make up for these portfolio shortfalls. Overall, UVA participants invest an average of 0.3 percent of their portfolio in real estate, while 98.2 percent of participants have less than 2 percent of their plan portfolios invested in real estate.[42]

We'll turn to the question of how fiduciaries might respond to the problem of asset class underweighting in Chapter 6. But for now, our

---

[39] *See, e.g.,* Christine W. Lai, *Determinants of Portfolio Efficiency Losses in US Self-directed Pension Accounts,* 27 J. FAM. ECON. Issues 601 (2006) (find that in evaluating more than 2500 self-directed retirement accounts that the "source of efficiency losses largely results from omitting the real estate holdings in portfolio choices").

[40] *See, e.g.,* Allen Taylor, *Real Estate Asset Allocation: How Much Is Enough?* SHARESTATES RESOURCE CENTER (December 12, 2016) www.sharestates.com/blog/2016/12/12/real-estate-asset-allocation-how-much-is-enough/. One notes that total value of real estate in the U.S. is more than a third the total value of the stock market (36.2 vs. 95 trillion dollars respectively).

[41] Nareit, *REIT Usage and Target Date Funds* (May 22, 2019), www.reit.com/news/blog/market-commentary/reit-usage-and-target-date-funds. ("eight of the top 10 fastest growing TDF managers feature meaningful allocations to listed REITs in their offerings, including Allianz Global Investors Solutions, American Century, BlackRock, J.P. Morgan, Lincoln National, Manning & Napier, MFS, and PIMCO").

[42] Although we find that 23 participants have more than 90 percent of their plan savings invested in this asset class and are thus presumptively overweighted.

case study of UVA's participants has shown that it does not require complicated statistical methods for fiduciaries to become apprised of likely diversification errors of either the fund overweighting or the asset class underweighting varieties. Simple descriptive statistics calculated by ubiquitously available Excel software can produce such information. The analysis of sector fund overweighting and the analysis of asset class underweighting (contained above in Tables 4.1 and 4.2, respectively) are within reach of all fiduciaries (and their advisors). Yet, plan advisors rarely provide anything close to this type of information, much less suggest its potential normative implications.[43]

4.4   How Fiduciaries Can Identify Potential Fee and Exposure Mistakes

In addition to using straightforward descriptive statistics to analyze the likelihood of diversification mistakes, this section shows the feasibility of creating analogous figures to analyze the likelihood of fee and exposure mistakes. For example, Table 4.3 shows the share of participants who held a substantial proportion of their portfolios in high-fee funds.

The table shows that, in 2016, 78 percent of participants held all of their assets in funds charging fees between 50 and 75 basis points a year. Most of these participants were invested in the Fidelity target date funds, which charged an average of 57 basis points.[44] Actively managed funds with annual expense ratios above 50 or even 100 basis points might generate gross returns that justify their high fees. However, abundant evidence suggests that most retail investors are not attuned to the possible return-reducing effect of high-fee funds and tend to achieve lower returns when they invest in these higher-cost options.[45] Fiduciaries should be particularly concerned about individuals who invest a large proportion of their portfolio in high-cost funds. Similar to investing in precious metals or

---

[43] Fidelity, for example, only includes an analysis of "single-investment option holders" which would let the fiduciary learn how many participants are invested in a non-lifecycle fund, but it fails to identify whether any of these funds are unreasonably narrow, or the extent to which other participants overweight fund investments or underweight important asset classes. East Bay Municipal Utility District, *401(K)/457 Advisory Committee Meeting* (March 6, 2013), www.ebmud.com/files/2714/3172/5392/401k-457-staff-report-03-06-13.pdf.

[44] The Fidelity lifecycle funds with target retirement dates had expense ratios ranging from 45 to 64 basis points.

[45] James J. Choi, David Laibson & Brigitte C. Madrian, *Why Does the Law of One Price Fail? An Experiment on Index Mutual Funds*, 23 Rev. Fin. Stud. 1405 (2009); James Kwak, *Improving Retirement Savings Options for Employees*, 15 U. Pa. J. Bus. L. 483 (2013).

Table 4.3 *Analysis of high-fee portfolios*

| | | Share of investors with over specified % of assets invested in expense ratio range | | | | | | | | | | |
Expense ratio	Any amount	Over 10%	Over 20%	Over 30%	Over 40%	Over 50%	Over 60%	Over 70%	Over 80%	Over 90%	All assets
0.25% or lower	0.28	0.26	0.25	0.24	0.22	0.20	0.19	0.17	0.15	0.13	0.12
0.26%–0.50%	0.19	0.17	0.14	0.11	0.09	0.08	0.06	0.05	0.05	0.05	0.04
0.51%–0.75%	0.78	0.75	0.72	0.70	0.68	0.67	0.65	0.63	0.62	0.61	0.60
0.76%–1.00%	0.09	0.07	0.05	0.04	0.03	0.02	0.01	0.01	0.01	0.01	0.00
>1.00%	0.03	0.01	0.01	0.01	0.00	0.00	0.00	0.00	0.00	0.00	0.00

Note: As of January 31, 2016.

sector funds, an argument can be made for allocating relatively small proportions of savings in higher-cost funds, but it is less prudent for a participant to put all of her eggs in a high-fee basket.

Savvy investors need not fetishize low fees as a few basis points annually
will not substantially impact retirement accumulations, but portfolio fees
above 50 basis points annually are concerning and fees above 100 basis
points (aka 1%) create a strong presumption that a participant made a fee
mistake. Analyzing the average portfolio expense ratios of individual participants, we find that:

- 69 percent of participants had average annual portfolio expense ratios
  above 50 basis points;
- 1.8 percent of participants had average annual portfolio expense ratios
  above 75 basis points;
- 0.2 percent of participants had average annual portfolio expense ratios
  above 100 basis points.

The proportion of participants with average expense ratios over 75 percent are not as pronounced as the proportions of participants identified as
making likely diversification mistakes. But the important takeaway is that
this kind of inquiry is straightforward to perform and is a type of analysis
that fiduciaries can, and ought to, conduct.

Finally, fiduciaries should assess whether participants are making
"exposure mistakes" in choosing their portfolio allocations. For fiduciaries to assess whether a participant is making an exposure mistake,
they must have some sense of what a non-mistaken exposure to stock
market risk would be. Reasonable people can differ over some range
of exposures.[46] But there is a consensus that it is unreasonable for participants in their twenties and thirties to have low exposure (less than
20 percent) to equities and unreasonable for participants in their six-
ties and seventies to have high exposure (greater than 80 percent). A
central advantage of target-date funds is that they automatically adjust
participant exposure to the stock market – reducing the exposure as the
participant ages.

Fiduciaries can assess the likelihood of participant exposure mistakes
by calculating the proportion of assets invested in equities for different
age groups. Figure 4.2 does this by assessing the proportion of participant
portfolios that is invested in equities for different age groups:

---

[46] *See* Ayres & Fox, *supra* note 14 (describing three different exposure rules: the Merton rule,
the birthday rule, and the leverage lifecycle rule).

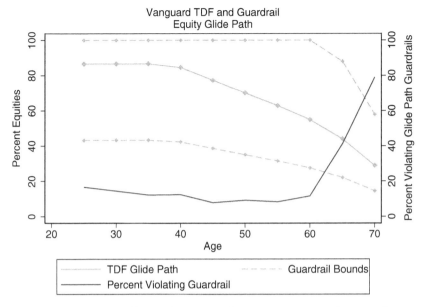

Figure 4.2   Proportion of target-date equities for participant ages, with potential upper and lower guardrail percentages

Table 4.4 suggests that exposure mistakes by older participants are in line with previous studies, but that exposure mistakes by young investors are not as pronounced as found in previous studies. For example, 41 percent of participants 70 or older held more than 80 percent of their portfolio in equities. Such large proportions in equities are presumptively problematic – especially because as discussed above, multiple studies suggest that people tend to hold similar proportions of equities inside and outside their tax-deferred plans.[47] The table also shows that less than 1 percent of participants under 30 had less than 20 percent of their portfolio in equities.

A natural way to assess the possibility of exposure mistakes for participants of every age is for fiduciaries to calculate the proportion of participants that depart substantially from the equity exposure found in the plan's target date funds. Figure 4.2 shows the equity exposure for UVA's Vanguard target date fund for different participant ages, and the two dotted lines represent equity portfolio proportions that are either half

---

[47] *See supra* note 71.

Table 4.4 *Analysis of equity exposure by participant age*

Age	Share of investors with X% in equities					
	No equities	< 10%	< 20%	< 80%	< 90%	< 95%
Under 30	0.3%	0.3%	0.3%	97.7%	4.1%	2.8%
30–39	0.5%	0.6%	0.6%	94.1%	8.4%	5.0%
40–49	0.7%	0.9%	0.9%	78.5%	18.2%	12.0%
50–59	1.7%	1.8%	2.0%	33.3%	22.2%	17.1%
60–69	3.1%	4.2%	4.2%	32.2%	24.6%	19.7%
70+	3.9%	3.9%	4.9%	41.2%	31.9%	27.9%

the target-date fund exposure (the lower bound) or twice the target date exposure (the upper bound, capped at 100 percent equity exposure).[48] In anticipation of our proposal to adopt limitations on plan allocations to curtail mistakes, we label these deviations from the target date exposure "guardrails." The figure shows that the Vanguard target-date funds would invest 87 percent of a 25-year-old's portfolio in stock, but only 44 percent for participants over 65 years old.

The orange line shows the proportion of participants of different age groups that have equity exposures that violate either the upper- or lower-bound guardrail. For example, the figure shows that 1.92 percent of 50-year-olds have less than the guardrail minimum exposure of 35 percent.[49] Overall, we find that 5.6 percent of participants have presumptively too little or too much exposure to the risk-premium offered by investments in equities. 2.2 percent of participants have allocations that fall below the reasonable lower bound and 3.4 percent of participants have allocations that exceed the reasonable upper bound. Restricting the upper-bound analysis to participants over the age of 60, who are the only participants who can violate our upper bound as it drops below 100 percent, we find that 34.3 percent of these participants violate the upper bound (and 5 percent violate the lower bound).

---

[48] The target-date funds are available in five-year increments so a participant targeting a retirement date halfway between the two available dates would need to split her portfolio between the two adjacent target date funds to achieve the exposure shown in the figure. The far right portfolio equity proportion is for the terminal "income" fund geared for participants who have retired.

[49] The maximum exposure guardrail for age 50 is 100 percent, so all violations in this age bracket are due to the minimum guardrail.

4.5 Assessing the Overall Prevalence (and Participant Characteristic Correlates) of Menu Misuse

Stepping back, our case study of the UVA plans has shown that straight-forward descriptive statistics about participant allocations can provide credible evidence of likely menu misuse. Table 4.5 summarizes the prevalence of diversification, fee, and exposure errors discussed above.

Because participants who stuck with target date funds avoid each and every error listed in the table, we focus on the percentage of non-TDF investing participants. With regard to diversification errors, we see that 11.8 percent of non-TDF participants have more than 10 percent of their portfolio invested in a narrow-gauged sector or regional fund, and that a whopping 65.4 percent of non-TDF participants have less than 20 percent of their equities portfolio invested in international stocks. With regard to fee errors, the table shows that 5.6 percent of non-TDF participants have portfolios with average annual expense ratios in excess of 75 basis points. And with regard to exposure errors, we find that 15.5 percent have equity allocations that fall outside the generous age-adjusted glidepath upper or lower bounds. Analyzed jointly, we find that 77.3 percent of all non-TDF participant portfolios make at least one of these four presumptive errors.

When it comes to the potential remedial actions that a fiduciary might take, it is important to keep in mind that 53.3 percent of UVA participants invest all of their plan savings in TDFs and thus do not fall prey to any of these errors. Looking across all UVA participants, we find that only slightly more than a quarter (27.1 percent) have portfolios making at least one of the four presumptive errors. Ignoring the participant failure to invest in the international equities asset class, we find that only 9.6 percent of participant portfolios are presumptively in error (by investing excess amounts in sector funds, having excessive portfolio expense ratios, or unreasonable exposure to equity risk). This is a substantial, but still limited percentage of participants. It becomes important when we consider guardrails later in Chapter 8 because it means that prophylactic portfolio limits can be instituted, which would leave almost 9 out of 10 participants' portfolio choices unaffected.

Before concluding, we briefly assess which types of participants are most likely to make the three core diversification, expense, and exposure errors (excluding, as before, the international equity underweighting). We do this by regressing various measures of error on the four participant attributes we observe in the UVA data for current employees: participant gender, participant age, participant plan balance, and UVA salary as of 2016.

Table 4.5 *Prevalence of likely diversification, fee, and exposure errors*

	% of non-TDF investors	% of all investors
Diversification Error: Single Sector Fund Overweighted	11.8	3.5
Diversification Error: International Equities Underweighted (Less than 20% Equities)	65.4	22.8
Expense Error: Average Expense Ratio Over 50 Basis Points	36.7	69.7
Expense Error: Average Expense Ratio Over 75 Basis Points	5.6	1.9
Any Non-International Error	27.9	9.6

Note: The shortfall in real estate is excluded because there is less consensus over what a reasonable allocation should be.

The table shows that men are 2.9 percentage points more likely than women to make at least one of the three allocation errors. Male participants might be disproportionately overconfident in their ability to pick investments that beat the market and accordingly are statistically more likely than women to overweight narrow-sector or region funds and are shown in the table to bear more uncompensated idiosyncratic risk.[50] Table 4.6 shows that older participants and those with higher plan assets also make more allocation errors.[51] Controlling for these other participant characteristics, higher-salaried people are more likely than lower-salaried

[50] This result that men are more allocatively error prone than women might at first seem surprising, given the national survey evidence that men are more comfortable than women in making financial decisions The 2019 Survey of Household Economics and Decision-making (SHED) found:

> Nearly 6 in 10 non-retirees with self-directed retirement savings expressed low levels of comfort in making investment decisions with their accounts…. Among those non-retirees with self-directed savings, women of all education levels, and men with less education, were not as comfortable as men with at least a bachelor's degree at managing their retirement investments.

supra note 19, at 4. In Chapter 9, we will learn that male, and higher educated employees disproportionately use and misuse the freedom of brokerage windows. When it comes to defined-contribution plans, having some discomfort might give women an advantage. Discomfort in affirmatively choosing retirement investments might disproportionately protect women by increasing the chance that they will stick with the better diversified QDIA.

[51] These results are highly statistically significant in most instances.

Table 4.6 OLS regression of presumptive errors on participant characteristics

	1	2	3	4	5
	At least one overweighted fund violation	Expense violation	Exposure violation	Any guardrail violation (1–3)	Idiosyncratic risk
Male	0.0116**	−0.00151	0.0216***	0.0292***	0.000247**
	(0.00581)	(0.00418)	(0.00664)	(0.00864)	(0.000118)
Age	0.000854***	0.000586***	0.00596***	0.00658***	−4.02e−06
	(0.000197)	(0.000142)	(0.000225)	(0.000293)	(4.01e−06)
Total assets	7.44e−08***	1.52e−09	2.24e−07***	2.86e−07***	−2.98e−10
	(1.99e−08)	(1.43e−08)	(2.28e−08)	(2.96e−08)	(4.05e−10)
Salary	9.16e−09	7.50e−08***	−4.22e−07***	−3.61e−07***	−1.31e−09
	(4.04e−08)	(2.90e−08)	(4.62e−08)	(6.00e−08)	(8.21e−10)
Constant	−0.0103	−0.0122*	−0.220***	−0.216***	0.00480***
	(0.00948)	(0.00682)	(0.0108)	(0.0141)	(0.000193)
Observations	6,628	6,628	6,628	6,628	6,628
R-squared	0.009	0.005	0.143	0.113	0.001

Standard errors in parentheses *** $p < 0.01$, ** $p < 0.05$, * $p < 0.1$.

people to invest in high-fee investments, which suggests some lower sensitivity to investment expenses. To be clear, we are not proposing that fiduciaries need to undertake this kind of regression analysis to correlate presumptive participant errors with participant characteristics. However, doing such analysis might allow a fiduciary to implement more effective soft guardrails, for example, by sending messages targeted at the concerns and situation of disproportionately affected participants.[52]

4.6   Conclusion

Two principal lessons follow from this chapter. First, there are good reasons for fiduciaries to be concerned that substantial minorities of participants will make substantial allocation errors. There is abundant evidence of diversification errors, fee errors, and exposure errors in multiple studies of allocations of individual retirement portfolios. Second, the types of tables laid out above simply showing the portion of participants over- or underinvested in particular types of funds are easily accomplished. While we argue that fiduciaries inform themselves of this type of analysis, the actual work of computation – like all the other plan analyses – will be completed by the plan advisors who provide plan information to fiduciaries on a quarterly basis. The marginal costs of providing such information would be close to nothing as advisors would incur one-off programming costs of producing a few more figures to be added to their quarterly reports. Table 4.6 by itself provides sufficient evidence to trigger fiduciary consideration of the streamlining and guardrailing remedies that we take up in Chapter 8. What is astounding is how utterly uninformed many fiduciaries are about the kinds of errors covered and uncovered in this chapter.[53] It does not take a Ph.D. in finance to see that something is terribly wrong with many retirement allocations.

---

[52] Soft guardrails are discussed below in Chapter 6.
[53] For example, an advisor like Fidelity fails to provide information on overweighting of funds or underweighting of assets. It provides no participant-level analysis of fees so one cannot access how many participants are paying in excess of particular benchmarks. Fidelity does a little better on exposure mistakes by telling fiduciaries the proportion of participants in various age ranges that fall outside the recommended stock exposure. *See, e.g., supra* note 45.

What More Fiduciaries Should Learn

Assessing Whether Participants' Portfolios Perform Poorly

While the weighting analysis of the last chapter can be sufficient standing alone to trigger a fiduciary duty to consider remedial actions, fiduciaries should also look to see whether individual participant portfolios produce persistently poorer performance than might have been obtained if they had made better allocation choices. The results of this analysis can strengthen fiduciary confidence that participant allocations are in error and that remedial interventions need to be considered. The last chapter focused on the inputs of participant choice, whereas this chapter focuses on the outcomes of that choice.

The central performance outcomes for an investment portfolio are risk and return. Accordingly, this chapter argues that fiduciaries should calculate the risk and return of each individual participant's portfolio. As in the last chapter, we show, using UVA data as a case study, that such an analysis can be done and can produce illuminating results. What's more, we'll show that it is within the capacity of plan advisors to provide such analysis. This chapter provides examples of such analysis that is already included in the materials advisors provide to plan fiduciaries.

This chapter is broken into four parts. First, we introduce the reader to risk and return scatterplot graphs, highlighting the competing advantages of ex ante and ex post analysis. Then we show how the scatterplots can be used to confirm that the portfolios identified in the last chapter are producing inferior performance compared to other, non-erroneous portfolios. The third part shows how risk and return can be combined into a summary measure of performance – the Sharpe ratio – to assess relative performance of different allocations. We conclude with an optional postscript on two additional performance measures that, while not necessary for fiduciaries to perform, could be used to further identify participants who have made substantial allocation errors.

5.1   Ex Ante vs. Ex Post Performance Analysis

Analyzing risk and return is a natural way to assess whether the presumptive mistakes uncovered in Chapter 4 lead to lower risk-adjusted returns than were achievable by plan participants who were not making erroneous allocations. We provide details on how to produce individual portfolio estimates of risk and return. Figure 5.1 shows the realized risk and returns of UVA participants for 2016.[1]

Each dot in the scatterplot represents the portfolio of a different participant. The annualized portfolio returns are plotted on the y-axis. Volatility of return can be measured with either the standard deviation or the variance of portfolio returns. The figure uses variance, displayed on the x-axis, as the measure of risk. The general upward slope of the mass of portfolio dots is a typical characteristic of such graphs because portfolios with higher risk tend to produce higher returns. In this risk/return graphical space, portfolios have superior outcomes if they have some combination of higher returns or lower risk – so graphically, portfolios appearing in the northwest are preferred to portfolios appearing in the south or the east.

Our analysis of Virginia plans is unusual for us as number crunchers because our own investments are included in the dataset. Quinn has been a participant in the plan since 2011 when he started teaching at UVA, and Ian has been a participant since 1990, when Ian was a visiting professor at the law school for a year. Quinn's plan balance is fully invested in the Vanguard 2045 target date fund, which corresponds to the scatterplot dot marked by a "Q"; while Ian's plan balance (which has grown to over $100,000) is fully invested in the Vanguard Total Stock Index. It shouldn't come as a surprise, given the last chapter's conclusions, that we have both invested in low-cost funds with broad exposure to U.S. equities. Ian's portfolio has a higher risk and return than Quinn's target date portfolio. Quinn's target date portfolio provides better diversification through its investments in bonds and international equities. When we identified participants with less than 20 percent of equities in international stock in the last chapter, Ian's portfolio was one of them. Ian's portfolio might also be criticized as having too much exposure to stock market risk given his age (63).[2]

---

[1] The figure uses the participant portfolios on January 1, 2016.

[2] However, it should be noted that Ian holds heterodox views about what types of exposure are reasonable for people at different ages and with different bequest intentions. *See* Ian Ayres and Barry Nalebuff, *Diversification across Time*, 39 J. PORT. MANAGEMENT 73 (2013).

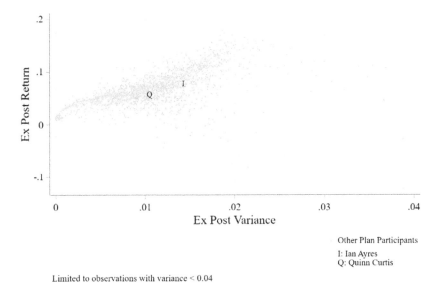

Other Plan Participants
I: Ian Ayres
Q: Quinn Curtis

Limited to observations with variance < 0.04

Figure 5.1   2016 Realized risk and return for UVA participants

Having introduced the end-product of risk and return analysis, let us turn to the question of *how* to actually produce the estimates underlying these kinds of figures. There are two widely used methods of estimating portfolio risk and return, which we refer to as the ex ante and ex post approaches. The ex ante approach uses what are called factor regressions to generate estimates of a portfolio's *expected* risk and return. The ex post approach calculates the *realized* risk and return of a portfolio for some period in the recent past. (The last figure was estimated using the ex post approach.)

Both types of risk and return analyses are standard tools of the trade – with ex ante estimates of expected risk and return more often undertaken by academics, and with industry participants more often implementing the ex post approach of calculating realized returns.[3] Both the ex ante and ex post approaches have distinct advantages. The principal advantage of the ex ante approach is that it avoids the possibility of non-representative

---

[3] For an example of the *ex ante* approach see Ning Tang, Olivia S. Mitchell, Gary R. Mottola & Stephen P. Utkus, *The Efficiency of Sponsor and Participant Portfolio Choices in 401(k) Plans*, 94 J. Pub. Econ. 1084 (2010) (estimating the mean and standard deviation of return for individual funds). For an example of the *ex post* approach, see Expert Report of Jonathan Reuter, Moitoso v. FMR LLC, No. 1:18-cv-12122-WGY (D. Mass. 2019) at ¶ 90 n.150, Exhibit 19a.

returns that can impact realized outcomes. The ex post approach tends to be calculated based on 3-5 years of monthly data. If, during that time period, a gold fund has an unexpectedly high return or low volatility, then the ex post analysis will inaccurately assess the prudence of overweighting this fund. The ex ante approach avoids this possibility by estimating the expected risk and return with less dependence on the particular realized returns over the past few years.[4] In contrast, the principal advantage of the ex post approach is that it is "non-parametric," in that it avoids relying on the parameters of a particular factor specification to predict expected risk and return. Factor models come in two broad classes: (1) models using Fama and French factors and similar variants, and (2) models using tradeable indexes.[5] Different factor specifications will lead to different predictions, and as Greg Mankiw has noted "expected returns are hard to measure precisely, even with a century or two of data."[6]

Happily, for the purposes of helping fiduciaries identify whether menu mistakes are producing suboptimal outcomes, both the ex ante and ex post approaches often produce similar conclusions. For example, Figure 5.2 shows examples of the ex ante and the ex post approach applied to UVA participant portfolios held in January 2016.

---

[4] The ex ante approach, which is also used to estimate fee and diversification losses in Chapter 2, begins by regressing monthly fund returns for each fund in a plan menu on certain factors that have been established as predictive of stock returns using up to 10 years of historic data. The coefficients from these factor regressions estimate the sensitivity of a fund's returns to particular factor effects. The approach then looks to average level of these factors over an even longer period often up to 25 years. Combining the estimated regression factor coefficients with the average factor levels allows the calculation of expected returns and risk of each portfolio. Formally, one can estimate the first and second moments for each fund: $\hat{\mu}_f = \hat{\beta}\hat{\mu}$, $\hat{\Sigma}_f = \hat{\beta}\hat{\Sigma}\hat{\beta}' + \hat{\Sigma}_{idio}$, where $\hat{\mu}_f$ is the vector of estimated mean excess return over all funds; $\hat{\Sigma}_f$ is the estimated variance-covariance matrix of excess returns over all funds; $\hat{\beta}$ is the vector of estimated factor coefficients from the factor regressions; $\hat{\mu}$ is the vector of mean excess returns for the factors; $\hat{\Sigma}$ is the variance-covariance matrix of the factors; and $\hat{\Sigma}_{idio}$ is the estimated idiosyncratic risk of funds estimated from the variance-covariance matrix of regression residuals. Based on the estimated mean and variance of returns over all funds, one can estimate moments of each participant portfolio: $\hat{\mu}_p = \omega'\hat{\mu}_f$, $\hat{\Sigma}_p = \omega'\hat{\Sigma}_f\omega$, $\hat{\Sigma}_{idio,p} = \omega'\hat{\Sigma}_{idio}\omega$, where ω is the weight vector over all funds in each participant's portfolio; $\hat{\mu}_p$ is each participant p's expected excess monthly return; and $\hat{\Sigma}_p$ is each participants expected variance in the monthly return. For details of such calculation see Tang, et al., *supra* note 71 at Appendix A; Ayres, *supra* note 97.

[5] Eugene F. Fama & Kenneth R. French, *Common Risk Factors in the Returns on Stocks and Bonds*, 33 J. FIN. ECON. 3 (1993); Expert Rebuttal Report of Ian Ayres, Moitoso v. FMR LLC, No. 1:18-cv-12122-WGY (D. Mass. 2019).

[6] Gregory Mankiw, *Budging (Just a Little) on Investing in Gold*, THE NEW YORK TIMES (July 27, 2013) at 3.

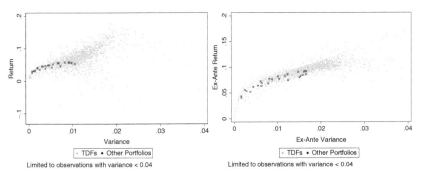

Figure 5.2 Ex ante and ex post estimates of risk and return
Note: Only portfolios with variance < 0.03 are shown.

The left side of the figure (Panel A) shows our ex ante estimates based on factor regressions using 8 index funds as the underlying factors, while the right side (Panel B) reports the ex post estimates from Figure 5.1 for the same participant portfolios for five years of realized returns.[7] Both analyses produce upward-sloping masses of dots, with some participant portfolios experiencing, expecting, and realizing higher risks and rewards. The ex post portfolio pattern is more diffuse than the ex ante pattern – as should be expected, given the idiosyncratic draws leading some portfolios to do better than expected and others to do worse.

The similarity in the approaches can also be seen in the estimated risk and return of the Fidelity target date portfolios (denoted by the symbol "X" in each panel). The target retirement dates that are further in the future have greater expected and realized risks and returns (due to their greater equity exposures). Both estimation approaches exhibit a substantial proportion of portfolios with higher risk and lower returns (to the southeast of the target date funds) than are achievable with the Fidelity target date funds – and both show some portfolios achieving superior risk/returns outcomes (to the northwest of the target date funds).

Our proposal allows fiduciaries to satisfy the requirement of assessing the risk and return by using either of these methods. The ex post approach avoids the need to justify a particular factor model and requires much less

---

[7] The following index funds are used as factors: iShares MSCI EAFE Index Fund, iShares Russell 1000 Value Index, iShares Russell 1000 Growth Index, iShares Russell 2000 Value Index, iShares Russell 2000 Growth Index, Vanguard Short-Term Bond Index Fund, Vanguard Total Bond Market Index Fund, and Vanguard Real Estate Index Fund.

sophistication.[8] Any reasonable sponsor can calculate the mean and standard deviation of monthly returns for the last 3 to 5 years. These types of charts are already created by plan service providers in various contexts,[9] including at least one financial firm's own employee plan.

5.2   Assessing the Performance of Problematic Portfolios

Risk and return scatterplots facilitate a visual comparison of different portfolios. By giving different types of portfolios a unique color, or shade, or character (e.g., Q or I), the viewer can more easily make out differences in performance. Fiduciaries should be concerned about groups of investors with risk/return combinations lying below or to the right of the risk/return combinations achievable by the default funds.

Assessing the risk and return of different portfolio groups can be usefully combined with the weighting analysis provided in Chapter 4. For example, Figure 5.3 shows in gold the ex post risk and return (for the period 2016–2017) of the participant portfolios that had more than 20 percent of their balance invested in the gold fund.

Even cursory examination of the figure confirms what theory suggests: participants sacrificed substantial opportunities for diversification. These goldbug portfolios are positioned to the south and east of what was achieved by peer participants, taking more risk for less return. The evidence of substantial overweighting, combined with this evidence of subpar performance measured by risk/return outcomes, creates a powerful basis for corrective action in the form of streamlining and/or guardrailing.

Distinguishing group markers can be used to evaluate other potential diversification and fee mistakes identified in Chapter 4. For example, the top panel in Figure 5.4 highlights portfolios that have more than 10 percent invested in a sector fund, and the bottom panel highlights the portfolios with average expense ratios in excess of 75 basis points.

---

[8] Fiduciaries relying on the ex post approach should qualitatively consider whether the realized risk and return of particular funds during the period analyzed have been historically anomalous and therefore might give inaccurate predictions of participants' likely future outcomes.

[9] Fidelity also provides such scatter plots to some of the outside plans that it advises. *See e.g.*, East Bay Municipal Utility District, *401(k)/457 Advisory Committee Minutes* (March 6, 2013). *See also* Aon Hewitt, *Customize DC Investments for Participant Success: How Custom Investment Options Improve Participant Outcomes* (2015) at 4, www.aon.com/attachments/human-capital-consulting/custom-dc-investments-for-participant-success-wp-july2015.pdf.

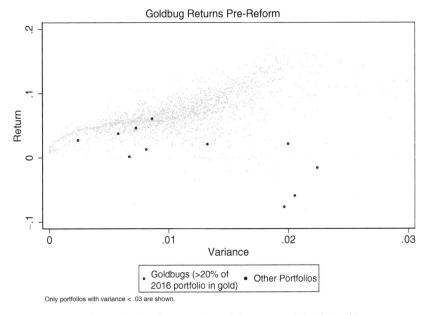

Figure 5.3 Analysis of risk and return of portfolios over-weighted in gold
Note: Only portfolios with variance < 0.03 are shown.

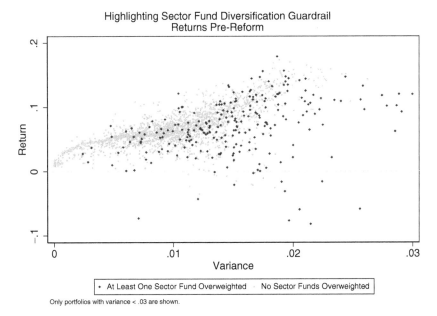

Figure 5.4 Risk and return analysis of portfolios with excessive sector fund or excessive fees
Note: Only portfolios with variance < 0.03 are shown.

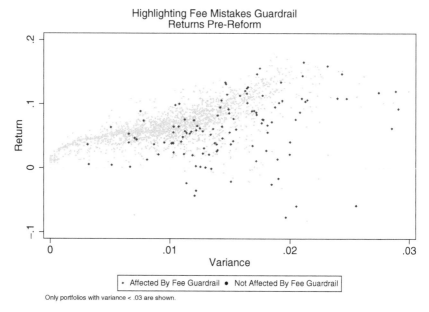

Figure 5.4 (cont.)

Both figures show a substantial number of portfolios lying to the right of and/or below those achievable with more diversified or lower-cost investments. The theory that overweighting sector investments sacrifices diversification is consistent with the portfolios with higher volatility – lying to the right of what was achievable. Similarly, the theory that excess expense ratios would drive down net returns is consistent with portfolios having lower returns – lying beneath what was achievable with non-presumptive investment mistakes.

A final point to emphasize about the foregoing figures is that the risk/return outcomes are not only inferior in that they lie to the south and east of what could be achieved with target date or more standard allocations, but the outcomes are themselves more dispersed. This greater volatility is another dimension of poor performance – risk-averse investors should be reluctant to take on allocations that increase the likelihood of wildly divergent risks and returns.

A less pronounced pattern can be seen when highlighting portfolios that are underweighted in international equities (less than 10 percent of the equity portfolio), as shown below in Figure 5.5.

The proportion of underweighted portfolios is so high that we display a random 10 percent subsample of such portfolios for ease of comparison.

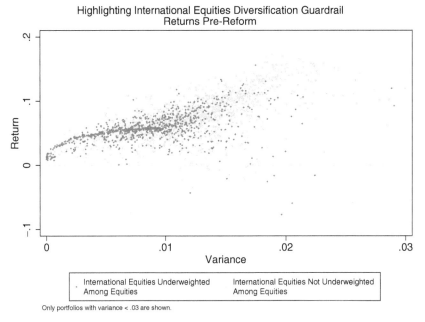

Figure 5.5   Risk and return analysis of portfolios with insufficient international equities
Notes: Only portfolios with variance < 0.03 are shown. TDFs are the black diamonds.
A 10 percent random sample of underweighted portfolios is displayed.

The comparison in Figure 5.5 suggests that international underweighting is not as substantial a concern. The underweighted funds have more dispersion in risk/return outcomes than other portfolios, but the dispersion is not decidedly worse than the self-directed portfolios that were not underweighted in international equities. This particular result might be driven by the unusually poor returns of international equities relative to domestic equities during this particular two-year time period.[10] Comparing the returns of two funds offered in the UVA menu at the beginning of 2016, we find that the Vanguard Total International Stock fund had an average annual return of 5.5 percent, while the Vanguard Total Stock Market Index (which almost exclusively consists of domestic equities) had an average annual return of 7.2 percent. The tendency of these two types of equities not to move in perfect lock step is the reason why international

---

[10]   We restrict our attention to this time period in order to compare the realized returns of the same UVA participants over the same time period after a new streamlined menu was implemented. *See infra* Chapter 8.

equities provide diversification benefits. These results show why fiduciaries might put less weight on the ex post risk and return analysis when the
performance analyzed is not representative of longer-term tendencies.

Finally, it is possible to analyze the position of portfolio allocations that
are presumptive exposure mistakes. Theory does not directly predict that
participants who make exposure mistakes will have inferior risk/return
outcomes, but rather that exposure mistakes are exemplified by young
participants holding too little stock and old participants holding too much
stock. Figure 5.6 highlights the risk and return of participants who either
fell below the minimum glidepath (top panel) or exceeded the maximum
glidepath (bottom panel) equity percentage tolerances discussed in the
last chapter.

Unsurprisingly, we see that young participants with too little stock market exposure have relatively low returns and that older participants with
too much stock-market exposure have relatively high returns. It is slightly
surprising to see the dispersion of risk associated with the low-exposure
portfolios (which is caused by some of these participants overweighting
non-equity asset classes such as real estate), as well as these portfolios' subpar returns (which are caused by overweighting money-market funds).
The bottom panel also shows a dispersion of risk and return among the
older participants with high-exposure portfolios (which is caused by their
overweighting of sector and region funds).

Stepping back, there is substantial evidence of inferior performance of
portfolios making diversification, expense, and exposure errors. One way
to summarize the shortfalls in performance is to estimate the proportions
of participant non-TDF portfolios that experienced better or worse risk
and return combinations relative to those produced by similarly aged TDF
investors. Table 5.1 does this by first dividing all participants into one of three
groups: (1) participants who were fully invested in TDFs; (2) non-TDF participants with allocations that make an expense, exposure, or (overweighting) diversification error[11]; and (3) non-TDF participants whose allocations
did not make one of these errors. We compare the realized risk and return of
each participant in the second and third groups to the risk and return they
would have realized had they been fully invested in their age-appropriate

---

[11] The underweighting of international stocks is not coded here as an allocation error
because scatterplots and Sharpe ratio analysis do not show that such underweighting
produced substantially inferior returns. An analogous version of the Table 5.2 which
includes underweighting this asset class as an erroneous allocation is included in our web
appendix.

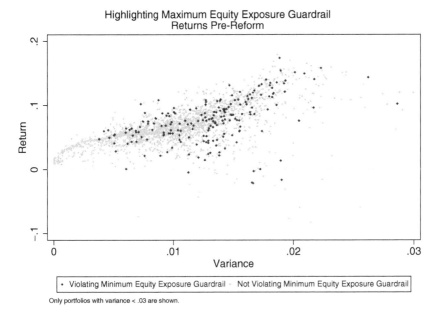

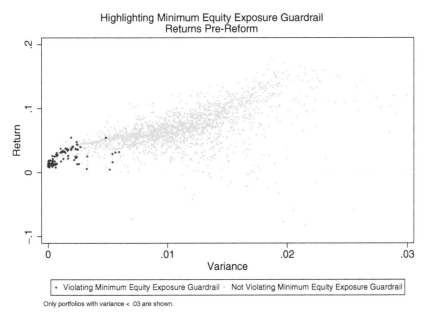

Figure 5.6 Risk and return analysis of portfolios with excessive or insufficient equity exposure

Note: Only portfolios with variance < 0.03 are shown.

Table 5.1 *Risk and return analysis of non-TDF portfolios with and without erroneous allocations in comparison to age-contingent TDFs*

Panel A. Non-TDF portfolios with erroneous allocations

	Category		Participants in each category, by age and overall					
TDF comparison	Risk	Return	25–35 (5.20%)	35–45 (14.33%)	45–55 (21.49%)	55–65 (21.63%)	65–75 (37.36%)	Overall
Better than TDF	Lower	Higher	2.7%	3.9%	0.0%	0.0%	0.0%	0.7%
Indeterminant	Lower	Lower	35.1%	34.3%	25.5%	27.9%	10.2%	22.1%
Indeterminant	Higher	Higher	45.9%	40.2%	42.5%	49.4%	73.3%	55.3%
Worse than TDF	Higher	Lower	16.2%	21.6%	32.0%	22.7%	16.5%	21.9%

Panel B. Non-TDF portfolios with non-erroneous allocations

	Category		Participants in each category, by age and overall					
TDF comparison	Risk	Return	25–35 (15.82%)	35–45 (25.22%)	45–55 (28.59%)	55–65 (24.30%)	65–75 (6.07%)	Overall
Better than TDF	Lower	Higher	6.1%	8.0%	1.7%	0.4%	0.6%	3.6%
Indeterminant	Lower	Lower	36.1%	49.9%	16.3%	13.0%	15.2%	27.0%
Indeterminant	Higher	Higher	18.6%	35.9%	66.6%	72.7%	67.8%	52.8%
Worse than TDF	Higher	Lower	39.2%	6.2%	15.4%	13.9%	16.4%	16.5%

Note: For each age bin, we compare participants to the Target Date Fund corresponding to the midpoint of the respective age bin – 2030 for 25–35, 2040 for 35–45, and so on. Participants below age 25 are mapped to the 25–35 bin and participants above 75 are mapped to the 65–75 age bin.

TDF (assuming they would retire at age 65) in Table 5.1. Individual portfolios with performance that lies strictly to the northwest (with lower risk and higher return) of TDF's risk and return are coded as having superior performance, while those portfolios lying strictly to the southeast (with higher risk and lower returns) are coded as having inferior performance.

The top panel of Table 5.1 analyzes the group of participants who chose non-TDF portfolios with at least one allocation error. It provides strong evidence that participants with erroneous allocations were far more likely to experience "worse than TDF" performance than to experience "better than TDF performance." Overall, 21.9 percent of participants with erroneous allocations experienced higher risk and lower returns than if they had invested in their age-cohorts' Fidelity TDF fund, while only 0.7 percent of these participants had higher returns and lower risk.[12] The results were particularly pronounced for those older than 45 – no one realized better-than-TDF performance, while 22.5 percent experienced worse-than-TDF performance. The bottom panel of Table 5.2 makes analogous comparisons for the group of participants with non-TDF portfolios that were not coded as erroneous allocations. This panel shows that even the non-erroneous allocations are more likely to underperform their age cohorts' TDFs. But the disparities are not nearly as pronounced. The ratio of "worse than" to "better than" proportions is 31.2 (21.9%/0.7%) for the portfolios with allocation errors, but only 4.6 (16.5%/3.6) for the portfolios without allocation errors.[13] Undertaking this kind of analysis is well within the reach of plan advisors. The structure of Table 5.1 is taken from an analogous table that Fidelity has provided on a quarterly basis to the fiduciaries of the plans that it advises.[14]

---

[12] Participants who experienced [lower risk and lower returns] or [higher risk and higher returns] cannot be characterized easily as better or worse than TDF performance because their performance is better on one dimension and worse on the other. Graphically, movements to the northeast or southwest are indeterminant. But again the substantial uncertainty across the "better than," "worse than," and "indeterminant" categories is itself a reason why target date investments might be preferred.

[13] Another way to interpret these results is to attribute all of the "better than" results to chance and to infer that the same proportion of "worse than" results were also a matter of chance. Non-random "worse than" portfolios might then be identified as the proportion in excess of the "better than" percentage. Under this interpretation, 21.2% of the erroneous allocations exhibited non-random "worse than TDF" performance (21.9%–0.7%), while only 12.9% of the non-erroneous allocations exhibited this non-random inferior performance (16.5%–3.6%).

[14] See East Bay Municipal Utility District, *401(K)/457 Advisory Committee Meeting* (March 6, 2013) at 68, www.ebmud.com/files/2714/3172/5392/401k-457-staff-report-03-06-13.pdf.

Table 5.2 *Analysis of Sharpe ratios for portfolios' likely allocation errors*

	Violating specific guardrail (mean)	All other portfolios (mean)	Delta (t-stat)
Diversification error: gold fund overweighted	0.040	0.546	−0.5058 (3.37)***
Diversification error: single-sector fund overweighted	0.496	0.550	−0.0536 (1.79)*
Expense error: average expense ratio over 75 basis points	0.381	0.555	−0.1743 (4.66)***
Diversification error: international equities underweighted (less than 20% equities)	0.634	0.399	0.2351 (13.40)***
Exposure error: equities share less than half or more than double benchmark TDF	0.352	0.593	−0.2408 (11.17)***
Any non-international error	0.398	0.612	−0.2140 (12.29)***
Any error	0.555	0.508	0.0474 (−2.23)**

*** $p < 0.01$, ** $p < 0.05$, * $p < 0.1$.

5.3 Analyzing the Risk-Adjusted Return of Portfolios with Sharpe Ratios

A standard way for financial economists to combine risk and return outcomes into a single statistic is to calculate Sharpe ratios.[15] The Sharpe ratio provides a measure of how much excess return an investor received for every increment of risk borne. The higher the ratio, the better the outcome. While the "better than"/"worse than" analysis of the last figure left more than half of the non-TDF participant allocation uncharacterized, Sharpe ratio analysis can help compare a broader swath of allocations. For example, it can help tell us whether a participant is experiencing sufficiently higher returns to justify the higher realized risk.

To calculate individual participant Sharpe ratios, all that is needed is to subtract the interest on government Treasury bills from the portfolio return and then divide by standard deviation of the portfolio return.

[15] *The Sharpe Ratio Defined*, MORNINGSTAR INVESTING CLASSROOM (2015), http://news.morningstar.com/classroom2/course.asp?docId=2932&page=4.

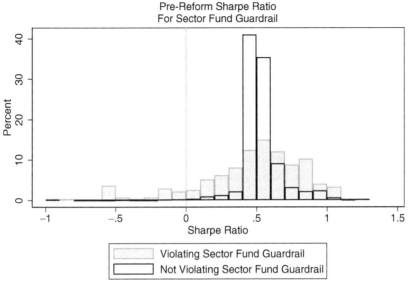

Sharpe ratios are bottom-coded at −1 and top-coded at 10.
With top- and bottom-coding, the Sharpe ratio for those violating the guardrail is and the Sharpe ratio for those not violating the guardrail is .

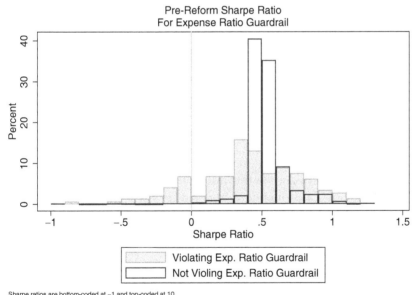

Sharpe ratios are bottom-coded at −1 and top-coded at 10.
With top- and bottom-coding, the Sharpe ratio for those violating the guardrail is and the Sharpe ratio for those not violating the guardrail is .

Figure 5.7   Analysis of Sharpe ratios for portfolios overweighted in sector funds and those with high fees

Note: Sharpe ratios are bottom-coded at −1 and top-coded at 10.

The resultant ratio can then be used as a kind of summary statistic for the portfolio's performance. One can assess whether different types of portfolios have different risk-adjusted returns. Figure 5.7 provides an example of this kind of analysis. It shows histograms of Sharpe ratios for the highlighted portfolio outcomes previously reported in Figure 5.6. The top panel compares the Sharpe ratios of portfolios that are over-weighted in sector funds to those that are not, and the bottom panel compares the Sharpe ratios of portfolios that have high expense ratios to those that do not.

Consistent with the visual scatterplots, these histograms show that portfolios suffering from diversification and fee mistakes experienced substantially lower and more dispersed risk-adjusted returns as measured by their Sharpe ratios.

It is also possible to simply compare the average Sharpe ratios for the problematic portfolios – making diversification, fee, and exposure errors – to the Sharpe ratios from portfolios not making these allocation errors. Table 5.2 does just this.

Table 5.2 shows that the Sharpe ratios for overweighted portfolios in narrow-sector or region funds have substantially lower and statistically different mean ratios than those that did not make this allocation error. The difference is even more pronounced for those portfolios that are overweighted in the gold fund. And as suggested by the foregoing histograms, we find statistically significant shortfalls in the average risk-adjusted returns of the portfolios that make expense errors or exposure errors. The only allocation error not giving rise to lower average Sharpe ratios relates to portfolios that underweight international equities. We find that portfolios underweighted in international stock outperformed those portfolios that did not underweight – probably because during this particular time period, international stock underperformed domestic equities.[16] Putting aside this international underweighting concern, Table 5.2 shows a pronounced and statistically significant shortfall in risk-adjusted returns (with Sharpe ratios of .44 vs. .54) for allocations that made a diversification, expense, or exposure error relative to those allocations that did not.

The weighting and risk/return analysis make a compelling case that a substantial proportion of participants were, as of January 2016, misusing the offered menu – particularly regarding overweighting narrow-gauged sector funds and incurring high-fee funds. While we have undertaken

---

[16] The Web appendix shows analogous histograms for the other dimensions of menu misuse.

more sophisticated analysis which we discuss in the Postscript to this chapter, we are cognizant of the costs of increased fiduciary process. For that reason, our proposal that fiduciaries assess the likelihood of menu misuse calls only for fiduciaries to calculate simple descriptive statistics. The weighting analysis discussed in Chapter 4 can answer straightforward questions:

- Are participants overweighting particular funds?
- Are participants underweighting important asset classes?
- Are participants overweighting high-cost funds?
- Are young participants investing too little in equities?
- Are older participants investing too much in equities?

The performance analysis, discussed in this chapter, simply asks fiduciaries to calculate mean and standard deviation of monthly portfolio returns and to use scatterplots to display these return and risk measures. It also calls upon fiduciaries to convert these risks and returns measures to Sharpe ratios to test whether problematic allocations produce inferior performance. All of this analysis – both the allocation weighting analysis and the performance analysis – can be done in any spreadsheet software such as Excel. Plan advisors, by incurring one-time programming costs, can automatically produce this analysis quarterly for all their plans at very low marginal cost. Our case study of UVA's participant data shows how powerful this type of analysis can be in producing actionable information and providing an impetus for corrective action. We have singled out UVA's plan not because it is an outlier, but precisely because its well-educated participants are likely, if anything, to make better choices than the participants of more representative, higher-cost plans. Indeed, as we show in the next chapter, participants in the UVA plan did substantially better when the university streamlined the menu in ways that made misuse less likely.

5.4 Postscript: More Sophisticated External and Regression-Based Assessments of Portfolio Performance

In this postscript, we discuss a variety of additional, more sophisticated assessments that might aid in determining whether remedial action is warranted. These assessments could be programmed, and thereby automated to scale across multiple plans every quarter. In part because these efforts require more contestable choices, and in part because the results maybe more difficult for fiduciaries to comprehend, we would not require that fiduciaries undertake them as a matter of course. However, fiduciaries may want to undertake these analyses on a contingent basis to provide themselves with additional information if the foregoing, less sophisticated analysis raises red flags concerning menu misuse. The results from these analyses should also be admissible in court to aid a trier of fact in determining whether a fiduciary acted imprudently in failing to mitigate evidence of participant allocation errors.

5.4.1   External Performance Comparisons

The performance analysis above has focused on internal measures of inefficiency. Figure 5.7, for example, compared the performance of participant portfolios making various allocation errors to the performance of portfolios that did not make these errors. Table 5.2 tests for shortfalls in performance relative to what might be achieved if the parties had allocated their retirement savings to the Fidelity TDFs, the plan's Default Investment Alternative (QDIA).

In addition to comparing the performances of different portfolios within the plan, it is possible to compare the performance of participant portfolios to that of what is available outside the plan. Such external comparisons are a standard part of the information that advisors provide to plan fiduciaries regarding the performance of individual funds within the plan's menu. For example, an advisor might provide "the fund's total-return percentile rank relative to all funds that have the same Morningstar Category."[17] An important limitation with the external competitors currently provided by paid advisors to plan fiduciaries is that they tend to include all the funds in the investment-style category – regardless of how excessive their fees and regardless of how little traction the funds have achieved in acquiring assets under management. The current information could be usefully supplemented by including performance comparisons to low-cost indexes and/ or funds with substantial assets under management.[18]

As applied to the UVA plan, our central concern with the foregoing analysis is that internal comparisons to the Fidelity TDFs limit the fiduciaries' ability to assess whether lower-cost TDFs might have produced even better risk and return combinations than the plan's high-cost target date funds. Charging more than 70 basis points for a target date fund QDIA is problematic and there are high-quality alternatives in the marketplace

---

[17] East Bay Municipal Utility District, *supra* note 20, at 35.
[18] Just changing the current analysis to "asset under management" weighted percentile might provide a much clearer competitive picture.

Table 5.3 *Sharpe ratio comparison (fidelity vs. lower-cost external options)*

Sharpe ratio is computed over a five-year period (2012–16) with monthly returns for the analogous Target Date Funds. The second row takes the average across Vanguard, TIAA, and Schwab, and the last column represents the equal-weighted average across the four TDFs.

	2010	2020	2030	2040	Overall
Fidelity	0.74	0.69	0.63	0.60	0.66
Vanguard/TIAA/Schwab	0.99	0.86	0.78	0.74	0.84

that have less than half the expenses of Fidelity's Freedom Fund TDFs. Table 5.3 compares the 5-year (2011–2016) Sharpe ratio of 4 Fidelity Freedom funds to the average TDF Sharpe ratios of three substantial, low-cost competitors: Vanguard, TIAA, and Schwab.

The figure shows that the external TDFs experienced sustained improvements in risk-adjusted return. This superior performance should be expected given that low-cost TDFs charge on average 20 basis points less annually than their Fidelity counterpart funds.

5.4.2   Regression-Based Performance Measures

Even though the technological capacity and human capital to execute regressions are becoming increasingly widespread,[19] we have shied away from calling upon fiduciaries (and their advisors) to undertake more sophisticated forms of econometric analysis. Thus, we would allow risk and return analysis to be accomplished with ex post computation of realized returns instead of an ex ante approach of estimating a Fama and French factor model to predict expected risks and returns.

However, if one takes on the difficulties of specifying a particular factor-model and estimating it, an additional payoff is that the residual mean square error of the regression constitutes a measure of the idiosyncratic risk of particular participant portfolios.[20] While this analysis is dependent on particular factor models,[21] it can provide a powerful measure of the

---

[19] One can, e.g., run ordinary least square regressions in Excel.

[20] Ning Tang, Olivia S. Mitchell, Gary R. Mottola & Stephen P. Utkus, *The Efficiency of Sponsor and Participant Portfolio Choices in 401(k) Plans*, 94 J. Pub. Econ. 1084 (2010).

[21] Because there is no single best-factor model for all situations, it is useful to show that the results are "robust" to alternative factor specifications.

Table 5.4 *Estimated mean idiosyncratic of participant portfolios with and without different types of allocation errors*

	Portfolios With Specific Allocation Error Mean	All other Portfolios Mean	Delta (t-test)
Diversification error: gold fund overweighted	0.0563184	0.004501	0.0518 (−67.02)***
Expense error: average expense ratio over 75 basis points	0.0158782	0.004392	0.0115 (−38.48)***
Exposure error: equities share less than half or more than double benchmark TDF	0.0044091	0.00462	−0.0002 (1.10)
Diversification error: international equities underweighted (less than 20% equities)	0.004808	0.004548	0.0003 (−2.47)**
Diversification error: single sector fund overweighted	0.0144126	0.004248	0.0102 (−48.47)***
Any non-international error	0.0080283	0.004246	0.0038 (−26.25)***

*** $p < 0.01$, ** $p < 0.05$, * $p < 0.1$.

risks borne by participants that go uncompensated. The earlier scatterplot and Sharpe analyses also provide evidence of under-performing UVA participant portfolios. However, analyzing the residuals of factor regressions can more readily distinguish between compensated and uncompensated portions of portfolio risk.

Using the same eight-index factors that we used above to produce Figure 5.2, we can assess whether portfolios with different allocations are estimated to have different expected idiosyncratic risk. Table 5.4 undertakes this analysis regarding the core allocation errors analyzed above.

Theory predicts that allocations that make diversification errors will be exposed to higher non-systematic (idiosyncratic) risk. That is exactly what our estimates find as well. Portfolios that are overweighted in the gold fund have an average expected risk that is tenfold larger than those that are not overweighted and this difference is highly statistically significant. The excess risk borne by a broader category of participants who overweight a narrow sector or regional fund is not as pronounced, but it is statistically significant. In contrast, participant portfolios that are underweighted in international equities are estimated to have a small increased uncompensated risk, but this difference is only marginally significant (p < 10%). Theory does not suggest that expense or exposure errors lead to increased risk-bearing. However, as shown in the scatterplots, participant allocations with expense errors were estimated to bear substantially higher idiosyncratic risk than those that did not make expense errors. This difference is statistically significant and on par with the extra risk borne by participants who overweighted sector and region funds. The high-expense portfolios were therefore hurting participants not just with reduced expected returns, but also with increased uncompensated risk.

Finally, it is possible to evaluate the efficiency of a participant's allocation by flipping around the factor regressions, and regressing the excess returns of each of the factors on the excess returns of the funds in the participant's portfolio.[22] The estimated intercept of each of these regressions is the Jensen's alpha for a particular benchmark. A finding of one or more statistically positive alphas is evidence that the set of funds in that participant's portfolio fails to "cover or span the global (liquid) capital markets."[23] A finding of portfolio inefficiency is an indication that the expected performance of a participant's portfolio could be improved by allocating some funds to the positive-alpha factor.[24] Spanning tests of this kind are yet another, more sophisticated way to bring in external benchmarks of efficiency – in this case, factor indexes that might have been beneficially added to participant portfolios.

---

[22] Frans DeRoon et al., *Testing for Mean-Variance Spanning with Short Sales Constraints and Transaction Costs: The Case of Emerging Markets*, 56 J. FIN. 721 (2001).

[23] Tang, *supra* note 26, at 7.

[24] As explained by Tang and her co-authors, the formal statistical test is:

$$\xi = \min_{(\alpha \le 0)} (\hat{\alpha} - \alpha)' \text{Var}[\hat{\alpha}]^{-1} (\hat{\alpha} - \alpha),$$

where $\hat{\alpha}$ is an 8*1 vector of estimated Jensen's alphas. For the critical value used in the test, we adopt the lower/upper bounds suggested by Kodde and Palm (1986) and run 1,000 simulations to see if the test statistic falls within the critical value bounds. The significance level of the test is 5%.

Tang et al., *supra* note 26, at 1084. *See* David Kodde & Franz C. Palm, *Wald Criteria for Jointly Testing Equality and Inequality Restrictions*, 54 ECONOMETRICA 1243 (1986).

6

What Fiduciaries Can Do to Remedy Menu Misuse

Different Ways to Implement Streamlining and Guardrailing

The foregoing two chapters have shown that it is possible for fiduciaries to identify menu mistakes and estimate the effect of those mistakes on the risk and return of plan participants. In this chapter, we describe two broad types of interventions that a fiduciary might use to address menu misuse. The first is streamlining, which in its simplest form is just the elimination of problematic funds from the plan menu. When eliminating a fund, fiduciaries must confront the questions of whether to replace it with another fund or simply shrink the menu, as well as how to handle existing allocations to the fund. Another option we examine is the more novel approach of guardrails – the judicious limitation of allocations over the plan menu to reduce the likelihood of mistakes. We describe in some detail the decisions that need to be made in implementing these interventions and the circumstances that are likely to make one intervention most appropriate.

6.1 Streamlining (and Mapping)

We tackle streamlining first. On its face, streamlining might solely imply reducing the number of funds available on a plan menu. However, we take the term to also comprise possibly substituting old funds with new funds on the menu, as well as design choices concerning the default "mapping" of existing fund balances to different funds (unless the plan receives alternative directives from the participant). Streamlining in the narrower sense of removing funds from a menu can provide obvious benefits with regard to both diversification and fee errors. For example, if a plan menu offers a fund in which no reasonable participant should invest because it is dominated by another menu fund providing similar investments with a substantially lower expense ratio, then fiduciaries can improve welfare by removing the dominated fund. In Chapter 2, we found that historically 52 percent of plans offered such "dominated" funds and that, when offered, 11.5 percent of plan assets were mistakenly allocated to these funds.[1] Removing dominated and other high-cost funds and mapping the existing balances in the dominating fund to lower-cost funds will likely reduce fee mistakes.

Removing narrow-gauged sector funds (and mapping existing balance to a broader-based fund) is likely to reduce diversification mistakes. Our ongoing example of the participants who sacrificed diversification by overweighting the Fidelity Gold Fund would likely achieve superior risk and return outcomes if this fund was simply removed from the plan menu and affected investments were by default transferred to one of the plan's QDIA target date funds.

While removing funds is a natural way to respond to the problem of the sector fund overweighting problem described above, redesigning menu options can also help mitigate the problem of asset class under-weighting. For example, if a substantial number of plan participants are underweighted in international equities, merely adding an additional international equity option to the fund menu may not overcome partici-pants' home-country bias.[2] But streamlining together with menu redesign can combat the problem of asset-class underweighting by substituting funds for the streamlined funds that include the underweighted asset class as part of the fund portfolio. AON Hewitt describes this stacking of asset classes within individual funds as "menu simplification" and provides an example of combining "three asset classes [Global Equity, Real Estate, and Hedge Funds] into a single diversified objective-based growth fund."[3] Participants who would not have been willing to invest in global equities or a real estate fund might nonetheless be willing to allocate some of their contributions to a fund labeled as having a "growth" objective.[4]

---

[1] Ian Ayres and Quinn Curtis, *Beyond Diversification: The Pervasive Problem of Excessive Fees and 'Dominated Funds' in 401(k) Plans*, 124 Y ALE L. J. (2014) at 1506.

[2] One superficial reason for home-country bias is the risk concern of foreign currency fluc-tuations. Few investors know that many foreign equity indexes hedge foreign currency risk with the use of derivatives. Chana R. Schoenberger, Currency Risk in Mutual Funds: Take It or Hedge?, W ALL ST. J. (August 4, 2013).

[3] Aon Hewitt, *Customize DC Investments for Participant Success: How Custom Investment Options Improve Participant Outcomes* (2015), at 7, www.aon.com/attachments/human-capital-consulting/custom-dc-investments-for-participant-success-wp-july2015.pdf.

[4] There is an ethical concern about labeling a fund as growth and then investing the under-lying assets in asset categories (global equities, and real estate) that might be well justi-fied on diversification grounds but are not in fact particularly growth-oriented. Fiduciaries might limit and guide participant choice through various forms of libertarian paternalism. For example, substituting a global equities fund (which invests in assets around the world including the home country) for an international equities fund (which invests exclusively

The decision to eliminate a particular fund from the plan's menu is far from an all-or-nothing decision for the fiduciary. For example, "Investment Policy Statements," which fiduciaries adopt to summarize their underlying philosophy and processes for the selection, monitoring, and evaluation of investment options, often call for the investment committee fiduciaries to consider the following six options:

1. Remove the fund from the probationary period if fund performance warrants.
2. Supplement the investment option(s) with one or more alternative investment option(s) for that category.
3. Close ("freeze") an investment option to new investments and future deferrals.
4. Replace the investment option with one or more alternative investment option(s) for that category.
5. Map future contributions to an alternative fund if the current fund has been closed to new investments ("frozen").
6. Eliminate the investment option.[5]

Merely freezing the fund to block future investments may reduce the backlash of investors who are psychologically anchored to their existing funds.[6]

Streamlining can powerfully respond to menu mistakes by dynamically remapping participants toward more suitable allocations. Launching a

---

in non-home-country assets) might induce participants to increase their holdings of international equities because they feel more comfortable with funds that include home country investments. *See* Norman Strong and Xinzhong Xu, *Understanding the Equity Home Bias: Evidence from Survey Data*, 85 REV. ECON. & STAT. 307, 312 (2003). *See also* Capital Insights, *How to Help Participants Make Better 401(k) Choices*, Capital Group (June 16, 2021). (suggesting a form of streamlining in which global dividend, U.S. large cap and non-U.S. equity asset classes are combined into a single "Global equity" fund). Guiding choice through misleading labels is more problematic. *See* Cass R. Sunstein & Richard H. Thaler, *Libertarian Paternalism*, 93 AM. ECON. REV. 175, 179 (2003).

[5] East Bay Municipal Utility District, 401(K)/457 Advisory Committee Meeting (March 6, 2013) at 136 www.ebmud.com/files/2714/3172/5392/401k-457-staff-report-03-06-13.pdf. Investment committee often only come to this point after establishing a probationary period that generally lasts two-three calendar quarter to continue review of underperforming fund. *Id.* Some investment policy statements say that during this probationary period the investment committee plans *may* "also include a review of the fund's utilization by Plan participants." But as emphasized above, participant-level information on the fund's utilization is rarely provided by the advisor to the investment committee and does not play a role in the decision to undertake various forms of streamlining.

[6] See the next chapter for a discussion of investor pushback to menu modifications, which can be a significant practical obstacle to streamlining.

new menu with only modest changes can produce profound reductions in diversification, fee and exposure mistakes if pre-existing balances are by default mapped toward low-cost, well-diversified target date funds. This is well understood by some plan advisors who characterize re-enrollment as "the Optimization Button" that can reset problematic allocations.[7] One could imagine a plan that periodically remaps assets toward more prudent allocations unless the participant periodically makes affirmative choices to the contrary. In other words, dynamic remapping of this kind need not be made contingent on changing the menu of fund offerings. We say more about this as a kind of guardrail in the next section.

The examples presented here show that streamlining can come in many varieties. A plan's menu can be redesigned to have fewer or different offerings. A particular fund can be closed to additional contributions, or it can be eliminated from the menu altogether. Moreover, mapping also comes in many shapes and sizes. Balances can by default be remapped to other funds even if there are no changes to the underlying menu. Most of these variants already exist in common practice, representing legally feasible forms of corrective action.

6.2 Guardrails

The basic idea of guardrails is to protect participants from engaging in menu misuse while preserving more of their allocative liberty. Instead of removing gold funds from the menu altogether, a guardrail intervention would merely cap the allocation that can be made to the fund. Guardrailing is attractive when a fund has a legitimate role in adding diversification but is presumptively inappropriate for a large allocation. By using a guardrail, a plan can preserve the potentially valuable option to use a fund menu appropriately, while avoiding misuse simply by ruling out problematic allocations.

The potential advantage of guardrailing relative to streamlining is that it preserves the freedom of rational investors to make a range of reasonably different allocation choices. Guardrailing represents a classic example of what George Loewenstein and coauthors call "asymmetric paternalism" in that it can be targeted to disproportionately protect participants with severe cognitive biases without substantially limiting the allocation choices of more rational participants.[8]

---

[7] Aon Hewitt, *supra* note 4.
[8] George Loewenstein et al., *Regulation for Conservatives: Behavioral Economics and the Case for Asymmetric Paternalism*, 151 U. PA, L. REV. 1211, 1254 (2003).

The introduction pointed out that guardrails already impact retirement accounts in one important dimension. Most plans adopt guardrails with regard to participants' choice of passwords to access their accounts online.[9] Requiring a minimum number of letters and characters and prohibiting certain sequences is standard practice. Password regulation is a useful metaphor we can draw on to suggest different types of guardrail protections. For example, just as password systems provide a range of softer and harder limitations, guardrail protections for participant allocations also can be softer- or harder-edged.

6.2.1   Informational Guardrails

At the softer end of the intervention, imagine a plan which merely provides allocation guidance (just as many platforms offer advice on the attributes of a strong password). Alternatively, plans might offer feedback to proposed allocations (just as some platforms will characterize proposed passwords as "very strong" or "weak"). Plans might go further and react to proposed allocations by suggesting an alternative, more reasonable allocation, that comes as close as possible to the participant's allocation without, say, sacrificing as much diversification. Showing how a participant's proposed allocation has fared in terms of return and risk over the past 5 years relative to the plan default or some alternative allocation might prove an especially useful disclosure. Feedback might also usefully deploy peer comparison, letting participants know how similar people have benefitted from allocating their savings differently.[10] Providing this kind of default counteroffer might nudge participants away from menu misuse just as some platforms suggest alternative passwords or user IDs.[11]

Informational guardrails are already in place with regard to company stock. The Pension Protection Act (PPA) of 2006 requires fiduciaries to send participants quarterly benefits statements that must include:

---

[9] Later in Chapter 8, we will also describe how many plans with company stock in their plan menu have capped the percentage of contributions that can be invested in that menu option to prevent overweighting of a single equity.

[10] Ian Ayres and Berry Nalebuff, *Peer Pressure*, FORBES MAGAZINE (April 11, 2005) www.forbes.com/forbes/2005/0411/118.html?sh=2ce23e8b33cd. *See also* Ian Ayres, Sophie Raseman and Alice Shih, *Evidence from Two Large Field Experiments that Peer Comparison Feedback Can Reduce Residential Energy Usage*, 29 J. LAW, ECON. AND ORG. 992, 1022 (2013).

[11] For example, Google suggests alternative Gmail usernames if a requested username is unavailable. *See* accounts.google.com/signup/v2/webcreateaccount?flowName=GlifWeb SignIn&flowEntry=SignUp.

[an] explanation, written in a manner calculated to be understood by the average plan participant, of the importance, for the long-term retirement security of participants and beneficiaries, of a well-balanced and diversified investment portfolio, including a statement of the risk that holding more than 20 percent of a portfolio in the security of one entity (such as employer securities) may not be adequately diversified.[12]

The Department of Labor has provided in a Field Advisory bulletin safeharbor language that includes the warning: "If you invest more than 20 percent of your retirement savings in any one company or industry, your savings may not be properly diversified."[13] While this admonishment helpfully goes beyond company stock to warn against investing in a single industry, its formulation ("may not be proper") is rather tepid and insufficiently prominent. It is also worth mentioning that this "warning" comes in the middle of more than 200 words. The PPA also quixotically requires the quarterly benefit statement to include "a notice directing the participant or beneficiary to the Internet website of the Department of Labor for sources of information on individual investing and diversification."[14] The materials at the Departments' website are worse than unhelpful. The first mention of portfolio allocation advises:

> Generally speaking, you should put some of your money in cash, some in bonds, some in stocks, and some in other investment vehicles.... [H]ow

---

[12] 29 U.S.C. §1025.
[13] Dep't of Labor, Field Assistance Bulletin 2006–03. www.dol.gov/agencies/ebsa/employers-and-advisers/guidance/field-assistance-bulletins/2006-03 The full model disclosure reads:

> To help achieve long-term retirement security, you should give careful consideration to the benefits of a well-balanced and diversified investment portfolio. Spreading your assets among different types of investments can help you achieve a favorable rate of return, while minimizing your overall risk of losing money. This is because market or other economic conditions that cause one category of assets, or one particular security, to perform very well often cause another asset category, or another particular security, to perform poorly. If you invest more than 20% of your retirement savings in any one company or industry, your savings may not be properly diversified. Although diversification is not a guarantee against loss, it is an effective strategy to help you manage investment risk. In deciding how to invest your retirement savings, you should consider all of your assets, including any retirement savings outside of the Plan. No single approach is right for everyone because, among other factors, individuals have different financial goals, different time horizons for meeting their goals, and different tolerances for risk. It is also important to periodically review your investment portfolio, your investment objectives, and the investment options under the Plan to help ensure that your retirement savings will meet your retirement goals. *Id.*

[14] 29 U.S.C. §1025.

> much of your retirement nest egg should you put into stocks: 10 percent …
> 30 percent … 75 percent? How much into bonds and cash? Your decision
> will depend on many factors …[15]

There is no discussion of different glide paths or of target date funds;
and the advice is implicitly skewed toward overly conservative options.
It begins its list of asset classes with cash (which many participants may
not understand to mean money market investments) and then anchors
on the possibility that investing only 10 percent in equities might be reasonable. Should a 25-year-old really be told that bonds and cash should
be among their retirement account allocations? Should 75 percent be the
highest listed commitment to equities? While these current disclosures
are unlikely to be effective in changing participant allocations,[16] the larger
point is that there is nothing radical about requiring participant warnings
that particular allocations may not be proper. The plan fiduciary, and not
the Department of Labor, has the information necessary to present this
type of information effectively. We believe they should do so.

6.2.2   Default Rule Guardrails

The enlightened use of defaults is one of the most powerful soft guardrails.
Establishing a high-quality target-date fund as the default investment is
in itself a soft guardrail that has produced substantial reductions in diversification and exposure errors. Scholars have found that the adoption of
QDIA funds have produced dramatic improvements in portfolio choice,
particularly with regard to diversification and exposure errors and that the
"adoption of low-cost target-date funds [as the plan default] may enhance

---

[15] EBSA, *Savings Fitness: A Guide to Your Money and Your Financial Future*, U.S. Department of Labor (2019) www.dol.gov/sites/dolgov/files/EBSA/about-ebsa/our-activities/resource-center/publications/savings-fitness.pdf at 17. This website booklet also includes a company stock warning: "Financial experts often recommend that you don't let your account get overloaded with company stock, particularly if the account makes up most of your retire-ment nest egg. Too much of a single stock increases risk." *Id.* However, this warning fails to advise how much is too much.

[16] James J. Choi, David Laibson, & Brigitte C. Madrian, *Are Empowerment and Education Enough? Underdiversification in 401(k) Plans*, BROOKINGS PAP. ECON. ACT. 151, 198 (2007). (finding scant empirical support for the "empower and educate" regulatory approach at reducing 401(k) employer stock holdings). *See* Olivia S. Mitchell & Stephen P. Utkus, *Company Stock and Retirement Plan Diversification*, PENSION RESEARCH COUNCIL WORKING PAPER No. 2002–4 (2002) (raising the possibility of more pervasive company stock warnings "incorporated in all communications media, whether print, telephone, meet-ings or the Internet.").

retirement wealth by as much as 50 percent over a 30-year horizon.[17] This impact is centered on new employees, but as mentioned above, streamlining combined with default mapping to target date fund can produce similar benefits for incumbent participants.[18]

6.2.3 Altering Rule Guardrails

An obvious limitation of informational warnings is that they might never be read. However, information feedback and defaults can be combined with a variety of "error-reducing" altering rules to enhance their prophylactic effects.[19] Just as operating systems often require confirmations ("Are you sure?") before certain non-reversible actions (e.g., reformatting a hard drive), plans might double-check that participants really want to choose an allocation that significantly sacrifices diversification. Alternatively, an altering rule might require a participant to make a representation that she has a certain level of sophistication or sufficient outside assets to render the plan allocation reasonable. A plan might even require participants to pass an objective test to establish that they have sufficient financial sophistication before allowing them to make an esoteric allocation.[20]

6.2.4 Dynamic Default Guardrails

An important new type of intervention we propose is to establish a default that periodically remaps presumptively erroneous allocations unless the

---

[17] Olivia S. Mitchell & Stephen P. Utkus, *Target-Date Funds and Portfolio Choice in 401(k) Plans*, JOURNAL OF PENSION ECON. AND FINANCE 1, 18 (2021).

[18] Hewitt, *supra* note 3. One might also consider the use of "active choice" guardrails which force employees to explicitly state their allocation preferences. Such systems are sometimes characterized as "default-free" even though as a formal matter they are penalty defaults in which by default the employees cannot enroll (or sometimes cannot be paid) unless they state their preferences. Choi, *supra* note 15, at 154. However, we are reluctant to propose "active choice" guardrails because we worry that many employees will choose poorly. "[D]efault-free systems will work only if employees are likely to make good decisions when forced to do so." *Id.*

[19] Ian Ayres, *Regulating Opt Out: An Economic Theory of Altering Rules*, 121 YALE L. J. 2032 (2012) (Altering rules "establish the necessary and sufficient conditions for displacing a default"). There are a "variety of altering interventions – including 'train-and-test' altering rules, 'clarity-requiring' altering rules, 'password' altering rules, and 'thought-requiring' altering rules – that might be deployed to reduce altering error." *Id.*

[20] *Id.*; Ayres & Curtis, *supra* note 1; Luis A. Aguilar, *Revisiting the "Accredited Investor" Definition to Better Protect Investors*, U.S. SECURITIES & EXCHANGE COMMISSION (2014), www.sec.gov/news/statement/spch121714laa.html.

participant explicitly objects to the remapping. For example, a plan might, on a quarterly or annual basis, move excessive allocations to a sector fund to the QDIA whenever the sector fund balance exceeds a certain percentage of the portfolio. Alternatively, the plan might remap the allocation to a likely less-erroneous allocation that resembles the status quo allocation, moving over-allocations from a tech sector fund to a more diversified growth fund, for example.

In Chapter 9, we will discuss how a dynamic default guardrail could be usefully applied to brokerage windows, where substantial proportions of invested funds can languish in zero-interest money market accounts. Plans might send participants with substantial money market balances notice that their funds will be remapped to the QDIA unless the participant objects. For allocations that seem clearly problematic (like holding money-market funds through a brokerage window subject to a 25 basis-point fee), it is reasonable for a fiduciary to require participants to repeatedly confirm across time that they really want to invest their savings in a heterodox way.

The idea of dynamic guardrails is closely related to the "Sell More Tomorrow" proposal of Nobel-prize-winning behavioral economist, Richard Thaler, and his frequent financial co-author, Shlomo Benartzi.[21] Their proposal takes aim at the diversification error that occurs when participants overweight company stock. They point to several reasons for this error, including overconfidence and "familiarity bias."[22] Moreover, for those who are already overinvested, it is difficult to overcome the power of inertia, and are reluctant to take actions they will regret if the stock price shoots up. Thaler and Benartzi suggest offering to employees the option of gradually selling their company stock over time. The proceeds of these sales could be invested in diversified assets, and the sales could continue until the participant's holdings are reduced to some targeted percentage. Thaler explained:

---

[21] Richard H. Thaler & Shlomo Benartzi, *Save More Tomorrow: Using Behavioral Economics to Improve Diversification in 401(k) Plans: Solving the Company Stock Problem*, 112 J. POL. ECON. 164, 187 (2004).

[22] They are particularly overconfident about the stability of investing in their own company's stock with "[n]ine out of ten plan participants believing that their company stock is at least as safe as a diversified fund with many different stocks." *See* Shlomo Benartzi, *Excessive Extrapolation and the Allocation of 401(k) Accounts to Company Stock?*, 56 J. FIN. 1747, 1764 (2001), and John Hancock Financial Services, *The Sixth Defined Contribution Plan Survey* (1999).

The idea is gradually to sell off stock automatically over several years until the participant divests down to a reasonable holding— say, a 10 percent cap. The money earned by selling company stock would be invested in the firm's default investment fund (unless the employee chooses something else).[23]

By allowing employees to keep a small (guardrailed) portion of company stock in their portfolio, the employer can still make the employees feel that they are part owners of the firm and reduces subsequent regret if the stock performs well, at a fraction of the risk associated with much large holdings. "This plan addresses plan sponsors' concerns of a sudden sell-off," Thaler said, "as well as the fear that removing it from the plan sends a negative signal about the stock."[24]

Benartzi and Thaler have even developed sample employee brochures showing how such an option can be presented to participants:

> If you simply think about your financial future and fill the Sell More Tomorrow reply card, you will enter a second $10,000 lottery. You will actually enter the lottery regardless of your investment decision, and you could change your mind at any time.
>
> ☐ No, I do not want to sell my XYZ holdings.
> ☐ Yes, I would like to have my XYZ holdings converted to the S&P500 immediately.
> ☐ Yes, I would like to join the Sell More Tomorrow program and have my XYZ holdings automatically converted to the S&P500 over the next 24 months.[25]

While the authors' primary focus is on reducing the overweighting of company stock, they are explicit that the same idea could be applied more generally to improve diversification:

> The Sell More Tomorrow program is not limited to company stock. In fact, it could be used to increase diversification in general. For instance, consider the late 90's when plan participants were thriving for Internet funds. The same approach of showing projected retirement income from a diversified portfolio versus an Internet fund could have been used to illustrate the risk of investing in a single sector.[26]

---

[23] Stacy L. Schaus & Ying Gao, Successful Defined Contribution Investment Design: How to Align Target-Date, Core, and Income Strategies to the Price of Retirement 74 (2017).
[24] Id.
[25] Thaler, *supra* note 20, at 7.
[26] Shlomo Benartzi & Richard H. Thaler, *Using Behavioral Economics to Improve Diversification in 401(k) Plans: Solving the Company Stock Problem* (working paper, 2003).

Benartzi and Thaler suggest implementing their proposal with a novel kind of "affirmative choice" default. By making an affirmative choice, participants are automatically enrolled in a $10,000 lottery.[27] It might be useful to go further and make Sell More Tomorrow a default that will automatically start selling company stock overtime unless the participant objects. Indeed, Thaler in a separate interview has suggested that "sponsors implement Sell More Tomorrow as an opt out."[28] Just like Sell More Tomorrow, this dynamic default could be applied periodically to any type of allocation error.

Dynamic guardrails could also be of an informational variety. For example, with regard to company stock, Olivia Mitchell and her co-authors have suggested that "[e]ducational messages and portfolio warnings might be *dynamic* – they could appear on statements and websites when a particular limit, such as 20 percent, is breached."[29]

6.2.5   Hard(er) Guardrails

The key requirement of these softer guardrails is that they preserve a pathway for participants to make unorthodox (i.e., presumptively mistaken) allocations, but nonetheless provide some prophylactic protection. In contrast, hard guardrails restrict freedom by eliminating some allocation possibilities without permitting an opt out. Hard guardrails come in many forms. Just as the streamlining elimination of a fund might or might not grandfather existing balances, a guardrail restriction might or might not apply to preexisting balances. For example, a pure contribution guardrail might limit the percentage of future contributions that could be allocated to a gold fund without correcting past imbalances. An obvious downside is that contribution guardrails fail to emulate the "reset button" effects of streamlining. Alternatively, one could combine a one-time rebalancing guardrail with ongoing contribution restrictions to better address allocation errors of the past. This approach might still allow some allocation drift if, over time, particular funds achieve sufficient returns to unbalance

---

[27] Affirmative choice defaults often prompt action by threatening what is naturally framed as a negative result if no affirmative choice is made. For example, a new hire might have to make affirmative choices in filling out various forms as a prerequisite to receiving a first salary payment; or students might have to affirmatively choose how they rate their professors before they can receive their grades. Here, however, making an affirmative choice qualifies them for entry in a lottery. Thus, we might think of it as a carrot affirmative-choice default rule, instead of the more common stick affirmative-choice default rule.

[28] *Id.*

[29] Mitchell, *supra* note 15, at 37.

a portfolio. A guardrail could also limit contributions to an overweighted fund (diverting those savings to other investments) until the overall proportion held in the portfolio is brought into compliance with some guardrail percentage.[30] Finally, and most restrictively, one might impose rebalancing on an ongoing basis to assure that portfolios abide by particular guardrail restrictions. This dynamic guardrail is similar to the softer dynamic default described above, except that participants would not have to freedom to opt out to stick with their unorthodox allocation. Many plans that offer company stock have already put in place this restrictive practice. Vanguard reported in 2020 for the plan it advises that "One in 5 organizations goes further and … redirect[s] contributions and/or account balances to the plan's qualified default investment alternative (QDIA), such as a target-date fund, when the company stock position exceeds the limit."[31]

Setting aside the timing of guardrail compliance, our previous analysis suggests the potential value of a variety of different (hard) allocation limits. Our analysis of sector funds suggests that a guardrail to cap the allowable percentage allocated to particular narrow-gauge funds. Our analysis of international equities suggests the possibility of guardrails that set floors for the minimum percentage allocated to certain asset classes. These asset-class floors would resemble the distributional requirements at many universities (which, e.g., might require a certain number of science or humanities courses to graduate).[32] Finally, our analysis of fees and glidepaths suggests that some guardrails may turn on the attributes of the portfolio taken as whole – such as requiring that the average portfolio expense ratio not exceed a certain amount, or that the portfolio's overall exposure to equities not fall below a certain percentage.

The contours of allocation limits should incorporate some tolerance for different participant tastes and circumstances. While we have provided a strong theoretical and empirical case for limiting participants' overweighting of the Fidelity Gold Fund, reasonable fiduciaries might disagree on

---

[30] As will be discussed later in Chapter 8, ForUsAll that will impose this kind of guardrail regarding investments in crypto currency. Anne Tergesen, *Coinbase Teams Up With 401(k) Provider to Offer Crypto*, WALL ST. J. (June 10, 2021) (If the balance in crypto holdings exceeds 5 percent of the participants over plan value, the system will block any more crypto contributions.) www.wsj.com/articles/coinbase-teams-up-with-401-k-provider-to-offer-crypto-11623317402.

[31] John A. Lamancusa & Jean A. Young, *Company Stock in DC plans*, VANGUARD RESEARCH (2020) at 10, https://personal.vanguard.com/pdf/ISGCSDC_122020_Online.pdf.

[32] Association of American Colleges & Universities, *Recent Trends in General Education Design, Learning Outcomes, and Teaching Approaches: Key Findings from a Survey among Administrators at AAC&U Member Institutions* 12, HART RESEARCH ASSOCIATES (2016).

whether the appropriate allocation cap should be, say, 5 percent or 10 percent of a participant's portfolio. But there is no world in which it would be reasonable for a fiduciary to allow participants to invest as much as 50 percent of their portfolio in a precious metal fund. The choice of a particular percentage cap or floor involves a basic tradeoff: tighter caps likely produce more prophylactic benefits for cognitively impacted participants, while reducing the freedom of rational investors to maximize their own welfare.[33]

Our proposal of encouraging plans with allocations errors to consider adopting multiple guardrails should be viewed as one means that a prudent fiduciary could use to construct a sound menu. Just as a prudent fiduciary is understood to breach a duty by including an obviously inappropriate investment option in a plan menu, so too a fiduciary should seek to avoid permitting obviously inappropriate allocations over the menu. ERISA does not demand perfection in eliminating all possibility of mistake, but instead requires that fiduciaries follow a rational, informed process in designing the menu. Adding guardrails to the mix is simply another tool that fiduciaries should consider in carrying out their duty.

6.2.6   Government Guardrails

The foregoing implementation analysis implicitly assumes that plan fiduciaries are in charge of deciding whether to deploy guardrails and how to craft them – just as they decide whether or not to streamline their menu, and if so how to implement streamlining. It is worth considering the possibility that the government itself could implement or encourage various forms of guardrails. This might be done by statute, by formal administrative rulemaking, or just by industry guidance. Hard allocation guardrails are already in place with regard to defined benefit plans. Under Section 407 of ERISA, defined benefit plans are subject to a 10 percent cap on investments in employer securities,[34] and several legislative proposals have attempted to extend the cap to defined contribution plans as well.[35]

---

[33] As a theoretical matter, there is likely to be a welfare maximizing percentage – as the prophylactic benefits are on the margin decreasing, while the liberty costs are on the margin increasing. We don't imagine that real-world fiduciaries would ever have sufficient information to estimate this optimum with precision.

[34] 29 U.S.C. § 1107.

[35] For example, Senators Boxer and Corozine introduced legislation that would have capped the share of DC plan assets invested in company stock at 20 percent. See Jeffrey Brown, Nellie Liang & Scott Weisbenner, *401(k) Matching Contributions in Company Stock: Costs*

Much of this book's analysis is a sustained argument for a more fulsome duty for fiduciaries to become better informed about participant menu misuse and, when appropriate, to ameliorate such misuse. But our discussion in Chapter 3 underscores the limitations of using the threat of litigation as the instrument to change fiduciary behavior. Most importantly, small and mid-sized plans face virtually no risk of being sued even if they offer plans with objectively poor menu options. Government guardrails establishing transparent allocation limitations are much more likely to induce broad compliance.

While centrally imposed rules would have to take into account the different needs of different plans and plan participants, the key concerns of diversification, expense, and exposure errors do not in fact vary substantially across plans. More specifically, consider the potential impact of the following five guardrails:

- QDIA guardrail: Plans must offer a QDIA with all-in expenses less than 50 basis points a year.
- Individual security guardrail: Individual participants cannot contribute more than 10 percent of their plan contributions to a single security (company stock, for example) (and at least quarterly balances in excess of 10 percent will be swept to the QDIA).
- Narrow fund guardrail: Individual participants cannot contribute more than 50 percent of their plan contributions to any non-QDIA eligible fund (and at least quarterly balances in excess of 20 percent will be swept to the QDIA).
- High-Expense Guardrail: Individual participants cannot contribute to an allocation with all-in-expense greater than 100 basis points a year (and at least quarterly if a participant's portfolio has expenses greater than 100 basis points, the funds with expenses greater than 75 basis points will be proratedly swept to the QDIA until the portfolio expenses fall below 100 basis points.

---

and Benefits for Firms and Workers, 90 J. PUB. ECON. 1315, 1346 (2006). The impulse to cap "both types of plans originated early in the Kennedy administration … The idea was then redebated in early versions of ERISA but it was blocked for DC plans after complaints from employers who sponsored profit-sharing programs that invested heavily in company stock. See Mitchell, *supra* note 28, at 22 (A "key opponent of a 10 percent cap on employer stock in DC plans was Sears Roebuck" whose stock had performed strongly through much of the 1950s and 1960s and whose participant/employees were reluctant to diversify.). *See* Michael S. Gordon, *The Employee Retirement Income Security Act of 1974: The First Decade: An Information Paper: Why Was ERISA Enacted?*, Special Committee on Aging, US Senate (1984).

- Exposure Guardrail: Individual participants cannot contribute to an allocation with an equity proportion that falls outside the maximum and minimum tolerances described in Chapter 5 (and at least quarterly, if the equity percentage in a participant's portfolio falls outside these tolerances, portfolio holdings will be sold pro-rata and swept to the QDIA until the portfolio falls within the exposure guardrail).

These guardrails respond to core allocation errors. The QDIA and high-expense guardrail work together to assure that participant allocations are not unduly costly – but retain enough flexibility so that participants can allocate some of their portfolio to higher cost and/or actively managed funds. The individual security and narrow fund guardrails work together to assure that participant allocations are not unduly undiversified. The individual security guardrail extents the defined benefit 10 percent cap on company stock to defined contribution plans and includes other securities (which as we will see later in Chapter 9 is important because some plan brokerage windows currently allow participants to invest all of their retirement savings not just in individual securities, but in cryptocurrency funds). Moreover, the quarterly sweep provisions to the QDIA further assist the diversification of participant portfolios. Lastly, the exposure guardrail works to assure reasonable exposures to equities with substantial tolerance for different levels of participant risk aversion: the upper-bound allows participants to remain 100 percent in equities until they are 65 (and the maximum percentage at age 70 is 88 percent), while the lower bound starts at 43 percent for younger employees and falls to 22 percent for 65-year-olds.[36]

Finally, the government might intervene by changing other fiduciary incentives regarding plan design. For example, some scholars have called

---

[36] Another rejoinder to the imposition of these government-mandated guardrails is that it might produce a fiduciary backlash of some employers choosing to curtail or eliminate employer matching programs. *See* Mitchell & Utkus, *supra* note 15, at 26 ("From a certainty-equivalent perspective, if employers did substitute smaller cash contributions for current stock contributions in the future [as a response to a new government-imposed cap limitation], this change may not necessarily be welfare-reducing for employees."). One response would be to only impose the guardrails on plans without meaningful employer contributions, where there is less of a worry that the guardrails will reduce employer beneficence. The IRS already has a safe harbor standard that exempts plans from non-discrimination testing if the employer contributions meet certain thresholds. ForUsAll: 401(k) Nondiscrimination Testing: A Simple Guide for Improving Your Results, www.forusall.com/401k-blog/401k-nondiscrimination-testing/. These same or similar thresholds could be applied to guardrails so that employers who made substantial contributions might be relieved from the need to enforce these prophylactic rules.

for legal changes to reduce or eliminate the affirmative tax incentives for employers to offer employees various vehicles for holding company stock.[37] One could imagine a variety of interventions that instead of mandating guardrail compliance, curtailed tax subsidies the more that participant allocations ran afoul of them.[38]

6.3   Legal Viability

As noted above, the decision to eliminate funds, map participants to other similar funds, or map participants into target date funds is a role that retirement plan fiduciaries carry out on an ongoing basis. Such streamlining interventions are commonplace in the existing market, and plan fiduciaries undertake these activities with the welfare of participants in mind. There is no question that they are legally permissible and fiduciary consideration of such interventions is an essential part of operating a plan.

The viability of guardrails as a legal matter is a more complex question. It should be noted that guardrails already appear in at least one form in existing plans: limits on allocations to company stock. Company stock is a highly questionable investment for any plan investors, as investing in a single stock entails a degree of under-diversification. Investing in one's employer stock effectively doubles down on the undiversifiable risk of one's own employment. If the company goes belly-up, one risks losing not only their job but also the portion of their retirement account invested in company stock. As such, financial advisors generally discourage holding company stock in a 401(k) plan, and many companies have started dropping the option.[39]

Some companies have elected to retain company stock, but cap employees' maximum allocation to it.[40] In doing so, they have essentially endorsed our argument that fiduciaries ought to be responsive to potential menu misuse. Whatever the appropriate role of employer stock in a retirement plan (we remain skeptical), it is surely the case that allocating more than

---

[37] Benartzi et al., *The Law and Economics of Company Stock in 401(k) Plans*, 50 J. LAW ECON. 45, 79 (2007).

[38] *See* Mitchell, *supra* note 15.

[39] Robert C. Pozen & Ming Liu, *Having Too Much Employer Stock in Your 401(k) Is Dangerous. Just Look at GE*, BROOKINGS (July 2, 2018), www.brookings.edu/opinions/having-too-much-employer-stock-in-your-401k-is-dangerous-just-look-at-ge/.

[40] Jacklyn Wille, *Target, Microsoft Lead Move Away from 401(k) Stock Investments*, BLOOMBERG LAW (March 16, 2018) https://news.bloomberglaw.com/employee-benefits/target-microsoft-lead-move-away-from-401-k-stock-investments.

a small percentage of one's portfolio to it is inappropriate. By capping the allocation, these employers provide the option to hold employer stock while mitigating the risk of misuse.

Similarly, Fidelity recently announced that it will create a cryptocurrency fund for retirement plans, subject to an employer-determined guardrail not to exceed 20 percent.[41] The guardrail can be understood as a response to the Department of Labor's skepticism as to whether cryptocurrencies are appropriate assets for retirement plans.[42] By adopting a guardrail, Fidelity presumably hopes to head off concerns that investors might overconcentrate in highly speculative assets. The proposed option illustrates the legal plausibility of a guardrail, and the willingness of sponsors to adopt guardrails when they perceive investment options as potentially liability-creating. Fidelity's approach also illustrates another potential benefit of guardrailing a risky option rather than excluding it – while we may be skeptical of Bitcoin as a retirement plan asset – making it available to investors (subject to a cap) may encourage retirement plan participation by crypto-enthusiasts who might otherwise seek exposure to the asset class elsewhere.

Our argument is that this sort of reasoning should be applied more broadly. However, we imagine that many plans might be initially reluctant to do so. One issue is the language of the 404(c) safe harbor, which foregrounds participant choice. To qualify for the safe harbor, employers must "provide an opportunity for a participant ... to choose, from a broad range of investment alternatives, the manner in which some *or all* of the assets in their account are invested."[43] Because a guardrail is an intervention that limits a participant's ability to invest all their assets in a particular fund, a guardrail falls outside the statute's protection. Why should a plan fiduciary proactively act to protect participants from allocation mistakes in ways that might increase the fiduciary's liability, particularly if they feel that the 404(c) safe harbor will relieve them from any liability for the mistakes that result? Perhaps in the case of company stock, which is already seen to carry legal risk for the fiduciary,[44] a guardrail is in the interest of the fiduciary, but other types of guardrails may seem less attractive.

---

[41] Tara Siegel Bernard, *Fidelity's New 401(k) Offering Will Invest in Bitcoin*, N. Y. Times B6 (April 26, 2022) www.nytimes.com/2022/04/26/business/crypto-401k-fidelity.html?searchResultPosition=1.

[42] *See* Tara Siegel Bernard, *The Labor Department Wants to Investigate Crypto in Retirement Plans*, N. Y. Times (March 10, 2022).

[43] 29 C.F.R. § 2550.404c–1(v)(ii) (emphasis added).

[44] Wille, *supra* note 40.

Our first response is the argument, outlined in Chapter 1, that the safe harbor cannot be used to establish the prudence of the menu because the fiduciary duty in menu construction is a precondition for the application of the safe harbor.[45] Guardrails might make prudent an investment option that could otherwise not be prudently included in a plan menu. Courts might find that adding a gold fund to a plan is only prudent if participants' allocations are capped.

The softer forms of guardrails, like simple indications of presumptive problems, and even heavier handed interventions like asking participants to make representations about their outside assets or sophistication are likely consistent with the 404(c) safe harbors emphasis on choice. For example, plans adopting a three-tier structure are already nudging plan participants in the direction of target date funds by segmenting off other types of funds in the presentation of the plan menu. More concretely, many plans require the affirmative submission of a form before participants can access the brokerage window. The softer set of guardrails we describe above preserve ultimate participant choice and are – at most – similar sorts of nudges.

If hard guardrails are unacceptable to fiduciaries because they believe guardrailing would jeopardize their safe harbor protections, then the Department of Labor (DOL) should make it clear that a guardrail on an item in the menu doesn't contravene the requirements of the safe harbor. Such regulation is well within the DOL's power, and we would argue that the best reading of the current law is that hard guardrails are already permissible (as their use in company stock indicates). If a fund in the plan could be completely excluded from the menu, then limiting the percentage allocated to that fund must *a fortiori* be consistent with the safe harbor as well. Any fear of litigation arising out of guardrails is overblown, and the DOL should settle the issue by making it explicit that they are a permissible tool of menu design.

Another potential concern relates to the non-discrimination provisions of the Internal Revenue Code. It is possible that restricting access to certain investments for some, but not all, plan investors might run afoul of Code requirements that retirement plans not discriminate between "highly compensated" and "nonhighly compensated" employees.[46] Regulations are

---

[45] *See* Chapter 2. Moreover, the provision says that to qualify participants must be given the opportunity to choose the manner in which "*some* or all" of the assets in their account are invested. Guardrails preserve the opportunity to choose how some of those assets are invested.

[46] Edward A. Zelinsky, *Is Bitcoin Prudent? Is Art Diversified? Offering Alternative Investments to 401(k) Participants*, 2022 CONN. L. REV. 520, 545 and accompanying notes.

explicit that the right to direct investments is subject to the nondiscrimination rules.[47] If a guardrail disproportionately limits "nonhighly compensated" employees, it may be problematic under tax rules.[48] These rules should not be a problem for soft or informational guardrails, and most of the hard guardrails we suggest would apply across the board, and so would be permissible. Nevertheless, if companies were to condition guardrails on outside assets or demonstrate financial sophistication, and these conditions correlated with compensation, these regulations could present an issue. In our view, the goals of the nondiscrimination rules could be achieved while permitting conditional guardrails that are correlated with income, so long as the intent is investor welfare, income is not directly a guardrail criterion, and no employees are excluded from the conditional test for the guardrail.

Finally, the concern might arise among plan fiduciaries that, in adopting hard guardrails, they must necessarily discount the interests of plan participants who have legitimate need for heterodox allocations. As we argued above, we think it's generally prudent for fiduciaries to consider plan assets to be most participants' primary retirement savings, and to ask those with significant outside allocations to make adjustments to holdings in non-plan assets in the interest of maximizing risk-return for plan participants as a whole. Nevertheless, there will be occasions when hard guardrails or streamlining entail real tradeoffs. In the next chapter, we consider how plan sponsors can approach those tradeoffs.

[47] *Id.* (citing Treas. Reg. § 1.401(a)(4)-4(b)(3)(iii)(B)–(C) (2001)).
[48] *Id.*

How Should Fiduciaries Trade Off Divergent Participant Interests?

Employers take different approaches to menu construction. While a small company might rely on the advice of a plan service provider and take it at face value, major employers might utilize investment committees with teams of consultants and lawyers to design their plan. In either case, the employer is under a fiduciary duty to run the plan prudently in the interest of employees, and as *Tibble*[1] makes clear, that duty is an ongoing one. Menu options must be regularly revisited and re-screened for inclusion in the plan. Fee lawsuits have produced some guidance as to what good plan management looks like, with employers tasked with considering the cost and performance of options included in the plan to eliminate inappropriate investment options, but years of litigation have left much unsettled in menu design.

When should a plan sponsor eliminate an option that is useful for some investors, but problematic for others? When shortening a menu, should investors in a specialized fund be offered a similar alternative or mapped into a target date fund appropriate for their age? When is it appropriate to refer an investor with specialized needs to a brokerage window and when should those needs be met within the plan menu? In answering these questions, it is inevitable that the interests of some plan participants will be balanced against the interests of others. The duty to run the plan in the interests of participants, of course, does not tell sponsors how to balance those competing participant interests.

This chapter provides guidance on these questions by drawing on fiduciary first-principles. Menu construction will always involve judgment calls, but it is possible to identify the types of questions sponsors should ask and the types of investor interests that should receive particular weight. Fundamentally, fiduciaries are required to give "due regard"[2] to the interests of all plan participants. In this chapter, we develop two frameworks

---

[1] 135 S. Ct. 1823 (2015).
[2] *See* notes 12–14 and accompanying text.

aimed at operationalizing this obligation. We also argue that the use of guardrails, can significantly reduce the need to make tough choices. As we explain below, by providing a middle path between eliminating an option from the menu and permitting unrestricted choice over the menu, guardrails enable fiduciaries to better balance the interests of plan participants.

7.1   Fiduciary Duties and Trading Off Interests in Menu Design

Recent trends in plan administration put plan sponsors in the position of trading off the competing interests of plan investors. Many employers have adopted streamlining as a best practice, rejecting the use of a kitchen-sink menu in favor of shorter menus divided into tiers that steer many employees toward presumptively appropriate target date funds. Moving to shorter, more tailored menus is a positive one, but there is a reason that menus have tended toward inclusivity: As any plan administrator will attest, cutting options from the menu can be controversial. While truly bad funds with high fees and recurrent poor performance will be cut to ensure compliance with the sponsor's fiduciary obligations, there are many funds featured in overly long menus that are unlikely to give rise to a fee lawsuit but are nevertheless candidates for removal for middling performance, highly specialized asset allocations, or simply because they are not very popular. Gold funds we've already discussed, but sector funds, regional funds, niche actively managed funds, and funds that have simply dwindled in popularity among plan investors may be on the chopping block.

Inevitably, the choice to remove a fund will frustrate an investor pleased with its performance or enthusiastic about a niche investment strategy, and plan administrators are likely targets for frustrated calls and emails. Some plan participants are so wedded to their past investments that it is as if they would only give up holding particular funds if they are pried from their cold, dead hands. These same administrators might reason that leaving a fund in the menu to please a few squeaky wheels does no real harm to investors who have plenty of other choices. Indeed, the 404(c) safe harbor affirmatively invites such an attitude.[3] Why court controversy, when it's so easy to leave one more fund in the menu?

In some cases, complaints about the removal of a fund might transcend unreasonable loyalty to a particular fund and reflect a genuine reduction in the welfare of an investor. For some investors, specialty funds giving

---

[3] 29 U.S.C. § 1104(c).

unusual exposure might fill what some participants perceive as an invest-ment need that the remaining funds in the menu don't address. As we have argued, though, this perceived need is usually seeking alpha (an urge to beat the market) and not a need to better diversify their non-plan savings. Such specialized funds can prove to be an attractive nuisance.[4] If investors made perfect decisions, adding to the menu could never leave them worse off, but we know that investors are imperfect and menu design has an effect on investor choice. It is clear enough that a fiduciary should remove truly bad options like dominated funds from the menu, but what should a fiduciary do when removing an option entails a real trade-off, because it will help many investors, but leave some worse off?

Streamlining a menu is likely not an unalloyed goods for all partici-pants. Take, for example, UVA's decision to eliminate the gold fund from its menu. Roughly half the investors in the pre-existing gold fund were making presumptively reasonable "small sliver" allocations of less than 12 percent of their plan savings.[5] Removing the gold fund option from the menu arguably hurt these participants by reducing their ability to diversify risk. While streamlining protected the goldbug participants from unrea-sonably overweighting gold in their portfolio, it potentially prevents other participants from making reasonable, diversifying allocations. Adopting a guardrail to cap allocation to the gold fund would mitigate, but not elimi-nate, this trade-off. For example, some participants might hold non-plan assets such that investing 15 percent of their plan portfolio in gold is a reasonable allocation but would be prevented from doing so if UVA had imposed a 10 percent cap in allocations to the gold fund.

Streamlining and guardrails will rarely represent a Pareto improvement. That is, it will often be the case that not every investor in the plan is left better off (or unaffected) by a change to the plan menu. When a menu change doesn't leave investors better off across the board, what should plan sponsors do?

The law offers surprisingly little guidance on this question. ERISA draws its framework for fiduciary duties from trust law.[6] A trustee is to avoid conflicts of interests and to operate the trust in the interests of the beneficiaries. For pension plans, where discretion in investment choices is fully in the control of the trustee, trust law is an apt source of guidance. A pension fund has reasonably predictable liabilities and the pension

---

[4] See Chapter 4, supra.
[5] Id.
[6] See 29 U.S.C. 1104(a); Central States, Se. & Sw. Areas Pension Fund v. Central Transp., Inc., 472 U.S. 559, 570 (1985).

manager can select an investment strategy in line with the projected future payouts.[7] But participant-directed retirement accounts pose the unique challenge of constructing a menu, and menus are a foreign concept to trust law, particularly when that menu construction involves trading off the interests of different participants.

While the notion of constructing a menu is foreign to trust law, the problem of multiple beneficiaries with competing interests is not.[8] In a trust, different beneficiaries may be entitled to income and principal, or there may be different risk tolerances between workers and retirees in a pension plan. A trustee has a duty of impartiality between multiple beneficiaries of a trust. The Restatement of Trusts frames this duty as follows:

> (b) A trustee has a duty to administer the trust in a manner that is impartial with respect to the various beneficiaries of the trust, requiring that:
>
> (a) in investing, protecting, and distributing the trust estate, and in other administrative functions, the trustee must act impartially and with due regard for the diverse beneficial interests created by the terms of the trust; and
> (b) in consulting and otherwise communicating with beneficiaries, the trustee must proceed in a manner that fairly reflects the diversity of their concerns and beneficial interests.[9]

The comments continue "impartiality does not require an equal balancing of diverse interests but a balancing of those interests in a manner that shows due regard for – that is, is consistent with – the beneficial interests and the terms and purposes of the trust."[10] As to investment duties, in particular, the Restatement makes clear that investing to balance the interests of different beneficiaries requires significant judgment on the part of the trustee.[11]

In short, the trustee, when beneficiary interests conflict, is placed in the role of impartially administering the trust in a way that gives due consideration to both parties' interests and is consistent with the goals of the trust. The question is how to operationalize this duty in the context of a retirement plan. Assuming a plan administrator is impartial as between plan participants, what does it mean to act with due regard to each investor?

---

[7] Even in the case of a pension fund there can be conflicts, as when the need for a secure cash flow of current retirees clashes with the need of future retirees for sufficient growth.

[8] For example, consider a trustee who is entrusted to manage an estate for the benefit of three siblings. If two of the siblings would like the trustee to build a basketball court, but the third believes it to be worse than a waste of money as it will detract from the aesthetic beauty of the trust property, should the trustee build the court?

[9] Restatement (Third) of Trusts § 79 (2007).

[10] Restatement (Third) of Trusts § 79 comment (c) (2007).

[11] Restatement (Third) of Trusts § 90 (2007).

7.2   Weighing Competing Interests in Menu Design

At the outset, we would note that allowing menu design decisions to be dominated by squeaky wheel complainers is not consistent with the fiduciary obligations of plan sponsors. Eliminated funds will have their adherents. Indeed, both of the authors have heard grumbling from colleagues about menu contraction decisions at our own institutions. To give too much weight to such complaints, and allow the menu to grow unchecked simply as a matter of comfort for the plan administrator is not consistent with the obligation to run the plan prudently and loyalty in the interests of *all* plan participants. Menu decisions need to be substantively defensible and in the interest of investors, not the inbox of plan fiduciaries.

Succumbing to marketing pressure from plan service providers is equally inconsistent with the fiduciary duties of a plan sponsor. Adding a hot new fund or to a plan or retaining a struggling option in response to sales pressure hardly serves plan participants.[12] Sponsors should be prepared to push back against aggressive tactics aimed at keeping plan menus long or giving another chance to clearly poor options.

So what to do? One option would be to discount the interests of investors who might make mistakes in favor of preserving choice for investors who might benefit from including additional options. There is an argument in favor of this approach: The overallocating investor can in principle choose to stop overallocating, but the investor whose useful fund is eliminated cannot so easily regain the investment exposure. Indeed, the 404(c) safe harbor seems to offer support for the view that participant choice is not a plan sponsor problem, and a plan sponsor might conclude that they should not weigh harms that result from participant choices against harms that result from menu omissions because the former, but not the latter, can be avoided by participants if they make better choices.

We've already made the case that this approach to menu design and this reading of the 404(c) safe harbor are both incorrect as a matter of law and inconsistent with current thinking about best practices in retirement plans.[13] If leaving choices up to participants were a safeguard against liability, then most of the excessive fee lawsuits would not have succeeded, because the *Hecker* large-menu defense that there were at

---

[12] Plan service providers have been shown to have considerable influence over whether options are included or excluded from plan menus. Veronika K. Pool, Clemens Sialm & Irina Stefanescu, *It Pays to Set the Menu: Mutual Fund Investment Options in 401(k) Plans*, 71 J. FIN. 1779–1812 (2016).

[13] *See infra*, Chapter 1.

least some good options would carry the day. And if employers gave no attention to the choices of their employees, they would simply throw the kitchen sink into the plan menu, leaving the hard choices to plan participants. This, again, is inconsistent with the law of menu design.

If disregarding the impact of participant choice when designing the menu is off the table that returns us to the question of how to trade off the interests of different plan participants. At the opposite extreme of unrestricted choice over a huge menu would be an approach that simply asks which menu options are likely to produce the most aggregate benefit to plan participants, conditional on the choices they are likely to make over the menu. While it is non-trivial to find a single metric of "aggregate benefit" our empirical analysis of the UVA plan provides some sense of how a plan administrator can track how participants are doing. Plan administrators might ask, with respect to a sector fund, "are more participants benefiting from this fund than appear to be making welfare-reducing choices by overcommitting to it?" If the answer is "no," then the fund should be dropped and the menu streamlined.

While this approach is better than letting participants fend for themselves over a huge menu, there may be circumstances where simply maximizing aggregate welfare fails to "give due regard"[14] to the interests of all plan participants. Consider the following scenario:

A tech startup has a relatively young workforce and offers a 401(k) plan with a generous match to its employees. Employees are defaulted into QDIA target date funds with target dates nearest their 65th birthdays when they enroll in the plan. Adopting the sort of monitoring approach we suggest, the plan fiduciary notes that a majority of plan participants who hold the 2025 target date fund are not the handful of older employees likely to retire in that timeframe, but instead a more numerous cadre of young employees attempting to time the market by moving money between aggressive and conservative allocations several times a quarter. Further analysis suggests that these employees are doing so with no evident market timing skill.

In our view, it would be inappropriate to drop the 2025 target date fund under these circumstances, even if the aggregate risk-return profile of the plan would be improved by pushing the market-timers into more appropriate funds. The reason is that the 2025 target date fund serves a clear need of the older employees: providing an age-appropriate target date funds is a core function of the plan menu. To drop the fund in the interest

---

[14] Restatement (Third) of Trusts § 79 (2007)

of improving the overall exposure of employees would discount the interests of the older employees in a way that is inconsistent with the duty to give due regard to all plan participants.

Neither ignoring employee choice nor simply maximizing plan performance net of choice is consistent with the fiduciary obligations of plan sponsors as articulated in the case law and the Restatement of Trusts. In the next section, we offer two frameworks for evaluating trade-offs in menus.

7.3   How to Weigh Trade-Offs in Menu Design

Whenever a fiduciary confronts a change to a plan menu, the fiduciary must balance the costs to those who benefited from the existing menu against the benefits to plan participants of the revision. The trade-off between individual liberty and the prophylactic effect of corrective action raises a foundational question of fiduciary duty. Should a fiduciary make a change that increases the overall welfare of the participants by improving the outcomes for a majority, but reduces the welfare of a minority of participant investors?

To state the problem in terms of classical economics, should a fiduciary make a change that is a Kaldor-Hicks improvement, but not a Pareto improvement?[15] For a change to constitute a Pareto improvement, no participant could experience reduced utility. So few policy changes satisfy this strict requirement that Guido Calabresi has characterized the Paretian welfare standard as "pointless."[16] The Kaldor-Hicks standard in contrast only requires that a change be a potential Pareto improvement, in that the people who are helped by the change are benefited sufficiently that they could hypothetically compensate the losers so that no one is made worse off by the change. However, the Kaldor-Hicks standard is criticized for ignoring the actual distributional consequences of the change.[17]

The question of whether fiduciaries should ever sacrifice the interest of the few in order to enhance overall well-being is raised by both streamlining and guardrailing. Dropping a gold fund (and other sector funds)

---

[15] Yew-Kwang Ng, *Quasi-Pareto Social Improvements*, 74 AM. ECON. REV. 1033 (1984).

[16] *See* Guido Calabresi, *The Pointlessness of Pareto*, 100 YALE L. J. 1211 (1990).

[17] For example, Robert Nozick concluded:

> Utilitarian theory is embarrassed by the possibility of utility monsters who get enormously greater sums of utility from any sacrifice of others than these others lose ... the theory seems to require that we all be sacrificed in the monster's maw, in order to increase total utility.

ROBERT NOZICK, ANARCHY, STATE, AND UTOPIA 41 (1974).

is likely to substantially improve the diversification of goldbug investors, but sacrifices the ability of more rational investors to use more modest gold allocations to diversify risk. Guardrailing provides fiduciaries more flexibility than simply dropping a fund from the menu, but as we show, even guardrailing will sometimes leave some investors worse off.

In considering whether to alter an existing plan menu – by stream-lining or by imposing soft or hard guardrails – the fiduciary should first determine that the proposed change would improve the general welfare of its participants. If the change does not represent at least a Kaldor-Hicks improvement, it should not be undertaken. Among this class of Kaldor-Hicks improvements, fiduciaries should further require that the change satisfy what we call an "enhanced Kaldor-Hicks" standard.

To pass the enhanced Kaldor-Hicks standard, a change must not only be Kaldor-Hicks efficient but also satisfy the fiduciary obligation that trade-offs between beneficiaries give due regard to the interests of all par-ties affected by the change. Specifically, *the menu should not be changed in ways that substantially disadvantage a substantial, identifiable groups of plan participants who are using the plan in an ordinary way to save for retirement.* That is, an otherwise efficient change should be rejected if there is a group of employees of a certain age, income level, or other char-acteristics who, in order to use the plan as their primary savings vehicle for retirement and achieve sufficient diversification rather than seek market-beating returns, would be required as a result of the change to clear sub-stantial investment hurdles that other investors would not.

This proposed standard for evaluating plan guardrailing and stream-lining is designed to operationalize the Restatement of Trusts approach to impartiality between beneficiaries. To give due regard to the interests of all plan participants means that a plan should provide a sufficiently extensive menu that participant that all participants seeking to use the plan as the primary vehicle for saving for retirement following a conven-tional approach to asset allocation will have sufficient options to meet their needs. These options should be available even if some investors in the plan might misuse them. On the other hand, the standard does not require the plan to offer options sufficient to meet the investment needs of every possible savings strategy. Our distinguishing conventional and non-conventional approaches to asset allocation are also consistent with the Restatement of Trust's reliance on the "purposes of the trust" when balancing divergent participant interests. As applied to the ERISA con-text, the purpose of 401(k) plans is not to facilitate the ability of individual participants to gamble with taxpayers' money. Employees with unusual needs or esoteric preferences can change the allocation of their non-employer brokerage accounts, whether tax-favored or not, if adapting the plan menu to meet their needs would create a high risk of menu misuse. Specifically, this standard does not require the plan to meet the needs of alpha-seeking or market-timing participants, if doing so reduces the overall welfare of participants.[18]

Consider the example above of a conservative target date fund used as a safe asset by young investors seeking to time the market. Suppose that the plan sponsor concludes that dropping the fund is a Kaldor-Hicks improving move, as the number of age-inappropriate investors in the fund is larger than the number of near-retirees and the cost to the market timers in terms of expected returns is bad enough to outweigh the benefits to the older investors holding the fund.

On the enhanced Kaldor-Hicks standard, the sponsor would then ask whether dropping the fund would substantially disadvantage a group of investors making ordinary use of the plan. The answer in this case would be "yes." The older investors investing in an age-appropriate target date fund are using the plan exactly as intended and in the same way as any other investor who chooses (or is defaulted into) the target date option. To remove that option in the interest of erecting an obstacle to aggressive market timing would unreasonably burden these investors: They would need to construct their own portfolio of funds approximating the target date exposure or move to the brokerage window just to achieve what other plan investors can do by default.

Contrast this hypothetical with the decision to streamline the gold fund in the UVA plan. There may well have been investors making appropriate use of the gold fund to address unique needs in the context of their household portfolio, and these investors may have been left worse off by the removal of that option from the menu. But these investors were using the flexibility of the plan to achieve something different than most participants. If they truly have unique financial needs, then it is not disregarding their interests to provide a plan that doesn't perfectly accommodate them. In failing to provide a specialized option, the plan is merely

---

[18] There may be other circumstances where it will be harder to decide whether a participant strategy should be given the protective convention treatment. For example, some participants have strong preference for menu options that allow them to hold funds that avoid investments in non-renewable energy or in Russia. *See* Quinn Curtis, Jill Fisch & Adriana Z. Robertson, *Do ESG Mutual Funds Deliver on Their Promises?* 120 MICH. L. REV. 292 (2021).

acknowledging that it is not possible to provide a menu that meets every conceivable need. There is a difference between singling out a group of investors with ordinary needs for worse treatment in the interests of a Kaldor-Hicks improvement and deciding that an option intended for investors with unusual needs is too risky to include in the menu.

Applying the enhanced Kaldor-Hicks approach to menu redesign poses some evident challenges. It is easier to assess the likelihood of menu misuse than to conclude with confidence that a particular corrective action will produce an aggregate benefit without disregarding the interests of investors with ordinary needs. This is especially true because the fiduciaries will not simply choose whether or not to keep the current menu, but must decide whether a particular variant of streamlining or guardrailing is most appropriate. In a horserace among multiple correctives, there at times will be no clear winner.

In such circumstances, enlightened fiduciaries might adopt a dynamic approach where they would favor a less restrictive approach (a soft guardrail over a hard guardrail or a hard guardrail over streamlining) when choosing among normatively unrankable peers and then monitor the effect of that guardrail to determine if a further change is warranted. A certain amount of dynamism is a natural attribute of the ongoing duty of fiduciaries to evaluate the prudence of their menu design. Evaluating after-the-fact the impact of a particular change leaves open the possibility of moving to a more restrictive alternative if fiduciaries find that likely menu misuse remains entrenched or moving to a less restrictive alternative if fiduciaries find that restrictions are degrading the risk/return outcomes of a substantial minority of participants.

While the enhanced Kaldor-Hicks standard requires plan sponsors to give weight to the interests of plan participants whose preferred options are being deprecated, some might object to the notion that a plan investor should ever be denied a choice in the menu merely because others might misuse it. But that logic would suggest doing away with any limits on plan menus. If we are to discount problems caused by investor's mistakes, then simply sending every investor to a brokerage window would be the logical outcome. That approach likely has advocates, but it is not the policy of retirement plans as we know them. Still, enhanced Kaldor-Hicks puts a thumb on the scale in favor of guardrailing over streamlining precisely because guardrailing might address the problems of menu misuse with minimal restrictions on investors who are using specialized options appropriately. Guardrails are attractive precisely because they enable plan fiduciaries to mitigate misuse while minimizing adverse effects to sophisticated plan investors.

7.4 Veiled Paretianism

While the enhanced Kaldor-Hicks approach to guardrailing and stream-lining provides a general framework, grounded in trust law, for making plan design decisions, it has some inherent limitations. Plan sponsors must still evaluate the welfare effects of different plan changes using the tools we have outlined in prior chapters and these evaluations will often produce ambiguous results. Moreover, the enhanced Kaldor-Hicks stan-dard itself impounds a degree of uncertainty by appealing to notions of "substantial disadvantage" and "identifiable group" that will also require plan sponsors to make judgment calls.

To offer a more concrete option for assessing the desirability of menu trade-offs, we propose a second standard, based in the notion of Pareto optimality, which we term "Veiled Paretianism." The notion behind veiled Paretianism is that there may be some plan changes that would be preferred by all plan investors, regardless of their selected investment risk, if those investors were asked to evaluate the desirability of the change based only on the changes impact on the distribution of expected risks and returns without knowing the particulars of the change itself.

Consider one of the risk-return scatterplots that are central to evaluat-ing plan outcomes (Figure 7.1). Divide the scatterplot into risk "bands" reflecting different levels of selected risk with the width of each band calibrated to include the same number of plan participants.

Now construct a second scatterplot showing the expected return of a proposed plan change: the streamlining or guardrail under consideration (Figure 7.2). The result of the change will be some shift in the distribution of the dots. If every dot moves up in return while holding risk constant, say because the change simply lowers fees on an existing fund while keep-ing everything else the same, then the change is literally Pareto approving and should be adopted.

But suppose that the change has more ambiguous effects, increasing the return for some investors within the risk band while reducing it for oth-ers. In the plot below, a hypothetical reform increases the performance of the worst-performing portfolios but also reduces the performance of the best-performing portfolios while increasing mean risk-adjusted returns. Should it be adopted?

The veiled Paretianism approach suggests that the plan sponsor should consider which of the two plan structures an investor who was aware of the risk band they belonged to, but not which dot represented her port-folio within that risk band would choose. If they were "veiled" from their

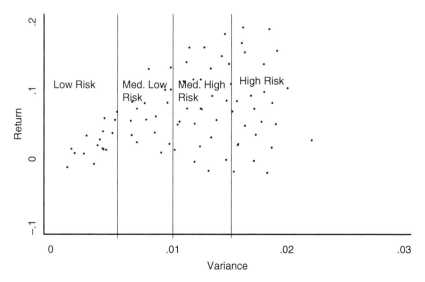

Figure 7.1   Risk-return scatterplots central to evaluating plan outcomes

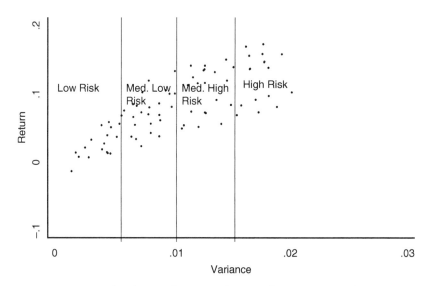

Figure 7.2   Scatterplot showing the expected return of a proposed plan change

particular expected outcome, would an investor in the risk band in question prefer the reformed plan? If the answer is "yes" for hypothetical investors in all risk bands, then the reform should be adopted.

The veiled Pareto standard has empirical support. Using data from UCLA's defined contribution plan, Benartzi and Thaler[19] presented plan participants with information about the distribution of returns they could expect from their own portfolio and from the median and average portfolios of plan participants. They found that investors were collectively indifferent between their own portfolio and the average portfolio but that a majority of investors actually preferred the median portfolio to their own portfolio selection.

This finding justifies the "veiled" aspect of the veiled Pareto standard. If investors on average prefer a typical portfolio to their own, then variation in a return within a risk band is less likely to be the result of careful planning to – for example – take advantage of cross-correlations with unobserved outside assets, but simply the result of noise in investors' varying approaches to making their portfolio choices. Even the investors in question might not regard their own choices as optimal when presented with full information. Put simply, if investors tend to prefer the average portfolio to their own, then paying attention to the average effect on returns should leave investors better off.

How should sponsors operationalize the hypothetical preferences of investors within a risk band? The most obvious answer is simply to look at average expected returns. If the average investor is getting increased expected returns conditional on their selected level of risk and investors at all risk levels are doing at least as well within their risk band, that ought to be sufficient for an investor to prefer the reformed plan within that risk band. We would go even farther, though, and suggest that a rational investor behind a veil of ignorance would also prefer a reform that merely reduced the variance of expected returns, that is the vertical distribution of outcomes. Risk-averse investors would reasonably be risk-averse about where they might end up on the scatterplot. Thus, a reform that reduces the variance of returns at each risk level, even while holding the average return constant, would be consistent with the veiled Pareto standard.

While this approach does not require reforms to be literally Pareto improving, it does require that reforms be beneficial to investors collectively at each risk level. Veiled Paretianism therefore a moderately more stringent standard than enhanced Kaldor-Hicks, which might permit trading off modest declines in risk-adjusted returns to some investors for sufficiently large improvements in expected outcomes for other investors.

---

[19] Shlomo Benartzi & Richard H. Thaler, *How Much Is Investor Autonomy Worth?*, 57 J. FIN. 1593–1616 (2002).

By closely linking the standard for adopting a reform to the expected risk-return plot, the veiled Pareto standard provides clearer guidance to plan sponsors in making menu decisions.

7.5   A Case Study: Northwestern University

Hughes vs Northwestern University,[20] discussed in Chapter 1, presents an interesting testbed for our suggested approaches to fiduciary duties in menu design. While the facts of the case are disputed, one of the plaintiff's claims is that the Northwestern plan agreed to maintain an allegedly high-cost and underperforming stock fund run by TIAA-CREF because TIAA-CREF would not agree to offer its annuity investment option in the plan unless the stock fund was included and TIAA-CREF was used as the record keeper. Northwestern has argued that eliminating the annuity option would have caused investors in the annuity to incur a surrender fee of 2.5 percent. Moreover, many investors strongly preferred the annuity option.

Let's assume that these facts reflect the reality of the situation that Northwestern faced: Either include an underperforming stock fund as an option or assent to the removal of the annuity, causing annuity investors to incur surrender charges. How should a plan sponsor, acting as a fiduciary for plan participants, assess that unpleasant choice? If the annuity adds value for some investors, and including the stock fund is a precondition of offering the annuity, the plan sponsor needs to trade off these outcomes.

As a threshold matter, a fiduciary should not discount the harm done by the underperforming stock fund simply because it is one of several choices in the menu. Taking the plaintiff's allegations at face value, the stock fund would be attractive nuisance, dominated by lower-cost choices elsewhere in the plan. Keeping it in the menu would only serve to create a risk of underperformance for investors who make the mistake of choosing it. A fiduciary should not discount this risk when constructing the menu simply because investors *might* avoid the pitfall.

How would the enhanced Kaldor-Hicks approach reconcile the competing interests of plan participants? Set aside for a moment the unusual feature of a surrender penalty. Suppose that the only trade-off is permitting investors to access the annuity option at the cost of including a clearly dominated fund. Participants' desire to hedge retirement risk with an annuity option would certainly constitute a conventional strategy in

---

[20]   No. 19–1401 (Sup. Ct. 2022).

our book. Doing so is the antithesis of trying to beat the market. The question then becomes whether eliminating the annuity option would substantially disadvantage a sufficiently-substantial, identifiable subgroup of investors.

To answer this question the plan sponsor should endeavor to understand why investors are choosing the annuity option and what alternatives could be provided in a reformed menu. We can attest anecdotally that annuities in university retirement plans have their fervent devotees, but an option should not be retained merely because investors will complain if it is eliminated. Instead, the plan sponsor should ask if investors are choosing the annuity because it genuinely provides risk and return characteristics that cannot be obtained elsewhere. Are there no close substitutes, such that these investors cannot be mapped into an option that doesn't carry the baggage of including a dominated fund in the menu?

Even if the annuity is a unique option in terms of its financial characteristics, a fiduciary should inquire whether those unique features really make it a superior investment option for an identifiable group of plan participants. Is there a specific reason for an annuity or – more to the point – this particular annuity to be part of the menu? The answer may well be "yes," but in applying the enhanced Kaldor-Hicks standard, while investors' expressed preferences should not be entirely discounted, it is important not to confuse the loud objections of a group of investors for actual financial harm.

If a sufficiently substantial minority of investors would be left worse off by the elimination of the annuity option, then the cost of including the stock fund must be considered as well. How many investors are choosing it, and how much worse are their outcomes than they would receive if mapped into a better-performing fund? The latter question is conventional in constructing the plan menu, but the former question is – we believe – unique to our approach: a fiduciary should give attention to how the option is actually being used in determining how much harm it is doing as an inclusion in the plan menu.

If the cost to plan participants of offering the stock fund outweighs the harm of removing the annuity, then the plan sponsor should consider the "enhanced" part of the enhanced Kaldor-Hicks analysis. Would an identifiable group of participants be *substantially* harmed by removing the annuity in order to keep the stock fund off the menu. If we now consider the surrender penalty, the answer would be "yes." Causing a sufficiently substantial group of investors to incur a significant financial penalty as a result of a menu reform would be inconsistent with the enhanced

Kaldor-Hicks standard, even if there would be offsetting gains to investors in the stock fund.

We hasten to add that the surrender penalty would be a reason not to agree to the bundled annuity and stock fund in the first place. Applying the enhanced Kaldor-Hicks analysis to the bundle in question, it should be impermissible to sacrifice the interests of stock-fund investors in order to make the annuity available.

But including the stock fund or not are not the only options. Could the stock fund be guardrailed? Perhaps allocations to it could be capped at a low level, or a soft guard rail could be used to steer participants to another option. (Of course, one wonders if TIAA's goal in including the stock fund would be achieved if a guardrail were applied.) Interestingly, one of the arguments made by the plaintiffs in the Northwestern case is that Northwestern, even if it could not eliminate the stock fund because of the surrender penalty, Northwestern could have closed it to new investments. In effect, the plaintiffs argue that, failing removal, a guardrail would have provided additional protection.

8

Can Streamlining and Guardrailing
Mitigate Allocation Error?

In this chapter, we explore empirically how to evaluate the two core interventions to mitigate allocation error: streamlining and guardrailing. As with our preceding analysis of menu misuse, we use data from the University of Virginia as a case study. We will analyze the actual effect of streamlining that was implemented at UVA in January 2017; and we then simulate the likely impact of guardrailing. Our core interest is to show *how* fiduciaries can assess whether an intervention ex ante is likely to enhance the risk-adjusted performance of participant portfolios, and ex post whether it in fact succeeded in ways that satisfy our enhanced Kaldor Hicks standard. But we begin by discussing the existing fiduciary trend toward the streamlining of menus and placing guardrail caps on company stock investments.

8.1   The Streamlining Movement

Over the last decade, there has been a marked and accelerating movement toward streamlining the core menus of retirement plans.[1] A 2019 study of 180 plan advisors who typically work with mid-sized 401(k)s with $10–$50 million in assets found that roughly half of advisors "agreed" or "strongly agreed" that they were moving toward smaller menus.[2] Plans that implement streamlining often do so by moving toward a tiered structure, with the first tier being the QDIA target date funds, the second tier being a much smaller core menu of diversified funds, and the third tier being a brokerage window.[3] At times streamlining also entails moving toward offering

---

[1] John Sullivan, *An Important Point about 401k Investment Menu Construction*, 401k Specialist (June 20, 2018) https://401kspecialistmag.com/an-important-point-about-401k-investment-menu-constructionl/.

[2] Ian Salisbury, *Your 401(k) May Soon Have Fewer Investment Choices – But That's a Good Thing*, Money (November 13, 2019) https://money.com/401ks-fewer-choices/.

[3] The tendency to streamline and establish target date defaults makes it harder to disentangle the effects of streamlining by itself, because QDIA setting can produce such pronounced benefits. *See* Olivia S. Mitchell & Stephen P. Utkus, *Target-Date Funds and Portfolio Choice*

"fewer choices but with broader diversification." For example, instead of a US equity and a non-US equity fund, a streamlined menu might offer a single global equity fund, or eliminate multiple fund style permutations of {small, mid or large cap} and {value or growth} and {domestic or international}, offering instead "a core menu of funds based on objectives such as growth, income, inflation, and capital preservation."[4]

More extreme versions of streamlining can even "eliminate the core lineup altogether."[5] For example, a large Midwestern state defined-contribution plan adopted this extreme form of streamlining, such that they only offer a set of QDIA-eligible target date and balance funds plus "a self-directed brokerage account, which very few use."[6]

This streamlining movement shows the impact and success of behavioral economics on the plan advisor community. There is an explicit consideration of "choice architecture" in plan design.[7] The advisor community is concerned about participant choice overload and how large menus can cause "analysis paralysis."[8] As plans increase the size of their menus, they tend to add funds with higher expense ratios.[9] Plans with larger menus have also been shown to have poorer average risk-return characteristics.[10]

In 401(K) Plans, J. PENSION ECON. FINANC. 1, 18 (2021) ("adoption of low-cost target-date funds may enhance retirement wealth by as much as 50% over a 30-year horizon").

4 Susan Czochara, *Streamlining 401(k) Plans to Improve Diversification*, Institutional Investor (June 24, 2015), www.institutionalinvestor.com/article/b14z9y86rzhdzf/streamlining-401k-plans-to-improve-diversification. See also Capital Ideas, *How to Help Participants Make Better 401(k) Choices*, Capital Group (June 16, 2021) www.capitalgroup.com/advisor/insights/articles/help-plan-participants-better-choices.html.

5 Pension & Investments, *Investment Lineup: Streamlining Continues* (October 28, 2019) https://supplements.pionline.com/trends-in-dc/2019-10-28/articles/investment-lineup-streamlining-continues.

6 *Id.*

7 Cerulli Associates, *U.S. Retail Investor Products and Platforms 2018: Defining Client Experience through Choice Architecture*, Annual Report (2018).

8 Sullivan, *supra* note 1.

9 Jeffrey R. Brown, Nellie Liang & Scott Weisbenner, *Individual Account Investment Options and Portfolio Choice: Behavioral Lessons from 401(K) Plans*, 91 J. PUB. ECON. 1992, 2013 (2007). ("the vast majority of the new funds added to 401(k) plans are high-cost actively managed equity funds," so as the number of option increases "average portfolio expenses increase, and average portfolio performance is thus depressed"). See also Tomas Dvorak, *Do 401k Plan Advisors Take Their Own Advice?*, 14 J. PENSION ECON. & FIN. 55, 75 (2015) ("[f]unds that are in clients' plans but not in their advisors' plans have higher expense ratios than the funds held by advisors").

10 David Goldreich & Hanna Halaburda, *When Smaller Menus Are Better: Variability in Menu-Setting Ability*, 59 MANAG. SCI. 2518, 2535 (2013).

In addition, larger menus have been shown to depress employee plan participation. For example, a 2004 cross-sectional analysis of 649 defined contribution plans managed by Vanguard found – after controlling for a variety of employee and plan attributes – that for every additional fund offered on the menu, participation rates dropped by about 2 percent.[11] This depressing effect of larger menus is particularly pronounced with regard to female employees.[12] Even when employees do participate, larger menus may also bias allocation decisions. Naïve diversification may lead participants to put more of their assets in asset classes that are disproportionately represented on the menu or in funds with which they are more familiar.[13]

Donald Keim and Olivia Mitchell have analyzed the impact of streamlining at a large US non-profit institution.[14] The plan eliminated 39 funds from its initial undifferentiated menu of 88 funds – culling funds "based on the funds' expense ratios, the similarity of return and risk characteristics with retained funds, the number of participants, and aggregate amounts invested in each fund."[15] The plan also moved to a tiered structure of 13 low-cost target date funds as the plan default, together with a second tier of four index funds, a third tier of 32 separate asset class funds, and a brokerage window as a fourth tier. The assets in deleted funds were automatically transferred to an age-appropriate TDF, unless the participant affirmatively choose a different investment option.

The authors found that the streamlined participants were "significantly older, more likely to be male, lived in higher-income households, and were more likely to have earned graduate-level degrees."[16] More importantly, the authors found that streamlining the plan into this tier structure

---

[11] Sheena Sethi-Iyengar, Gur Huberman and Wei Jiang, *How Much Choice Is Too Much? Contributions to 401(k) Retirement Plans*, Wharton Pension Research Council Working Papers 426 (2004). *See also* Maureen Morrin, Susan Broniarczyk, and Jeffrey J. Inman, *Fund Assortments, Gender, and Retirement Plan Participation*, 29 INT. J. BANK MARK. 433, 450 (2011). (When Oregon University expanded its menu from 10 to 19 fund choices in July 2007, the percentage of participants sticking with money market QDIA increased from 21 percent to 34 percent).

[12] *Id.* at 433 ("larger fund assortments tend to reduce participation among women but increase it among men").

[13] Richard H. Thaler & Shlomo Benartzi, *Naive Diversification Strategies in Defined Contribution Saving Plans*, 91 AM. ECON. REV. 79, 98 (2001). *See also* Innovest Portfolio Solutions, *Investment Menu Simplification*, A Retirement Plan Whitepaper (2005).

[14] Olivia S. Mitchell & Donald B. Keim, *Simplifying Choices in Defined Contribution Retirement Plan Design: A Case Study*, 17 J. PENSION ECON. & FIN. 363, 384 (2017).

[15] *Id.* at 367.

[16] *Id.* at 369.

tended to improve the quality of participant allocations. They estimate that the uncompensated, idiosyncratic risk fell significantly after streamlining – indicating a reduction in diversification errors. What's more, the streamlined group experienced a statistically significant reduction in the average portfolio expense ratio of 4 basis points – indicating a reduction in expense errors.[17] Their analysis establishes that, by focusing on affected participant portfolios, it is feasible to assess whether streamlining has positively impacted portfolio performance.[18]

8.2   Evaluating the Impact of Streamlining

The University of Virginia data provides important information about the impact of corrective menu redesign because in January 2017 the plan also implemented a substantial streamlining of its menu. As shown in Table 8.1, the plan went from offering 303 options to just 50 options after.

The discontinued funds were not just closed to additional investments; existing balances in the discontinued funds were, by default, mapped to either TDF default funds or to broad-gauged indexes within the same asset class.[19] The redesign was targeted at the three core allocation mistakes discussed earlier in Chapter 4.

The new menu targeted the problem of diversification errors by completely eliminating all sector funds and country- and region-specific international funds. The default mapping of several eliminated funds to low-cost, target-date funds could also mitigate the diversification mistake of underweighting particular asset classes, the exposure mistakes of too much or too little equity allocations, and the fee mistakes of bloated portfolio expense ratios.

Table 8.2 shows the proportion of assets held in various types of funds *before* streamlining for participants who would subsequently be streamlined as well as for participants whose portfolios were not impacted by streamlining.

The non-streamlined portfolios were dominantly invested in target date funds while the streamlined portfolios were more likely to be invested in

---

[17] *Id.* at 378. The authors also found that the streamlined group on average increased the proportion of their portfolio invested in equities but did not analyze age-appropriate exposure to assess whether this increase was a normative improvement. *Id.* at 371.

[18] Assessing UVA's streamlining change, the next section of this chapter emulates a great deal of their analytic approach.

[19] TDF funds for mapping were based on the age of the employee. Specific mapping were based on the eliminated fund and communicated to employees in advance of the redesign.

Table 8.1 *Describing UVA menu pre- and post-reform*

Fund type	Pre-reform	Post-reform
Domestic equities – broad	82	7
Domestic equities – sector	43	0
International equities – broad	16	2
International equities – region funds	12	0
TDFs	22	23
Balanced	19	0
Bonds	34	5
Real estate	4	1
Money market	8	1
Other Funds	39	11

Table 8.2 *Types of assets held by streamlined and non-streamlined participants*

Fund type	Streamlined	Non-streamlined
Domestic equities – broad	45.7%	3.1%
Domestic equities – sector	5.1%	0.0%
International equities – broad	3.8%	0.2%
International equities – region Funds	1.7%	0.0%
TDFs	16.00%	96.90%
Balanced	14.70%	0.00%
Bonds	7.50%	0.10%
Real estate	2.00%	0.10%
Money market	4.00%	0.00%
Dominated	7.10%	1.00%
N	2324	5383

broad domestic equity funds and every other asset class. The table also shows that streamlined portfolios were much more likely to be invested in the 31 funds which we coded as dominated funds – because of their high expense ratio and similar investments to other menu offerings.[20] Streamlining impacted the portfolios of 30.2 percent of participants and

---

[20] For the UVA plan, we code funds as dominated if the fees of the fund exceed the fees of the mean fund in the Lipper Objective code by 25 basis points in the cheapest fund in the same Lipper Objective code by 50 basis points.

Table 8.3 *Demographics of streamlined and non-streamlined participants*

Differences in streamlined individual characteristics	Streamlined group Mean	Non-streamlined group Mean	t-Test Difference
Age under 30	0.02	0.14	−0.12***
Age 30–39	0.13	0.36	−0.23***
Age 40–49	0.25	0.24	0.01
Age 50–59	0.32	0.16	0.16***
Age 60–69	0.22	0.09	0.13***
Age 70+	0.06	0.01	0.05***
Female	0.22	0.24	−0.02**
Male	0.3	0.24	0.06***
Salary 50,000 or under	0.05	0.11	−0.05***
Salary 50,000–100,000	0.23	0.25	−0.01
Salary 100,000–150,000	0.14	0.08	0.06***
Salary over 150,000	0.09	0.04	0.05***
No. funds per person	4.46	1.12	3.34***
Observations	2324	5383	7707

Statistics are for January 2016 portfolios of individuals that appear in both 2016 and 2017. Individuals with all assets invested in TDFs or in funds that were still available after reforms are included. Ages are as of November 2016. * $p<0.10$, ** $p<0.05$, *** $p<0.01$.

42.2 percent of plan assets. The redesign had the potential to dramatically impact the affected portfolios. These affected "streamlined" portfolios on average had 63.7 percent of their assets in funds that were eliminated and 38.1 percent of these portfolios had more than 90 percent of their plan savings in eliminated funds.[21]

Table 8.3 compares the demographics of participants who were and were not streamlined[22]:

In line with Keim and Mitchell's findings, this table shows that streamlined participants were disproportionately older, male, and with higher salaries. The streamlined group invested in 4.5 funds on average while the non-streamlined group held on average just 1.1 funds.

---

[21] *See infra* Appendix Figure 5.

[22] Gender is missing from the data for a significant subsample of participants.

Table 8.4 *Average allocation changes in fund types for affected participants*

Fund type	Streamlined: active choice	Streamlined: passive choice	Non-streamlined
Domestic equities – broad	−0.074***	0.006***	0.005***
Domestic equities – sector	−0.061***	−0.047***	0.000
International equities – broad	0.029***	0.005***	0.000
International equities – region funds	−0.015***	−0.017***	0.000
TDFs	0.142***	0.216***	−0.016***
Balanced	−0.097***	−0.162***	0.000
Bands	0.048***	−0.005***	0.004***
Real estate	−0.008*	−0.001**	0.001***
Money market	0.033***	0.001***	0.002***
N	549	1775	5383

* $p < 0.05$, ** $p < 0.01$, *** $p < 0.0$.

After streamlining took effect, a substantial majority (71.6 percent) of affected portfolios kept their savings fully invested in these plan default funds (as well as unaffected previous allocations), with less than a fifth of streamlined participants making affirmative choices to invest in non-mapped funds offered in the streamlined menu.[23] The stickiness of the default mapping remained somewhat persistent across time with 93.4 percent of participants who were initially plan defaulted remaining with the default funds a year later.[24] New employees hired after January 2017 also tended to stick with the default portfolio allocation: 80 percent of them remained in a single Vanguard TDF and over 90 percent kept all of their assets in TDFs.

Table 8.4 shows the average change in allocation for the participant portfolios that were affected by the streamlining redesign for both the participants who initially stayed with the default mapping funds (passive choice) and for those who affirmatively chose alternative allocations

[23] *See infra* Appendix Figure 6. Participants are considered to be streamlined and plan-defaulted if, in January 2017, they only hold TDFs or funds to which their January 2016 holdings would have been mapped, regardless of the proportion of their 2016 and 2017 holdings in each fund.
[24] *Id.*

(active choice), as well as for those participants whose portfolios were not streamlined.

This table shows that participants whose portfolios were unaffected by streamlining experienced no substantial change in the proportion of their portfolios invested in various asset classes. By contrast, the substantial reductions in sector funds and country-specific international funds were a hard-wired result of the redesign, forcing these allocation percentages to zero. The streamlined participants who stayed with the default mapping funds held 4.7 percent of their portfolios in sector funds pre-reform and 0 percent afterward. More generally, these passive choice streamlined participants experienced a 21.6 percentage point increase in exposure to target-date funds (with the allocation shift coming largely from sector funds, country-specific international funds, and balanced funds reductions), while the active choice streamlined participants experienced a more modest increase of 14.2 percent.

A possible concern raised by the table is that participants who made affirmative allocation choices after the menu redesign ended up with a bit more savings (3.3 percentage points) in the plan's money market fund and shifted 7.4 percentage points of their allocations away from broad domestic equity funds. Even though the passive choice streamlined allocations were well designed to reduce diversification, fee, and exposure mistakes, the streamlined participant's active choices regarding the streamlined menu might still produce suboptimal outcomes.

To more directly assess the extent to which streamlining improved the quality of participant allocations, Table 8.5 reports the proportion of various errors that were eliminated by the streamlining process.

This table shows dramatic declines in all three core errors.[25] All of the participants who held more than 10 percent of the portfolios in narrow sector or region funds were no longer overweighted following the streamlining reform. The same holds true for portfolios that had overall annual expenses of more than 75 basis points. While the streamlined menu still included one high-cost fund, the Fidelity Diversified International Fund, with an expense ratio of 81 basis points, no participant was so heavily invested in the fund to have a high-cost portfolio overall. The streamlining also dramatically reduced the prevalence of exposure mistakes. Post-streamlining there were no participants below the minimum exposure

---

[25] The table does not report the underweight of international equities as an error but streamlining also corrected 100 percent of this error.

Table 8.5 *The proportion of error correction due to streamlining*

Guardrail violation	Number of portfolios with allocation errors prior to streamlining	Proportion of portfolios that stopped making errors after streamlining	Number of new violators
Expense error	145	100%	0
Diversification error	271	100%	0
Exposure error	429	62%	1
Any non-international error	732	77%	0

discussed in Chapter 5 and only a few older participants (>65 years old) clung to portfolios with large equity exposure.

8.3   Impact on Risk and Return Performance

This substantial reduction in allocation errors by itself is a good reason to judge streamlining as a success. But as before, it is also possible to complement this analysis by looking at portfolio performance. To undertake this additional analysis, we calculated the ex post (realized) risk and return of the portfolios that the participants actually held in 2016 just after the redesigned menu took effect and compared it to the realized risk and return for that participants would have experienced if they had continued to hold their prior portfolios over the same period (from 2017 to 2018). For example, the scatterplot in Figure 8.1 uses vectors to show how streamlining impacted the realized risk-and return outcomes of goldbug investors who initially held more than 10 percent of the portfolio balances in the Fidelity Gold Fund.

This figure dramatically illustrates the potential prophylactic good that constraining menu choice can produce. In virtually every case, the participant experienced higher returns and lower risk than they would have had if their plan balances had continued to be invested in the pre-reform portfolio. Figure 8.2 undertakes an analogous exercise for all participants. Instead of displaying arrows connecting each portfolio pair, the scatter plot displays the same array of risk and return outcome for the pre-redesign allocations as well as the outcomes of the post-redesign allocations for the same participants over the same time period.

Two things become immediately apparent from this figure. First, the risk/return outcomes of the post-redesign portfolios are much less dispersed than those portfolios held by the same participants just before the

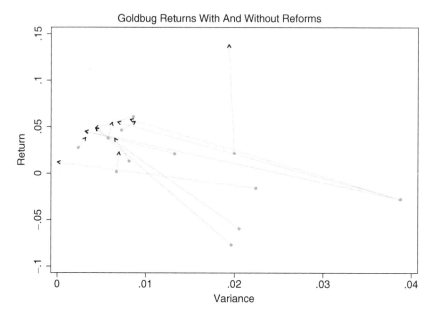

Figure 8.1 Impact of streamlining on risk and return of participants over-weighted in gold

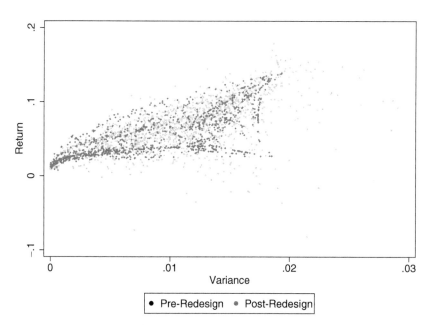

Figure 8.2 Comparison of risk and return for streamlined portfolios and what pre-reform outcomes would have been

Note: Only portfolios with variance <0.03 are shown.

menu redesign. In particular, the figure shows far fewer post-redesign outcomes in the southwest portion of the graph – which represents higher risk and lower returns. A participant with even moderate risk-aversion would likely prefer an outcome drawn from the post-redesign's more concentrated, distribution. These patterns suggest that streamlining represents a Kaldor-Hicks improvement.

Second, the figure shows that some participants would have experienced superior risk/return outcomes during this time period had they been allowed to continue to hold their pre-streamlining portfolio. The blue dots lying above and to the left of the cluster of post-streamlining orange dots are the portfolios of participants who were made worse off by the menu redesign. Part of this outperformance is an artifact of luck that one should expect for a few portfolios, even if they had inferior expected risk and returns. Yet, part of the overperformance may be due to streamlining constraining savvy participants from investing in better performance. If true, this means that the elimination of funds did not produce a Pareto improvement in expected risk/return outcomes, thought the change might have still met the veiled-Pareto concept as we described in the previous chapter. Before analyzing whether streamlining met the enhanced Kaldor-Hicks standard, we turn to an analysis of how guardrails might, alternatively, have mitigated menu misuse.

8.4 Evaluating the Impact of Guardrails

As mentioned above, hard guardrails capping the proportion of assets invested in company stock have already been implemented by fiduciaries for several plans. In June 2020, Vanguard conducted an analysis of retirement plans that it advises. Vanguard found that roughly two-thirds of plans that offer company stock restrict participant contributions and/or exchanges into company stock.[26] Most plans restrict the allocations of both employer and employee contributions, with the most common cap being 20 percent. One in five plans go further than contribution limits and redirect account balances to the QDIA target date fund when "the company stock position exceeds the limit."[27] These restrictions – along with the elimination of company stock plan offerings[28] – have dramatically reduced

---

[26] John A. Lamancusa and Jean A. Young, COMPANY STOCK IN DC PLANS, Vanguard Research (December 2020).

[27] *Id.* at 10.

[28] The percentage of participants nationally who were offered company stock fell from 40 percent in 2005 to 19 percent in 2020. *Id.* at 5.

the number of participants across the country who hold concentrated positions in company stock. In 2005, 14 percent of Vanguard participants had
company stock portfolio concentrations greater than 20 percent, but by
2020 this proportion had gone down to only 4 percent.[29] The movement
away from such overweighting is almost certainly salutary, given that the
failure to diversify retirement portfolios overinvested in company stock has
been estimated to sacrifice as much as 42 percent of the portfolio certainty-
equivalent values, while the theoretical incentive benefits to employers of
such employee holdings are empirically much smaller.[30]

In this section, we go beyond company stock guardrails to assess the
impact of three different guardrails that were suggested in the discussion
of menu misuse in Chapter 6:

- To mitigate diversification mistakes, we impose a sector guardrail
  that caps the amount that can be allocated to any individual sector or
  regional stock fund at 10 percent.[31]
- To mitigate fee mistakes, we impose a fee guardrail that caps the average
  fund expense ratio of a portfolio at 0.75 percent, and finally.
- To mitigate exposure mistakes, we impose a (lower- and upper-)
  glidepath guardrail which mandates that the percentage of a portfolio
  allocated to equities must be at least half and no more than twice the
  percentage for that participant's default target date fund glidepath.

The freedom-preserving advantage of guardrails relative to streamlining is particularly evident with regard to these guardrail restrictions. As
we previously analyzed in our discussion of menu misuse, about 9.6 percent of UVA portfolios at the beginning of 2016 violated at least one of
these three guardrails. In contrast, the streamlining redesign of the UVA's
menu impacted almost three times as many (30.1 percent) participant
portfolios. Guardrailing also impacted fewer underlying assets than the

---

[29] *Id.* at 5. *See* also Olivia S. Mitchell & Stephen P. Utkus, *The Role of Company Stock in Defined
Contribution Plans*, NBER WORKING PAPERS 9250 (2002). ("Today an estimated 11 million participants have concentrated stock positions exceeding 20% of account assets.").

[30] Lisa Meulbroek, *Company Stock in Pension Plans: How Costly Is It?*, 48 J. LAW ECON. 443,
474 (2005). *See* also Benartzi et al., *The Law and Economics of Company Stock in 401(k) Plans*,
50 J. L. & ECON. 45, 79 (2007). While the costs of failing to diversify are substantial, they
must be traded off at times against the cost of excess plan fees. One upside of investing in
company stock is that it is normally purchased without transaction costs or annual expense
ratios. We found earlier in Chapter 1 that the high expenses of some plans made it rational
for participants to hold non-trivial proportions of company stock in their portfolios.

[31] A participant could hold 10 percent in each of several different sector or regional equity
funds without violating this guardrail.

Table 8.6 *Demographics of guardrailed and non-guardrailed participants*

	Non-guardrailed group	Guardrailed group	*t*-Test
	Mean	Mean	Difference
Age under 30	0.11	0.02	0.09***
Age 30–39	0.31	0.10	0.21***
Age 40–49	0.25	0.17	0.08***
Age 50–59	0.21	0.22	−0.01
Age 60–69	0.11	0.30	−0.19***
Age 70+	0.01	0.19	−0.18***
Female	0.24	0.17	0.07***
Male	0.25	0.33	−0.09***
Salary 50,000 or under	0.09	0.05	0.04***
Salary 50,000–100,000	0.25	0.22	0.03*
Salary 100,000–150,000	0.10	0.12	−0.02
Salary over 150,000	0.05	0.09	−0.03***
No. funds per person	1.97	3.53	−1.56***
Observations	6968	739	7707

Statistics are for January 2016 portfolios of individuals that appear in both 2016 and 2017.

Ages are as of November 2016. Many participants had missing gender information.

Note: *p<0.10, **p<0.05, ***p<0.01.

streamlining interventions. Streamlining forced the reallocation of 63.7 percent of the assets in the portfolios that it impacted, while our three guardrails would have only forced the reallocation of 32.7 percent of the portfolios impacted. Thus, guardrailing targets and disables the most troublesome forms of diversification, fee, and exposure mistakes more precisely without disturbing the choices of most participants. The more precise targeting can be seen if we recall from Table 8.5 that streamlining only succeeded in eliminating 77 percent of these three errors, while these guardrails would definitionally eliminate all of them.

Table 8.6 is analogous to Table 8.3 and reports the demographic differences between those portfolio holdings that would be subject to one of the guardrails and those that would not.

This table shows that, similarly to our streamlining analysis, participants who are older, male, and with higher salaries are significantly more likely to have 2016 portfolios that hit one of the guardrail constraints.

Table 8.7 *Portfolio holdings of guardrailed and non-guardrailed participants and how guardrailing changed some allocations*

Fund type	Non-guardrailed	Guardrailed	Guardailed delta
Domestic equities – broad	0.142	0.321	−0.063***
Domestic equities – sector	0.002	0.144	−0.086***
International equities – broad	0.012	0.023	−0.004***
International equities – region funds	0.000	0.048	−0.033***
TDFs	0.784	0.166	0.292***
Balanced	0.040	0.081	−0.023***
Bonds	0.016	0.093	−0.033***
Real estate	0.005	0.023	−0.002***
Money market	0.002	0.103	−0.047***
N	6968	739	739

$^* p < 0.05, ^{**} p < 0.01, ^{***} p < 0.0.$

Like streamlining, any guardrailing intervention that attempts to correct existing allocation errors must also specify how allocations that violate a guardrail will be remapped.[32] To address this issue, we simulate a program that by default maps non-complying assets to a participant's age-appropriate target date fund. For example, if a participant has more than 10 percent in a particular fund, only the allocation in excess of the guardrail is reallocated to the TDF.[33] Our algorithm reduces just the parts of a participant's portfolio that violate a guardrail and increases the age-appropriate TDF until none of the guardrails are violated.

Table 8.7 serves two different purposes. First, it reports the different holdings of the portfolios that will be guardrailed and those that will not. Second, in the final column, it shows how much guardrailing shifts those holdings.

In the table, we see that the non-guardrailed portfolios had over 75 percent of their portfolios invested in target date funds with their second largest holdings (14.2 percent) in broad domestic equity funds. In

---

[32] A less intrusive guardrail might only apply to future contributions and would leave intact pre-existing menu misuse.

[33] The appendix describes the details of the TDF mapping as well as a second mapping approach.

contrast, portfolios subject to the guardrail algorithms began with less than 20 percent of their assets in TDFs and 19.2 percent invested in the narrow sector and regional equity funds. Guardrailing reduces the holdings in sector and regional equity funds from 14.4 percent and 4.8 percent to 5.8 percent and 1.5 percent, respectively. Our simulation indicates that guardrailing would increase the target date fund holdings nearly three-fold, by 29.2 percentage points. This kind of remapping toward target date funds would tend to improve the allocation quality on a number of fronts. A remapped portfolio due to overweighting in a narrow technology sector fund would – through the target date fund – be exposed to more international stock and a more balanced exposure to equities.

There is always the possibility that some participants would opt out of our TDF default by affirmatively choosing alternative portfolios that comply with the guardrails. However, given that 76.1 percent of participants affected by streamlining stayed with plan-defaulted funds, there is good reason to believe that a substantial majority of participants whose portfolios are partially remapped because of guardrails would stick to the TDF mapping defaults. The following simulations examine the effect of our proposed guardrails assuming no affirmative choice alterations. Even if participants affirmatively switched away from guardrail default allocations, any alterations that did occur would have to independently comply with the guardrails. For example, a participant with a portfolio that exceeded the fee cap might choose not to let its highest fee funds be mapped to TDFs but, in choosing an alternative portfolio, the participant would still have to bring the resulting average expense ratio below 75 basis points. Therefore, even with affirmatively chosen portfolios, none of the resulting portfolios would run afoul of the diversification, excess fee, or exposure standards.

To assess the likely impact of guardrails, we compare the 2017–2018 realized risk and return for the portfolios with guardrails in place to the same outcomes for the unconstrained portfolios that the same participants held in January of 2016. Figure 8.3 visually accomplishes this with a scatter plot that is the guardrail analog to the streamlining analysis shown in Figure 8.2.

As we found with streamlining, the imposition of guardrails is effective at eliminating many of the worst risk/return outcomes. Figure 8.3 shows that many of the outcomes with high risk and low return are shifted to the northwest. But we also see that guardrailing does not represent a Pareto improvement as some portfolios after the imposition of guardrails realize reduced returns and/or higher risk.

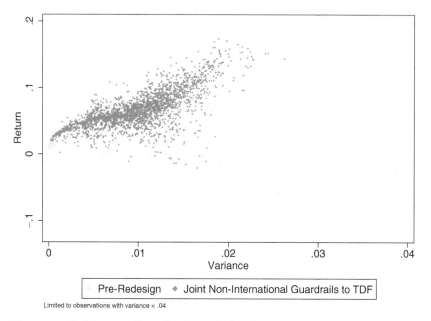

Figure 8.3   Risk/return effect of hard guardrails with target date mapping
Note: Only portfolios with variance < 0.04 are shown.

8.5   Do Streamlining or Guardrailing Correctives Produce Enhanced Kaldor-Hicks Improvements?

The failure of both streamlining and guardrailing interventions to meet the stringent Pareto improvement requirement that not a single participant experience a reduction in utility does not mean that fiduciaries must cling to the status quo or remain agnostic between the two competing correctives. This is particularly true given the foregoing evidence that both streamlining and guardrailing applied to the UVA plan would substantially reduce or eliminate the prevalence of diversification, fee, and exposure errors.

Table 8.8 explores the impact of these interventions by regressing various measures of changes to allocation quality and portfolio performance on whether the portfolio was subject to streamlining and guardrailing as well as various participant demographics.

The first specification shows that streamlining reduces the idiosyncratic risk of the streamlined portfolios by statistically significant amounts. The idiosyncratic risk of the streamlined passive choice participants fell by 0.184 percent, and the idiosyncratic risk of the streamlined active choice participants fell even more (by 0.253 percent).[34] The second specification analogously tests the impact of guardrail simulations and finds that portfolios subjected to guardrail remapping experienced an even larger reduction in idiosyncratic risk. Because there is no way for participants to choose alternative allocations in our simulations, the guardrail regressions, unlike the streamline regressions, do not distinguish between the active and passive choice participants.

Specifications 3–6 report analogous regressions testing the impact of streamlining (in the odd specifications) and guardrailing (in the even specifications) on expense ratios and the percentage of the participant allocation invested in dominated funds. In specification 3 we see that streamlining reduces the expenses of active and passive choice streamlined portfolios by 21.7 and 20.3 basis points, respectively, and that these reductions are highly significant (p. < .01). Specification 4 shows a similar, but somewhat smaller expense reduction of 12.5 basis points for guardrailed portfolios. Following Keim and Mitchell, we estimate that if similar "savings could be achieved on an ongoing basis over 20 years and reinvested at 5% annually,"[35] the accumulated benefit per participant would amount to about $8,000 for the streamlined portfolios and $5,000 for the guardrailed portfolios.[36] The fifth and sixth specifications show analogously statistically significant declines in percentage of portfolios invested in (high-cost) dominated funds. Streamlining reduces the holdings of dominated funds by more than 8 percentage points for passive streamlined portfolios, and by 3.5 percentage points for active streamlined portfolios; while our simulation shows guardrailing reducing dominated fund allocation share by 3.7 percentages points.

The final two specifications estimate the impact of streamlining on the prevalence of exposure errors and whether a portfolio had any of the three guardrailed errors. [Unlike the other specifications, these regressions do not have guardrail analogs because portfolios that are impacted by guardrails perfectly predict the portfolios that correct errors in the simulation.] Specification 7 shows that streamlining is associated with statistically significant reductions in exposure errors – especially for passive choice participants. The results presented in Table 8.8 provide strong evidence

---

[34] The participants who opted out of the default remapping are estimated to have larger drops than the passive choice participants, not because active choosers ended up with less diversified portfolios, but because their initial portfolios had more idiosyncratic risk to being with.

[35] Mitchell, *supra* note 14 at 378.

[36] In comparison, Keim and Mitchell estimated that a 4 basis point reduction in expense caused by streamlining might lead to an accumulated benefit of around $4,000 per participant.

Table 8.8 *Effects of streamlining/guardrailing on allocation quality and portfolio performance*

	Mean	(1) Delta idiosyncratic risk (streamlining)	(2) Delta idiosyncratic risk (guardrailing)	(3) Delta expense ratio (streamlining)	(4) Delta expense ratio (guardrailing)	(5) Delta % dominated funds (streamlining)	(6) Delta % dominated funds (guardrailing)	(7) Delta exposure error (streamlining)	(8) Delta any error (streamlining)
Streamlined: active choice	0.230	-0.00253*** (0.000172)		-0.217*** (0.00580)		-0.0348*** (0.00379)		-0.104*** (0.00811)	-0.231*** (0.0115)
Streamlined: passive choice	0.071	-0.00184*** (0.000251)		-0.203*** (0.00946)		-0.0837*** (0.00782)		-0.0434*** (0.0118)	-0.177*** (0.0192)
Guardrailed	0.096		-0.00407*** (0.000403)		-0.125*** (0.00654)		-0.0370*** (0.00518)		
Age as of 2016	45.182	9.64e-05*** (1.97e-05)	-7.83e-05*** (2.41e-05)	-0.00174* (0.000894)	-0.000656 (0.000531)	-0.00182*** (0.000612)	-0.000814** (0.000364)	0.0382*** (0.00171)	-0.0153*** (0.00203)
Age-squared	2198.658	-9.68e-07*** (2.19e-07)	8.48e-07*** (2.69e-07)	1.04e-05 (9.89e-06)	6.37e-06 (5.98e-06)	1.62e-05*** (6.90e-06)	8.02e-06* (4.09e-06)	-0.000455*** (1.98e-05)	0.000176*** (2.35e-05)
Male	0.255	-0.000312*** (0.000107)	-0.000217*** (7.88e-05)	0.00255 (0.00442)	-0.00344** (0.00147)	-0.00281 (0.00276)	-0.000234** (0.00102)	-0.0150** (0.00612)	-0.0130 (0.00857)
Gender unknown	0.508	-0.000395 (0.000249)	-0.000266 (0.000203)	-0.00145 (0.0106)	0.00473 (0.00608)	-0.00616 (0.00631)	-0.000632 (0.00321)	0.0899*** (0.0229)	-0.00579 (0.0264)
Total assets (100,000 USD)	0.474	0.000194*** (3.95e-05)	0.000111*** (3.03e-05)	0.00414** (0.00205)	0.00208** (0.000893)	0.000317 (0.00128)	0.00151*** (0.000412)	-0.000873 (0.00365)	0.00368 (0.00475)

	(1)	(2)	(3)	(4)	(5)	(6)	(7)	(8)
Salary 50,000 or under	0.091	0.000629 (0.000450)	0.000697* (0.000359)	-0.00770 (0.0174)	0.00667 (0.00577)	-0.00177 (0.0122)	0.00312 (0.00402)	-0.0392 (0.0249)	-0.0379 (0.0359)
Salary 50,000–100,000	0.243	0.000505 (0.000430)	0.000661* (0.000339)	-0.0142 (0.0171)	0.00443 (0.00568)	0.00222 (0.0120)	0.00508 (0.00382)	-0.0462* (0.0243)	-0.0474 (0.0354)
Salary 100,000–150,000	0.100	0.000877** (0.000406)	0.000721** (0.000321)	-0.00503 (0.0156)	0.00751 (0.00513)	-0.00249 (0.0113)	0.00476 (0.00332)	-0.0261 (0.0228)	-0.0265 (0.0331)
Salary over 150,000	0.057	0.000347* (0.000186)	0.000254** (0.000125)	0.00290 (0.0127)	0.00508 (0.00379)	-0.00488 (0.00963)	0.00179 (0.00193)	-0.0364* (0.0186)	-0.0281 (0.0277)
Salary data missing	0.534	0.000849* (0.000479)	0.000795** (0.000385)	-0.00610 (0.0196)	-0.00114 (0.00815)	0.000650 (0.0133)	0.00237 (0.00474)	-0.137*** (0.0326)	-0.0373 (0.0429)
Constant		-0.00338*** (0.000629)	0.00110* (0.000599)	0.0497* (0.0260)	0.0112 (0.0122)	0.0446** (0.0183)	0.0161* (0.00824)	-0.703*** (0.0439)	0.354*** (0.0569)
N		7,707	7,701	7,707	7,707	7,707	7,701	7,707	7,698
R-squared		0.075	0.131	0.358	0.342	0.069	0.069	0.288	0.126
Diff(β?(Streamlined, plan-defaulted) – ?(Streamlined, non-plan-defaulted))		-.00068**		-.01402		.04881***		-.06026***	-.05334**
Mean of dep var		-.001	-0.0003678	-.076	-.012	-.02	-.003	-.057	-.063

t statistics in parentheses; * $p < 0.05$, ** $p < 0.01$, *** $p < 0.001$.

that both streamlining and guardrailing reduce participants' menu mis-use. Guardrailing by design eliminates specific allocation errors, and specification 8 shows empirically that streamlining reduces the preva-lence of portfolio allocations with weighting, expense, or exposure errors. Both interventions reduce our estimates of idiosyncratic risk and expense ratios and these results are all highly significant (p < .01).

The regressions also suggest that these prophylactic interventions are particularly helpful for male participants. For example, the guardrail regres-sions suggest that male participants had even larger reductions in idiosyn-cratic risk and fund expenses than women (the reference gender category). This is consistent with much of the literature suggesting that men are more likely to be "cowboy" investors who believe they can beat the market and are less willing to stick with tried and true approaches to investing in low-cost, well-diversified, and well-exposed investments. The coefficients on age and age squared that are precisely estimated imply intermediate ages between 36 and 56 where the specification outcome reaches an extreme value. For example, the change in idiosyncratic risk caused by streamlining is increasing in the participant's age until 50 and then declines, while the change in idiosyncratic risk caused by guardrailing is estimated to decrease in age until the participant reaches 46 and then it increases.

Lastly, it is possible to look at realized risk and return performance to assess whether guardrailing or streamlining can satisfy the enhanced Kaldor-Hicks standard. Table 8.9 makes this comparison for both the actual streamlining redesign that UVA effectuated and for the three guardrails we have simulated.

The first row of the table summarizes the impact of the streamlining redesign. Making a pairwise evaluation of the portfolios with and without a particular intervention, we find that streamlining failed to increase the average Sharpe ratio – only increasing the risk/return outcomes of less than half (33.39 percent) of the affected portfolios. While streamlining helped the small set of investors who were overweighted in gold, Table 8.9 suggests more generally that streamlining (as measured by realized returns in this relatively short period) did not produce a Kaldor-Hicks improvement.

In contrast, the third row of the table makes a much stronger case for imposing our targeted guardrails as corrective action for participants' menu misuse. As previously mentioned, the guardrail intervention is more targeted than streamlining – impacting 9.8 percent vs. 30.4 per-cent of participant portfolios. Most importantly, guardrailing produces improvements in risk/return outcomes (again, as measured by realized

Table 8.9 *The impact of guardrails and streamlining on portfolio Sharpe ratios*

	% of investors affected	% of assets affected in affected portfolios	% of affected with increased Sharpe	Mean change for affected	5th percentile of change for
Streamlined	30.4	66.8	33.9	−0.06 (−0.204)	−0.51 (−1.731)
Any guardrail	9.8	32.8	58.5	0.08 (0.211)	−0.15 (−0.380)
Diversification guardrail	3.8	34.9	64.6	0.08 (0.201)	−0.19 (−0.486)
Expense guardrail	2.2	10.5	72.8	0.02 (0.041)	−0.02 (−0.054)
Minimum equity exposure guardrail	2.1	38.7	55.7	0.21 (0.422)	−0.15 (−0.297)
Maximum equity exposure guardrail	3.3	30.7	46.4	−0.00 (−0.012)	−0.10 (−0.326)

Note: Changes in Sharpe ratios are bottom-coded at −1 and top-coded at 1. Parenthetical numbers indicate standardized changes measured in standard deviations.

Sharpe ratio increases) for about 3 out of 5 (58.5 percent) affected participants. The average change in Sharpe ratio for the targeted guardrails was positive whereas the average change for streamlining was negative (0.08 vs. −0.06). The table provides confirmatory evidence that guardrailing would produce a Kaldor-Hicks improvement in risk/return outcomes.

What's more, the table provides evidence that guardrailing would meet the enhanced Kaldor-Hicks standard. During this period, 40.6 percent of affected participants would have experienced diminished risk and return outcomes, but the lowest 5th percentile of outcomes was relatively minor (less than four-tenths of one standard deviation of the pre-reform variation in Sharpe ratios). In contrast, streamlining imposed a reduction in performance of more than one and a half standard deviations on the lowest 5th percentile of affected portfolios.

The remaining rows report analogous results for guardrail alternatives. The table shows that three guardrails (the sector, fee, and the upper glide-path) if individually imposed produced Sharpe ratio improvements for more than half of the participants and caused less than a half standard

deviation drop in Sharpe ratio for the fifth percentile of affected investors. These analyses show that variants of guardrails can avoid the distributional concern of imposing unusual losses on a substantial subset of
beneficiaries. Together, the table provides support for the idea that the
diversification, expense, and exposure guardrails or some variations of
them could satisfy the enhanced Kaldor-Hicks requirements.

It is important to note that the analysis of Sharpe ratio changes is based
on the realized returns of five years of data. The failure of the maximum
guardrail to produce performance improvements might be due to our
analysis occuring during a period of unusual stock market results. As discussed above, prudent fiduciaries would want to qualitatively consider
whether the realized performance was representative of general market
tendencies or not.

We think it's likely that our proposed guardrails satisfy the veiled
Pareto standard. While not every investor subject to the guardrail did
better than they might have otherwise, these investors would have difficulty predicting what kind of allocations would fall into the category
of portfolios doing worse in Table 8.9, suggesting that the 5 percent who
were most harmed by the guardrailing were just unlucky in that their
realized returns for the particular market performance over the time
period could have been better without a guardrail. Behind a veil of ignorance, looking only at ex ante information, we think investors would
have likely preferred the guardrailed approach, despite the small risk of
reduced realized returns.

* * *

This chapter has empirically evaluated the impact of streamlining and
guardrailing on the University of Virginia retirement plan as a case study
for showing how fiduciaries might evaluate these two interventions. There
is strong evidence that removing the gold fund improved the risk/return
outcomes of goldbug investors. But guardrailing more clearly satisfies the
enhanced Kaldor-Hicks standard which we have argued should guide
ERISA fiduciaries. First, we have shown that our proposed guardrails are
more targeted than the streamlining menu redesign that UVA actually
undertook – leaving more participant portfolios unaffected and mapping a smaller percentage of assets of the affected portfolios. Thus, our
proposed guardrails preserve more freedom than the streamlining intervention. Second, we have shown that our proposed guardrails produce
improved outcomes for most participants without imposing outsized
losses on a substantial subgroup.

As before, our analysis of the UVA plan shows it is feasible for fiduciaries to analyze the likely impact of a streamlining or guardrail corrective in advance of an intervention. Fiduciaries have the capacity not only to assess whether participants are misusing an existing menu but also to assess whether streamlining or guardrailing restrictions are likely to improve or have in fact increased participant outcomes. We do not believe it is necessary for fiduciaries to run regressions and estimate idiosyncratic risks and the tests of statistical significance included here. But fiduciaries and their advisors can monitor the impact on participant expenses of streamlining or guardrailing high-fee mutual funds. Fiduciaries and their advisors can monitor the impact these interventions (combined with mapping balances toward participant target date funds) have on diversification. Fiduciaries and their advisors can monitor the impact of streamlining and guardrailing on the prevalence of young participants eschewing equity and the prevalence of old participants eschewing bonds.

One of the benefits of guardrails is that they directly attack specific kinds of menu misuse. Hard guardrails, by design, completely eliminate extreme forms of diversification, expense, and exposure errors. There are strong theoretical and empirical justifications for taking action. Just by continuing to monitor the kinds of weighting and performance analysis outlined in Chapters 5 and 6, fiduciaries can evaluate over time whether particular changes have improved participant outcomes.

The Growing Misuse of Brokerage Windows

In this chapter, we apply the book's central claims to the growing phenomenon of self-directed brokerage accounts (SDBAs). SDBAs, commonly referred to as brokerage windows or "open option" plans,[1] are features of plans that give participants the option to transfer some or all of their plan balances to brokerage accounts where they are free to invest in a wider universe of funds and exchange-traded funds (ETFs). Although estimates vary, most evidence indicates that between 30 and 50 percent of employer retirement plans include a brokerage window and that between 1 and 5 percent of employees with access to a brokerage window make use of it.[2] Window offerings are more prevalent in plans with more than 5000 participants and in plans serving professional groups such as physicians, lawyers, accountants, and architects.[3]

Brokerage window investments are emblematic of the core problems this book is trying to address because they offer almost unconstrained choices. Brokerage windows seem to put these problems on steroids: when investing in brokerage windows, participants make even more substantial

---

[1] Susan J. Stabile, *Freedom to Choose Unwisely: Congress' Misguided Decision to Leave 401(K) Plan Participants to Their Own Devices*, 11 CORNELL J. LAW PUBLIC POLICY 361, 385 (2002).

[2] *See* VANGUARD, *The Brokerage Option in DC Plans* (May 2018), https://institutional .vanguard.com/iam/pdf/CIRBOP.pdf (finding that 20 percent of plans administered by Vanguard include a brokerage window and 1 percent of eligible employees use them). *See also* Anne Tergesen, *Why More 401(k) Plans Offer "Brokerage Windows,"* WALL ST. J. (July 1, 2016), www.wsj.com/articles/why-more-401-k-plans-offer-brokerage-windows-1467391672?ns=prod/accounts-wsj. (finding that 40 percent of plans offer brokerage windows and that 3–4 percent of eligible employees utilize the windows). *See also 2019 Defined Contribution Trends Survey*, CALLAN INSTITUTE (2019), www.callan.com/uploads/2020 /05/8d05737f54f9edfccfb9db29d070ff67/callan-dc-trends-survey-2019.pdf. (finding 49.6 percent of plans included brokerage window within their fund line up).

[3] *See, e.g.,* Stacy L. Schaus and Ying Gao, SUCCESSFUL DEFINED CONTRIBUTION INVESTMENT DESIGN: HOW TO ALIGN TARGET-DATE, CORE, AND INCOME STRATEGIES TO THE PRICE OF RETIREMENT 74 (2017). ("The 58th Annual PSCA Survey reports that 29 percent of all plans have brokerage windows; notably, 39 percent of the largest DC plans (i.e., those with more than 5,000 participants) offer brokerage windows as an option.").

allocation errors and fiduciaries are even more in the dark about these mistakes. Plan fiduciaries are routinely given no information about how the individual participants are using brokerage windows or whether those portfolios are producing reasonable risk-adjusted returns. Indeed, fiduciaries often only know the total amount of funds that are being invested in brokerage scheme.

Some courts have treated the availability of brokerage windows as evidence that employers have satisfied their fiduciary duties by providing a wide range of investment options. This "large menu defense" should be rejected, just as it is rejected in plan menu construction. Fiduciaries' duty to select prudent investment options should extend to their decision to offer a brokerage window. The decision to offer a brokerage window should be subjected to the same prudential analysis as the decision to offer a menu of "designated investment alternatives."

Moreover, we will argue here that this duty should include analogous obligations to become informed and to take action. To become informed, fiduciaries should assess whether plan participants are misusing their plan brokerage window features. The previously discussed weighting and risk/return analysis can be conducted just as readily on these portfolios as on the menu portfolios. There is good reason to believe that participants utilizing the brokerage windows fall prey at times to diversification, fee, and exposure mistakes. For example, it is likely that some participants who invest via a brokerage window are overconfident and recklessly sacrifice diversification in order to "beat the market" by overweighting narrow-gauged investments. Other participants pay excessive fees as many brokerage window plans require participants to take on extra transaction costs to buy and sell funds in their brokerage accounts. And we will later detail how brokerage windows cause substantial assets to languish in money market accounts – causing participants to insufficiently expose their retirement savings to the age-appropriate equity premium.

Informed fiduciaries who learn of substantial window misuse should be obliged to take action to curb the abuse in ways that mirror our earlier analysis. At times, plan sponsors should streamline the plan by shutting down the window. At other times, they should put on soft or hard guardrails. Brokerage windows are typically opt-in, and some involve additional paperwork to access, creating a sort of soft guardrail, but these minor obstacles should at the very least be more carefully calibrated to ensure that brokerage window users are aware of the risk, and harder guardrails are likely warranted in many cases. Some plans already have a form of hard guardrail by capping the proportion of assets that can be invested in

the brokerage account.[4] We describe a variety of other fiduciary actions –
including periodically repatriating brokerage money market investments
(unless the participant objects) to reduce the exposure mistake of having
retirement assets languish in cash equivalents.

9.1   The Promise and Perils of Brokerage Windows

In 2014, the Department of Labor's request for information about brokerage windows presented three competing arguments. First, the Department
noted that some industry articles assert that brokerage windows allow
sophisticated participants to create "a better customized, more diverse
portfolio":

> Brokerage windows may, for example, provide access to a specialized asset
> class or classes not available through the plan's core designated investment
> alternatives. Sophisticated investors may be less likely to be overwhelmed
> by a large number of investment options and may benefit from the flexibil-
> ity that brokerage windows offer.[5]

Second, the Department's request noted that brokerage windows
might be good for plans' unsophisticated participants by enabling plan
administrators to provide a set of streamlined funds to less knowledgeable
investors in the plan's main menu:

> Some articles … assert that many plans over time have increased the
> number of designated investment alternatives they offer in response to
> demands from company owner-employees, senior executives, and other
> potentially sophisticated employee-investors for access to more diverse
> investment opportunities. This results in some plans having a very large
> number of designated investment alternatives, which may confuse less
> knowledgeable participants.[6]

According to these views, brokerage windows are a win-win. They allow
more sophisticated participants to satisfy their "idiosyncratic needs" while
simultaneously allowing plan administrators to offer a menu with a more

---

[4] *See*, e.g., Mass Mutual Statement, *The Iowa 457 Employee Contribution Plan*, MASS MUTUAL 2
   (April 21, 2021), wwwrs.massmutual.com/retire/plp/iowa/pdfs/iowaperf_457_participant_
   fee_disc.pdf. ("The maximum percentage of your account that can be transferred to the
   SDBA is 50.00%").
[5] Department of Labor, Request for Information Regarding Standards for Brokerage
   Windows in Participant-Directed Individual Account Plans, 79 Fed. Reg. 49469, 49473
   (August 21, 2014), www.govinfo.gov/content/pkg/FR-2014-08-21/pdf/2014-19832.pdf.
[6] *Id.* at 49471.

limited set of core funds that benefit the less sophisticated, rank-and-file participants who are less interested in managing their accounts.[7]

Brokerage windows have become the final tier in a three-tier system of investment offerings adopted by an increasing number of plans. The first tier consists of only target date funds, the default investment option.[8] This tier is especially well suited for investors who wish to have someone else make the investment choices – so called "do it for me" investors. The second tier consists of the broader menu of designated investment alternatives, which tend to offer more specialized exposure to broad asset groupings for "help me do it" investors who want some control over the asset mix in their portfolio. Finally, plans often make a third tier available in the form of a brokerage account that must be separately activated, for "let me do it" investors who wish to have total control over their investments.[9] The rosy picture paints brokerage windows as providing motivated participants with maximal autonomy while economizing on the choice costs for participants who prefer increasing tiers of guidance.

There is, however, a less rosy picture of SDBAs. The Labor Department also requested information pertaining to a third vision of brokerage windows:

> Other articles, however, counter that brokerage windows may present undue risks for many retirement plan participants, because plan fiduciaries do not engage in a deliberative process to affirmatively review and select each of the investment options available through brokerage windows. Thus, they say in the absence of a deliberative review and selection process by an ERISA fiduciary, participants may not have adequate or any protections against potentially costly or unsuitable investments made through the brokerage window.[10]

Under this view, brokerage windows are bad for participants who utilize them and end up making poor allocation decisions.

9.2   What Is Known about Participant Allocation Errors

There is limited information about how individual participants invest their funds in brokerage window accounts. This is in part driven by DOL regulations which allow plans with brokerage windows to report just an aggregate amount invested in all accounts and dispense with even

---

[7] *Id.*
[8] Callan Institute, *supra* note 2.
[9] Schaus, *supra* note 3.
[10] Request for Information, *supra* note 5.

aggregate descriptions of types of assets held.[11] Although some investment brokerages publicize information about the defined contribution plans they administer,[12] "there is no current data for the number of self-directed defined contribution participants who opt for open-brokerage window investment allocations nor for the amount of money invested in these vehicles relative to all defined contribution dollars."[13]

However, surveys of plan sponsors indicate that in 2010 "of those offering a brokerage window, 71% offered a full window (vs. the 29% offering a more limited mutual fund window)."[14] A full window of offerings means that participants can invest not only in a broader range of mutual funds and ETFs but also in individual securities. These expanded options give participants the freedom to sacrifice diversification by overweighting individual securities. Unfortunately, there is substantial use of this freedom. Charles Schwab reports that in 2020 about one-third of brokerage window assets were invested in individual equities. There is no mechanism in place stopping brokerage window participants from day trading their tax-subsidized retirement savings in GameStop. SDBA participants might incur the transaction costs of high-security turnover. Or they might invest all their savings in the next Enron. Participants might even invest all their savings in their employer's shares and thus recreate the tragic scenarios that have occurred when plans have included company stock on the core menu of investment offerings. The brokerage window options in most plans also include esoteric investments such as cryptocurrency funds. Charles Schwab reports that Greyscale Bitcoin Trust was one of the primary equity holdings of millennial brokerage window investors (along with meme stocks like Alibaba and Tesla).[15] Yesterday's goldbug is today's cryptocurrency enthusiast.

---

[11] The DOL's 2014 Request for Information explained: "the Schedule H [of the Form 5500] allows plans to report certain classes of investments made through a brokerage window as an aggregate amount under a catch-all "other" category rather than by type of asset on the appropriate line item from the asset category, e.g., common stocks, mutual funds, employer securities, etc." *Id.* The Department asked respondent whether "this special provision be changed to require more detail and transparency regarding these investments." *Id.* at 49473.

[12] Tergesen, *supra* note 2.

[13] Anne Tucker, *Retirement Revolution: Unmitigated Risks in the Defined Contribution Society*, 51 Hous. L. Rev. 153, 227 (2013).

[14] Callan Institute, *supra* note 2.

[15] Business Wire, *Schwab Report: Self-Directed 401(k) Balances Hold Steady; Millennials Allocate More to ETFs and Cash Than Gen X, Boomers* (December 4, 2019), www.business wire.com/news/home/20191204005172/en/Schwab-Report-Self-Directed-401-k-Balances-Hold-Steady-Millennials-Allocate-More-to-ETFs-and-Cash-Than-Gen-X-Boomers.

In June 2021, ForUsAll Inc., a 401(k) provider moved forward with a plan that would "allow workers in plans it administers to invest … 401(k) contributions in bitcoin, ether, litecoin, and others."[16] The firm's affirmative case for opening up such investments is two-fold: diversification and participation. Electronic currencies are just another asset class that held in proper proportion, like gold, might help diversify a portfolio and reduce idiosyncratic risk. And allowing employees to invest in meme stock and esoteric investment plays might increase participation. Paul Selker, president of Spark Street Digital, a ForUsAll client, said he was attracted to the brokerage window cryptocurrency option because he believes his "employees – many in their 20s and 30s – will 'be more engaged'" with the 401(k) plan.[17]

Crucially, ForUsAll is limiting the investment amount to 5 percent of a participant's contributions. This cap is explicitly described as a "'guardrails' [that] ForUsAll has built into the service [to] help his employees invest prudently." As Mr. Selker colorfully explained, the window is "not going to let my people YOLO Dogecoin to the moon." The ForUsAll example suggests that imposing guardrail caps is legally feasible, given that they are in the process of rolling out plans with such caps. It also shows that there is market interest in designing plans that offer *but limit* the amounts that can be invested in esoteric assets. Finally, the example provides insights into how a hard guardrail might be beneficially imposed. The ForUsAll plan combines three different kinds of guardrails. In addition to imposing the 5 percent limit on contributions (hard guardrail), the plan also includes soft warnings by sending "alerts to participants when the value of their crypto investments exceeds 5% of the balance, urging them to sell some crypto and transfer the profits into stocks and bonds" (soft guardrail). Lastly, if the balance in crypto holdings exceeds 5 percent of the participants' plan value, the system will block any more crypto contributions (hard guardrail).[18]

Concerns about the lack of diversification and elevated fees have led to disagreements among plan consultants over whether plans should offer SDBAs. In PIMCO's 2016 Defined Contribution Consulting Support

---

[16] Anne Tergesen, *Cryptocurrency Comes to Retirement Plans as Coinbase Teams Up with 401(k) Provider*, WALL ST. J. (June 10, 2021), www.wsj.com/articles/coinbase-teams-up-with-401-k-provider-to-offer-crypto-11623317402.
[17] *Id.*
[18] *Id.*

and Trends Survey, "25 percent recommend a mutual-fund-only window, and 22 percent suggest full brokerage, while over a third (35 percent) advised against offering either type of window."[19] While many in the plan-advisor industry paint the picture of brokerage window participants as sophisticated, one might alternatively view brokerage window participants as "cowboy" investors who overconfidently believe they can pick stocks that will beat the market. We know that brokerage window users are disproportionately male – Vanguard found that 80 percent of brokerage participants were male, while only 58 percent of all participants were male.[20] We also know that professionals such as physicians, architects, and lawyers disproportionately lobby for and utilize plans with brokerage windows.[21] Physicians have absorbed a great deal of medical information, but there is some evidence that they are not as a group sophisticated investors, adept at picking stocks that will beat the market. For example, we were struck at the large number of physician plans that we identified as part of the letters we sent to high-cost plans.[22] In this laissez-faire landscape, it should not be surprising that some participants who overestimate their ability to pick stocks would fail to adequately diversify or economize on fees and transaction costs. Brokerage window freedom is for some the freedom to chase "'hot' stocks or funds ... buying high and selling low."[23]

In purchasing these investments from the brokerage window, plan participants incur additional fees, as brokerage window mutual funds are often available only at retail prices[24] and brokerage window transactions typically incur per-transaction commission fees and annual account fees that erode potential returns.[25] We know that brokerage window users are more active traders than non-brokerage window users; and some brokerage window participants are likely harmed by excessively moving in and

[19] Schaus, *supra* note 3.
[20] Vanguard Research Note, *The brokerage option in DC plans*, Vanguard (May 2018).
[21] Department of Labor, *Study of 401(k) Plan Fees and Expenses*, Pension and Welfare Benefits Administration 19 (April 13, 1998). ("Typical plans offering self-directed brokerages would be professional corporations such as law firms, accounting firms, and medical practices.").
[22] Mark P. Cussen, *The Rise of 401(k) Brokerage Accounts*, INVESTOPEDIA STOCK ANALYSIS (September 26, 2018), www.proquest.com/docview/2251496730.
[23] *Id.*
[24] Bloomberg, *Managing 401(k) Plans*, BUREAU OF NATIONAL AFFAIRS at 3 (September 2012) ("Investments in brokerage window more expensive because employees generally pay retail prices instead of institutional prices"); *See also* John Keefe, *Through the 'Window'*, STRATEGIC INSIGHT (September 2019).
[25] Cussen, *supra* note 22.

out of particular positions. Charles Schwab's 2020 analysis of its own brokerage accounts found that the *average* brokerage participant made an eye-popping 13.6 trades per quarter.[26]

Gregory Kasten is one of the few analysts to publish a study of the returns of individual brokerage window accounts. Using data from Unified Trust's retirement plan, Kasten examined 61 participant brokerage accounts with a collective market value of $12.5 million during the 2002–2003 period.[27] He found the investment performances of accounts with brokerage windows are "generally inferior to managed model portfolios," with lower rates of return.[28] In particular, he found that 76 percent of the accounts he examined underperformed the S&P 500 and that 72 percent of the brokerage accounts were "below the core fund model portfolio for their plan" (with equivalent asset allocations).[29] Compared with these core fund portfolios, "the asset-weighted performance lag was 4.70 percent, and accounts greater than $250,000 lagged by 5.18 percent."[30] He connected this poor performance of brokerage window accounts to fees, active trading, trading overconfidence, and poor asset allocation.[31]

An illustrative example of some troubling aspects of brokerage windows can be found in the SDBA that Fidelity offered its own employees, which it called "BrokerageLink."[32] Three aspects of the BrokerageLink design are concerning: its funding default, its altering rules, and the framing of its investment menu, as discussed in Ayres's public expert report assessing the prudence of the Fidelity plan.[33] As Ayres stated in his expert report:

> Transfers and contributions into BrokerageLink are automatically invested in the Fidelity Government Cash Reserves Fund until participants gave Fidelity instructions to allocate those funds to other investments. Transfers to BrokerageLink are typically accessible for trading two business days

---

[26] Charles Schwab, THE SCHWAB SELF-DIRECTED BROKERAGE ACCOUNT INDICATORS, Charles Schwab & Co., Inc. (2020)

[27] Gregory W. Kasten, *Self- Directed Brokerage Accounts Tend to Reduce Retirement Success and May Not Decrease Plan Sponsor Liability*, 12 JOURNAL OF PENSION BENEFITS 48 (2005).

[28] *Id.* at 43.

[29] *Id.* at 48.

[30] *Id.* at 49.

[31] *Id.* at 47–48.

[32] The analysis for this discussion is taken from the paid expert report of one of the authors. Expert Report of Ian Ayres, Moitoso v. FMR LLC, No. 1:18-cv-12122-WGY (D. Mass. 2019).

[33] *Id.*

following the transfer. The process of investing in BrokerageLink involves extra steps and extra time beyond what is required to make investments in funds in the Plan's core menu.[34]

There is evidence that this default of funding the account via the money market fund combined with an altering rule regarding transfers (having to wait two days before directing the funds to a non-money market investment) created a kind of friction that kept substantial brokerage account funds languishing in the cash reserve fund.[35] Between September 2014 and March 2019 between 17.5 percent and 37.4 percent of Brokerage Link funds were invested in this Cash Reserve fund.[36] Moreover, as of June 2017, more than a third of participants using the brokerage window (603 out of 1,781 participants) were identified as having 100 percent of their brokerage account balance invested in the Cash Reserve Fund.[37] The assets of these participants represented 15 percent of all BrokerageLink assets at the time, and these investor participants had been invested 100 percent in this cash reserve fund for an asset-weighted average of 9.1 consecutive months.

This evidence of large cash holdings points to an exposure mistake. As Ayres noted:

> It is unlikely that such a large percentage of BrokerageLink participants would specifically take the extra steps to enroll and invest in BrokerageLink if their actual preferences were to fully invest those funds in the cash reserves fund....[38]

This is especially true because the default funding mechanism was a money market that had twice the expense ratio of money markets available on the plan's core fund menu (37 vs 14 basis points).[39] The high fees in this default fund eat up most of the expected return on these assets. Indeed, as we write this in June 2021, the year-to-date return on Fidelity's Cash Reserve fund has been 0.00 percent. Investing for retirement in vehicles that pay such low returns is massively imprudent.

---

[34] *Id.*

[35] Having to wait two days before directing funds to a non-money market fund can cause participants who want to continue to invest in a streamlined fund that has been discontinued from the plan menu to bear the risk that the discontinued fund will appreciate in value during the period after the fund is redeemed and before it is repurchased as a brokerage window holding.

[36] See Ayres, *supra* note 32, at 6.

[37] These participants were identified as investing solely in the cash reserve account because their monthly account return that was within 5 basis points of the monthly return of the cash reserves fund.

[38] See Ayres, *supra* note 32.

[39] *Id.*

The substantial presence and duration of participants fully invested in the brokerage window's high-fee cash account is likely due to the cognitive biases related to the default funding mechanism and frictional altering rules for changing those cash investments. Many brokerage windows participants fail to attend to the cash in their account. After funding the brokerage account, they fail to later instruct the broker to use the cash reserves to buy some other investment. Or after selling a position or receiving dividends from an investment, the participant fails to reinvest in a non-cash fund. The Fidelity brokerage plan is not alone in stranding a substantial proportion of brokerage assets in cash. Gregory Kasten's analysis of Unified Trust's SDBA found that 30 percent of brokerage assets were held in cash.[40] Schwab reported in 2020 that 15.9 percent of its brokerage assets were held cash equivalents (paying a paltry 0.1 percent annual return).[41] As we discuss further below, enlightened fiduciaries might take action against such stranded cash scenarios by periodically transferring these funds to a QDIA investment – unless the participant objects – or by changing the default sweep account to a QDIA investment itself.

Ayres's analysis of Fidelity's brokerage window menu also suggests that investment options were presented in a way that might have contributed to participants making fee mistakes. Fidelity's materials categorize the available funds in brokerage window offerings into three classes: "no transaction fee" (NTF) funds, transaction fee funds (which charged participants a $20 fee to purchase the funds), and load funds (which passed onto participants any sales load charges imposed by the load funds). Fidelity's brochure listed the NTF class of funds first and emphasized that these funds had no transaction fee. Although Fidelity did not charge plan participants a transaction fee for NTF funds, Fidelity regularly received "remuneration" equal to 0.4 percent of assets invested in an NTF fund. This remuneration was paid for by the participants out of NTF expense ratios that were systematically higher than those for the transaction fee funds. As of March 31, 2019, 33 percent of BrokerageLink assets were invested in NTF funds. The weighted average net expense ratio for the

[40] Kasten, *supra* note 28, at 48.
[41] Charles Schwab, *Schwab Intelligent Portfolios® Sweep Program* www.schwab.com/legal/ sip-sweep-current-interest-rates. *See also* Schwab, *supra* note 27. In the past, the proportion invested in cash was even higher. *See* Mark Coffrini, SELF-DIRECTED BROKERAGE ACCOUNTS: A FIRST LOOK AT PARTICIPANT INVESTMENT BEHAVIOR, Sage Publications at 62 (2002) (24 percent of Schwab brokerage windows assets in cash and cash equivalents in 2001).

NTF funds was 1.21 percent, whereas the weighted average net expense ratio for all other funds was 0.67 percent – a whopping 55 basis points lower than the NTF average expense ratio.[42]

There is a reason for concern that the presentation and framing of the NTF funds predictably led participants to make fee mistakes. This possibility is borne out by articles in the popular press warning retail investors "Don't Be Fooled by No-Transaction-Fee Funds." One anonymous fund manager noted: "We'd like every dollar possible in the [lower-cost] institutional share class…. But you need a no-transaction-fee share class to get traction in this business. Investors would rather pay no transaction fee because they don't do the math."[43]

Stepping back, it is evident that there are good reasons for fiduciaries to worry that participants will make substantial allocation errors when using self-directed brokerage accounts. Often fiduciaries choose to offer SDBAs as a kind of squeaky-wheel response. A small, but vocal group of participants who are intensely dissatisfied with streamlined choices might be mollified by the opportunity to invest in the larger universe of brokerage window investments.[44] Some of these participants may have a reasonable basis for seeking these alternative investments, but many brokerage window advocates will be overconfidently sacrificing diversification and taking on needless transaction costs and supra-competitive fees in a quixotic attempt to beat the market. Others will make substantial exposure mistakes by allowing their brokerage balances to languish in cash investments. The next section considers whether fiduciaries should be allowed to indulge the preferences of these 'cowboy' investors as the price to sustain a safer fund menu for rank-and-file participants. But for now, we have shown that there is a likelihood that a substantial proportion of brokerage window investors are misallocating their retirement investments by making diversification, fee, and exposure mistakes.

---

[42] *See* Ayres, *supra* note 32.

[43] *See* John Rekenthaler, *Will the Fund Industry Ever Come Clean?*, MORNINGSTAR (November 14, 2017), www.morningstar.com/articles/836421/will-the-fund-industry-ever-come-clean.html ("Would that investor pay $1250 for the NTF platform's services, if billed for them directly?").

[44] Offering brokerage windows might be especially effective at mollifying participants who lose the ability to invest in funds that are eliminated by streamlining. *See also* Schaus, *supra* note 3 ("Some plans may lessen the concern of a "take away" by offering access – possibly even transferring allocations – to favorite brand-name mutual funds via a brokerage window."). Yale University added a brokerage window as part of its menu streamlining in part to avoid some of the "take away" effect.

9.3 What Should Fiduciaries Do?

Let us begin simply. A fiduciary's decision to offer a brokerage window and to continue to offer a brokerage window is a fiduciary decision. Therefore, the same requirements of prudence should apply to this decision. There is no reason why the requirement to engage in a deliberative process to affirmatively review each investment option available in a plan should not include brokerage window investment options. While industry participants tacitly recognize the fiduciary nature of this decision,[45] the Department of Labor should make this duty explicit and provide better guidance on what kinds of processes fiduciaries should undertake in making this decision.[46]

---

[45] *See, e.g.,* Fred Reish and Bruce Ashton, OFFERING A BROKERAGE WINDOW: A DISCUSSION OF THE FIDUCIARY CONSIDERATIONS, TD Ameritrade Institutional (2015) (writing that "[d]eciding to offer a brokerage window is a fiduciary decision, but there is little guidance on the considerations a fiduciary should use in making the decision.").

[46] On May 15, 2012, the DOL published a Field Assistance Bulletin that required plans with brokerage windows to "monitor the investments made through the brokerage window and … to provide disclosure information on a certain percentage of the investments made through the brokerage window." Gayle M. Meadors, *Supreme Court Upholds Health Reform Law; Participant Must Cooperate in Claims Review; Stop Loss Concerns; and Brokerage Windows in Defined Contribution Plans,* 28 J. MED. PRACTICE MANAGEMENT 203, 205 (2012). This FAB advised:

> If, through a brokerage window or similar arrangement, non-designated investment alternatives available under a plan are selected by significant numbers of participants and beneficiaries, an affirmative obligation arises on the part of the plan fiduciary to examine these alternatives and determine whether one or more such alternatives should be treated as designated for purposes of the regulation.
>
> Pending further guidance in this area, when a platform holds more than 25 investment alternatives, the Department, as a matter of enforcement policy, will not require that all of the investment alternatives be treated, for purposes of this regulation, as designated investment alternatives if the plan administrator—

(1) makes the required disclosures for at least three of the investment alternatives on the platform that collectively meet the "broad range" requirements in the ERISA 404(c) regulation, 29 CFR § 2550.404c-1(b)(3)(i)(B); and

(2) makes the required disclosures with respect to all other investment alternatives on the platform in which at least five participants and beneficiaries, or, in the case of a plan with more than 500 participants and beneficiaries, at least one percent of all participants and beneficiaries, are invested on a date that is not more than 90 days preceding each annual disclosure.

FAB 2012-02, FAQ 30 (May 15, 2012). After loud objections from the plan sponsor community, the DOL issued a superseding Field Assistance Bulletin 2012-02R rescinding many of the brokerage window disclosure requirements, but instead advising in part: "[F]iduciaries

Our goal in this section is to suggest a blueprint for such guidance. At a minimum, fiduciaries of plans that have brokerage windows should inform themselves of whether participants using the SDBAs are making probable allocation errors, so they can better assess the welfare tradeoffs involved in offering this feature. The quarterly reports that plan advisors provide to fiduciaries are routinely bereft of even the most rudimentary information about how the brokerage window is used. Fiduciaries are told only the total value of assets invested in their plan's window and the number of participants that have window investments. Currently, fiduciaries do not usually know the identity of specific securities in which their participants are investing. They might not even know what asset classes are being held.[47] Plan fiduciaries are not given sufficiently individualized information to assess whether participants are investing all their plan savings in a bitcoin fund.

[of] plans with platforms or brokerage windows, self-directed brokerage accounts, or similar plan arrangements that enable participants and beneficiaries to select investments beyond those designated by the plan are still bound by ERISA section 404(a)'s statutory duties of prudence and loyalty to participants and beneficiaries who use the platform or the brokerage window, self-directed brokerage account, or similar plan arrangement, including taking into account the nature and quality of services provided in connection with the platform or the brokerage window, self-directed brokerage account, or similar plan arrangement." See John J. Canary, *Field Assistance Bulletin No. 2012-02R1*, U.S. DEPARTMENT OF LABOR (July 30, 2012), www.dol.gov/sites/dolgov/files/ebsa/employers-and-advisers/guidance/field-assistance-bulletins/2012-02r.pdf. The same FAQ made clear that a broker window investment is not a designated investment alternative under the participant fee disclosure rule. "Nonetheless, in the case of a 401(k) or other individual account plan covered under the regulation, a plan fiduciary's failure to designate investment alternatives, for example, to avoid investment disclosures under the regulation, raises questions under ERISA section 404(a)'s general statutory fiduciary duties of prudence and loyalty." See also DOL, *supra* note 5, at 49470. One of the reasons for the legal uncertainty about whether the decision is fiduciary in nature is the possibility that will construe the decision to be a pre-fiduciary, "settlor" decision made by the employer in setting up the plan. For example, Dana Muir and Norman Stein argued:

> Arguably, a fiduciary that makes a decision to provide a brokerage window has an obligation to consider its value and cost to the plan population before selecting a window. But if the window is written into the terms of the plan, the decision to include it would be a settlor decision, even if the fiduciary believed it would be an attractive nuisance to many or even most employees.

See Dana Muir and Norman Stein, *Two Hats, One Head, No Heart: The Anatomy of the ERISA Settlor/Fiduciary Distinction*, 93 N.C. L. REV. 459, 524 (2015).

[47] DOL, *supra* note 5. The DOL's 2014 request for information explicitly asked whether "plan fiduciaries have access to information about specific investments that are selected or asset class or allocation information."

Our central claim is that the process for evaluating the appropriateness of brokerage window options should follow what we outlined above with regard to evaluating the investment options on the core menu. Fiduciaries should assess on an ongoing basis whether participants are misusing the window. They should determine the extent to which participants are making diversification, fee, and exposure mistakes. Should fiduciaries learn that a substantial number of brokerage window participants are misusing the window, the fiduciaries should take action by imposing soft or hard guardrails or by streamlining or eliminating the window option.

We reject what might be called the "squeaky wheel" justification for brokerage windows – the idea that by accommodating the vocal and intense demands of some employees for particular investment options, plan fiduciaries can maintain a more pristine core menu of designated investment alternative.[48] As part of their duties, fiduciaries should, when appropriate, resist the call to provide unrestricted brokerage options *and* also resist the urge to include inappropriate options on their plan's core menu.[49]

Fiduciaries should be required to undertake the same overweighting and performance analysis that we discussed above in Chapter 6. Such an inquiry can supplant the more traditional analysis of historical returns. It is not a useful exercise to compare the historic returns and fees of each and every brokerage option to analogous investments. However, fiduciaries should periodically produce risk and return scatter plots to assess whether the brokerage window users are systematically falling behind their non-brokerage peers in terms of risk or reward. Even more simply, fiduciaries should produce the overweighting analysis to learn the extent to which brokerage users are putting all or most of their plan retirement nest eggs in just a handful of stocks or exotic investments. To be clear, both the

---

[48] See Lori Lucas, *Meeting the Financial Planning Needs of a Diverse and Paradoxical 401(k) Population*, BENEFITS Q., Fourth Quarter 2002, at 15, 19; David Pratt, *Focus On ... Recent Developments Affecting ERISA* Section 404(c) *and Brokerage Windows*, J. OF PENSION BENEFITS, Spring 2015, at 21–24 (brokerage window may benefit "rank-and-file participants by limiting the number of [default investment alternatives]" that sophisticated investors would demand in a plan's main menu if they could not purchase these investment vehicles through the brokerage window).

[49] The squeaky wheel argument would be stronger if fiduciaries were confident that including the brokerage window allowed the brokerage participants to cross-subsidize the non-brokerage participants. There is no credible evidence that the supra-competitive profits earned by advisors on the brokerage windows redound to the non-brokerage participants benefit. At least one spokesperson for the advisor industry has also suggested, without any credible evidence, that providing brokerage windows might somehow increase plan participation. Bloomberg, *supra* note 25, at 1 ("having a brokerage window can increase participation").

scatterplot analysis and the overweighting analysis should evaluate participants' entire plan portfolios, not just their brokerage window portfolio. Brokerage window investments that, by themselves, would seem unreasonable might become non-problematic if they form a relatively small part of a participant's plan savings or compliment the investments made from the core menu. Enlightened fiduciaries should also want to know whether such individuals have offsetting non-plan savings to balance seemingly undiversified brokerage holdings.

Much of the empiricism of Section B of this chapter was aggregated at the plan level. This aggregate information is by itself troubling. Individualized allocations within the data might be less or (much) more troubling. It is theoretically possible that plans exist where the brokerage window users only use the window to invest a reasonably small proportion of their overall savings in individual stocks, or only use the window to invest in mutual funds or ETFs that keep them reasonably diversified, or only use the window to counterbalance overweighted savings outside their plan account. But it is also most certain that there are other brokerage windows in which a substantial proportion of participant users make grievous diversification and exposure mistakes and pay excessive fees to boot for the privilege of so doing. As we speak, these substantial allocation errors persist, while their supposed fiduciaries remain blissfully ignorant.

Armed with information about substantial allocation errors by a minority of brokerage users, faithful fiduciaries should consider the same kinds of actions that we have discussed previously: soft and hard guardrails or streamlining of brokerage window options (including possibly eliminating the brokerage window altogether). The specifics of each intervention might play out differently when applied in this context.

The three-tiered approach to structuring retirement plans can already be seen as deploying default and altering rules as a form of soft guardrails. Altering rules are the necessary and sufficient conditions for opting out of default. The tiered plans make it easiest to stick with the QDIA (the first-tier default). Tiered plans make it slightly harder to invest in one or more of the core menu items (the second-tier designated investment alternatives) because the participant needs to affirmatively choose portfolio proportions. Lastly, these plans make it most difficult to invest in a brokerage window (the third-tier) because a participant must engage in a multi-step process often lasting over several days: agreeing to create a brokerage account, funding the account, waiting for the funds to clear, and then instructing the broker on how to invest those funds. These existing altering rules reduce the equilibrium usage of the brokerage windows.

Fiduciaries learning of substantial window allocation errors might begin by implementing new altering rules that would go further in dissuading window usage. Providing participants with information about the historic lags in returns and excessive volatility of brokerage results compared to the QDIA would constitute a soft guardrail. Or the platform might be programmed to give more individualized information showing how a participant's proposed window portfolio would have done historically.

Instead of (or in addition to) providing information, fiduciaries might require participants to answer a few questions before being able to qualify to use the window. For example, fiduciaries might require participants to warrant that they own sufficient non-plan savings to counter-balance the seemingly undiversified brokerage portfolio. Alternatively, as discussed in Chapter 6, fiduciaries could require participants to pass a sophistication test before investing in the window, or at least pass a test indicating that they have some understanding of what the risks associated with window usage.[50]

Fiduciaries could go further and require sustained affirmations of choice across time when they notice a participant in a presumptively inappropriate allocation. For example, they might, by default, remap misallocated funds out of the brokerage account and back to the QDIA unless the participant affirmatively objects. Remember the brokerage balances in the Fidelity plan that were languishing in zero-return money market funds? A default that periodically repatriates these dollars back to a QDIA would increase participant risk-adjusted returns. An even simpler default change would be to change the sweep account of brokerage window accounts to be the participant's age-appropriate QDIA. Using money market accounts as the sweep account in non-retirement funds can make it easier to keep track for tax purposes of dividend income. However, in retirement accounts, where taxes are not paid until withdrawn and there is no need to account for investment bases, there is no credible financial reason as to why a target date fund couldn't serve as the brokerage sweep account.

In addition to these varying "soft" guardrails, fiduciaries might consider a range of "hard" guardrails.[51] Commentators have already suggested the

---

[50] Ian Ayres and Edward Fox have suggested testing for knowledge of by how much a portfolio's return must beat the market's return in order to justify non-diversification or excess fees. *See* Ian Ayres and Edward Fox, *Alpha Duties: The Search for Excess Returns and Appropriate Fiduciary Responsibilities,* 97 TEXAS L. REV. 445 (2019).

[51] Some commentators have suggested that softer nudges are likely to fail. Jacob Hale Russell, *The Separation of Intelligence and Control: Retirement Savings and the Limits of Soft Paternalism,* 6 WM. & MARY BUS. L. REV. 35 (2015) (criticizing "soft paternalism" techniques such as nudging and disclosure as being unable to improve retirement portfolio allocation decisions).

possible benefits of capping the amounts that can be contributed to brokerage window accounts and some plans have imposed such caps.[52] While many plans already impose minimum balances,[53] allocation errors provide a powerful rationale for imposing maximum amounts. Or windows might cap the proportion of contributions that could be invested in individual equities or more exotic commodity or currency funds.

Finally, if all else fails to sufficiently remediate the problem allocation errors, fiduciaries should consider adopting some version of streamlining. Many plans already limit the range of investments available in the brokerage window. Just as UVA eliminated its gold fund from its core menu of investment options, a strong argument can be made for eliminating any investments where a substantial number of participants invest unreasonably large proportions of their portfolios. Fiduciaries should consider excluding all individual equities as potential investments. Given that there are more than 8,000 mutual funds and more than 2,000 ETFs,[54] there is no compelling reason why individual equities would appreciably aid even sophisticated participants. There are, however, strong reasons to expect that their inclusion could hurt the faux sophisticated window user.

At the end of the day, we predict that an analysis of brokerage window investments will routinely uncover substantial and unjustified allocation errors that needlessly sacrifice diversification and returns. Requiring fiduciaries to inquire about allocation errors will likely result in many windows being completely closed and forcing participants to invest in either QDIAs or the core menu offerings. This will undoubtedly anger many incumbent brokerage users who have intense preferences to maintain their higher-cost, undiversified and idiosyncratic investments. But taxpayer money should not facilitate day-trading on Gamestop or trying to

---

[52] Ron Lieber, *Seeking Investment Flexibility In a 401(k)*, NEW YORK TIMES (July 8, 2011), www.nytimes.com/2011/07/09/your-money/401ks-and-similar-plans/a-401k-window-to-more-investing-choices-your-money.html. *See also* ABA Retirement Funds, *Important Information Regarding the Self-Directed Brokerage Account*, (August 2019), www.cdstudio host.com/ABA/2019/2019_07_SDBA_Fee_Change/admin_sdba.html. ("a maximum 95% of a participant's future contributions" to be deposited into a participants SDBA).

[53] *See, e.g.*, Michigan Office for Retirement Services, *State of Michigan 401(k) and 457 Plans*, TD AMERITRADE https://stateofmi.voya.com/csinfo/fundinfo.aspx?cl=MICHIGAN& pl=640001PU&page=investment_informationfundinformationtheself&domain=stateo fmi.csplans.com&s=xpfpxy45t1omev2zktkeoo55&d=56a9d6cf52ffcef177cb8c9fcd1f30643 12ae5bd.

[54] INVESTOPEDIA, *Mutual Fund vs. ETF: What's the Difference?* www.investopedia.com/ articles/exchangetradedfunds/08/etf-mutual-fund-difference.asp#:~:text=According%20 to%20the%20Investment%20Company,assets%20for%20the%20same%20period.

ride Dogecoin to the moon. Workers who want to speculate are free to save their money outside of a tax-deferred account and pursue alpha. But fiduciary law should force fiduciaries to stop facilitating such shenanigans.

Reining in the worst impacts of brokerage windows will not be easy. A vocal minority of participants want them. Plan advisors also want them. The proliferation of brokerage windows is a profit center for plan advisors,[55] so much so that they may be willing to reduce the costs of some other plan expenses to help incentivize fiduciaries to adopt plans with brokerage windows. At the very least the law should not have its thumb on the scale tilting fiduciaries toward windows. Yet, until very recently, that is exactly what the law did. The misguided Seventh Circuit decision in *Hecker v. Deere & Co.* found that offering thousands of investment options though a brokerage window tended to immunize fiduciaries from liability and undermined their duty to affirmatively review and select prudent investment options.[56] There should be no "large menu" defense

---

[55] *See* Jacob Hale Russell, *The Separation of Intelligence and Control: Retirement Savings and The Limits of Soft Paternalism*, 6 WM. & MARY BUS. L. REV. 35 (2015). ("a public-choice or capture theory could explain why brokerage windows – which charge higher fees and are more prone to lucrative churning – are allowed."). *Id.* at 85.

[56] *Hecker v. Deere & Co.*, No. 06-C-0719-S (W.D. Wis. Dec. 8, 2006). Industry publications also have explicitly claimed that brokerage windows immunized fiduciaries. For example, in describing an "invest in the world" brokerage window where participants "have the opportunity to choose whatever investments they prefer," one commenter in 1997 opined: "The plan sponsor bears no liability for investment selection, since no funds are selected or otherwise endorsed." Jon C. Chambers, *Unrestricted Investment Accounts in Participant-Directed Plans: Problems and Solutions*, 52 EMPLOYEE BENEFIT PLAN REVIEW 42, 42 (Aug. 1997). *See* also, David Albertson, *Self-directed 401(k) Accounts Give Participants Greater Choice*, EMPLOYEE BENEFIT NEWS (June 1, 2000), link.gale.com/apps/doc/A62405315/ITOF?u=29002&sid=ITOF&xid=2220e396. ("[O]nce you let your participants invest in virtually any mutual fund or public security available through a brokerage account, you suddenly take some of the pressure off the responsibility to monitor particular funds and fund performance. You assume the menu of choices is appropriate because the menu is almost infinite.") *Id.* at 1. *See* Susan J. Stabile, *Freedom to Choose Unwisely: Congress' Misguided Decision to Leave 401(K) Plan Participants to Their Own Devices*, 11 CORNELL J. LAW PUBLIC POLICY (2002). ("[open option] plans, by freeing the employer from the need to determine the prudence of particular investment options, go a long way towards removing what little protection the law gives employees.") *Id.* at 386. *See* also Morton A. Harris, *Working with Participant Directed Investment Options Under ERISA §404(c)*, SE02 ALI-ABA 893, 919, (July 5, 1999) (noting open option plans are "an attractive approach to an employer who wants to reduce its fiduciary burden in connection with the selection and monitoring of the investment fund alternatives since an employer can avoid this process altogether"); *See* also Hewitt Associates, *Survey Findings: Self-Directed Brokerage Accounts and Fund Windows in 401(K) Plans* 1, 27 (2001) (reporting survey findings that one reason plans offer brokerage accounts is to avoid monitoring funds). *Id.* at 27.

to claims of fiduciary imprudence.[57] Allowing participants to invest all of their retirement savings in a single stock, if anything, should militate toward a finding of liability. It is worth emphasizing that we are not proposing a *de facto* ban of SDBAs. Instead, we propose that fiduciaries offering such options should only be required to reduce or eliminate brokerage assets if and only if they learn that their window is hurting a substantial minority of their participants.

---

[57] Louis Cusano, *The Rise the Duty of Prudence and Demise of the Large-Menu Defense: An Update on Recent ERISA Litigation and Divane v. Northwestern,* (2019) http://dx.doi .org/10.2139/ssrn.3506849.

~

Conclusion

This book has argued that guardrails can be useful menu limitations that preserve participant freedom more than streamlining interventions while still powerfully discouraging diversification, fee, and exposure mistakes. Regardless of whether ERISA embraces harder or softer variations of guardrail remedies, our more fundamental process claim is that fiduciaries should start assessing the likelihood and extent to which their participants are making menu mistakes. Fiduciaries' failure to assess whether participants are overweighted in narrow-gauged funds or underweighted in important asset classes is tragically imprudent – all the more so because information on how participants' funds are allocated across the plan menu is readily available to the fiduciaries. It is much harder for a toaster manufacturer to know whether its customers are misusing its products' options once the device is in the privacy of the consumer's home. Even this distance is being bridged by the internet-of-everything with its increased connectivity of devices. One of us recently received an email from Subaru warning that one of our tires needed inflating. If a car manufacturer can warn us when we are likely misusing our car, a retirement fiduciary should be able to warn us when we are likely misusing the plan menu.

Stockbrokers and investment advisors are required to "know thy customer" to make sure that investment strategies align with a particular individual's investment objectives.[1] Yet, bizarrely, ERISA fiduciaries aren't required to undertake even the most rudimentary analysis to find out whether participant investment strategies are well suited to diversify idiosyncratic risk, or expose investors to age-appropriate amounts of systemic

---

[1] Ian Ayres & Alan Schwartz, *The No-Reading Problem in Consumer Contract Law*, 66 STANFORD L. REV. 545, 609 (2014). (arguing that mass contractors should use surveys to become informed of contract terms customers find unexpectedly harsh); *See* also, Jonathan Macey, et al., *Helping Law Catch Up to Markets: Applying Broker Dealer Law to Subprime Mortgages*, 34 J. CORP. L. 789, 816 (2009) (discussing the New York Stock Exchange's "Know Thy Customer Rule").

risk. Our case study of UVA's participant data shows that this analysis is well within the capacity of today's fiduciaries. Assessing the likelihood of menu misuse by participants is by no means burdensome. The weighting and risk/return scatter plots described in Chapter 5 can be automated and produced by plan advisors at a negligible marginal cost.

Most 401(k) menus today succeed at giving participants *the opportunity* to avoid diversification and exposure mistakes. Plans that offer broad-based stock and bond funds, and target dates funds in their menu lineup provide participants the option of avoiding these mistakes. However, many plans still charge unavoidable excessive fees. As reported in Chapter 1, average excess fees in 2008 were more than 40 basis points, with many plans charging unavoidable fees in excess of 100 basis points annually. There is still important work that fiduciary law can do to reduce this problem of unavoidable across-the-board plan fees.[2] However, our analysis of UVA participant allocations, combined with several other studies discussed above, suggest that participants' "menu misuse" is a larger problem. Substantial numbers of participants fail to diversify idiosyncratic risk, expose themselves to unreasonable amounts of systemic risk, and overweight funds with excessive fees. As unavoidable plan fees subside, it will become increasingly important to take action to address the harmful allocations that participants choose.

In medicine, there is now an understanding that patients are routinely harmed by their own behavioral choices. Non-adherence to pharmaceutical treatments can account for "up to 25% of hospitalizations each year in the United States" and over 100,000 deaths.[3] Changing individual behavior to reduce "six modifiable risk factors … could prevent more than 37 million premature deaths over 15 years."[4] More importantly, public health officials understand that system design can powerfully effect these behaviors. It is far too easy for fiduciaries to wash their hands of the problem by arguing that it's not their fault if participants choose to overweight gold or bitcoin or keep all their savings in money market investments. Traditional

---

[2] For example, we have proposed that fiduciaries be required to label certain plans as "high cost" and allow participants in such plans to roll over their assets to low costs IRAs. *See* Ian Ayres & Quinn Curtis, *Beyond Diversification: The Pervasive Problem of Excessive Fees and 'Dominated Funds' in 401(k) Plans*, 124 YALE L.J. (2014), at 1522.

[3] Jennifer Kim, et al., *Medication Adherence: The Elephant in the Room*, 43 U.S. PHARMACIST 30 (2018).

[4] Vasilis Kontis, et al., *Contribution of Six Risk Factors to Achieving the 25 × 25 Non-Communicable Disease Mortality Reduction Target: A Modelling Study*, 384 THE LANCET 427 (2014).

menu design choices including streamlining and mapping can powerfully reduce the prevalence of menu misuse. More innovative correctives in the form of hard or soft guardrails can protect those most in need while preserving substantial investor freedom.

* * *

While this book has focused on improving participant allocations, there are also important issues in making sure that employees participate and save enough and that they withdraw their savings in appropriate ways. We conclude our narrative by briefly taking on these important inflow and outflow problems, and we describe a bonus proposal that we believe can simultaneously ameliorate both.[5]

The inflow predicament begins with the problem of coverage. Roughly half of employers fail to offer any retirement benefits.[6] This problem is particularly pronounced among small employers, for whom the fixed costs of administration can make providing defined contribution plans prohibitively expensive. Then, there is the problem of non-participation. Even when employers have plans, many employees fail to either participate or save a sufficient amount.[7] One of the biggest issues with 401(k)s is that a majority of workers are not actively contributing to a plan, and those that are participating rarely contribute enough to provide for their retirement.[8]

One counterargument to our proposals to reduce "excess" plan fees is that these fees are necessary to encourage and educate employee participation. Advisors are fond of arguing retirement savings aren't purchased, they're sold. But there is no credible that higher fees lead to

---

[5] Our analysis here grows directly out of ad quotes extensively from Ian Ayres & Jacob Hacker, *Social Security Plus*, 26 ELDER L.J.261 (2019).

[6] *See* Eli R. Stoltzfus, *Beyond the Numbers. Defined Contribution Retirement Plans: Who Has Them and What Do They Cost?*, 5 BUREAU OF LAB. STAT. 3 (2016) (referencing Chart 1), www.bls.gov/opub/btn/volume-5/pdf/defined-contribution-retirement-plans-who-has-them-and-what-do-they-cost.pdf; *See also*, Warren Cormier, *Who Are Uncovered Workers, and Why Should We Care about Them?*, NATIONAL ASSOCIATION OF PLAN ADVISORS (November 30, 2017), www.napa-net.org/news-info/daily-news/who-are-uncovered-workers-and-why-should-we-care-about-them.

[7] Paul Schott, *Helping Working Americans Achieve a Financially Secure Retirement How the 401(k) System Is Succeeding*, Independent Directors Council (July 28, 2011), www.idc.org/speeches-opinions/11_pss_ayco_401k.

[8] Alicia H. Munnell, *401(k)/IRA Holdings in 2013: An Update from the SCF*, 14–15 CENTER FOR RETIREMENT RESEARCH AT BOSTON COLLEGE 4–5 (2014), https://crr.bc.edu/wp-content/uploads/2014/09/IB_14-151.pdf.

better participation or better participant decision-making more generally. In fact, using the massive plan dataset from Chapter 1, we tested testing whether employee participation is higher in plans with higher costs. After controlling for industry groups, employer matching, and other factors that might directly be related to employee participation, we found evidence that expensive plans actually have significantly lower employee participation. We also found that expensive plans have lower contributions per employee and that employees in expensive plans allocate their portfolios less effectively even before accounting for fees. Plan advisors often defend their fees by claiming that they educate employees about the importance of retirement savings. But our results suggest that high-cost plans are not inducing more employees to participate more or to contribute more. In fact, our data hint that the opposite may be the case: it may be that costly plans discourage investor participation, reduce investor contributions, and produce poorer allocation decisions.

The outflow problems begin with leakage. The problem with leakage is that employees have too often *disinvest* their savings before retirement. Munnell's analysis of Vanguard retirement accounts, for example, suggests that more than 1.5 percent of assets annually "leak" from the balances – not because of high fees but because of various forms of withdrawals.[9] Over time, these leakages can reduce the size of a participant's nest egg at the time of retirement by more than 25 percent.[10] The largest source of the leakage is account cash-outs, which can occur when employment with a particular plan employer ends and the former employee, instead of maintaining an account with the plan or rolling the balance over to an IRA, directs the plan to cash out their balance.[11] The temptation to grab the cash happens even though most of these cash-outs are subject to a 10 percent early withdrawal penalty. Other sources of leakage include hardship withdrawals, post-age fifty-nine-and-a-half withdrawals, and loan defaults.[12]

The final outflow problem is the failure of most participants to annuitize their retirement savings. And with good reason. Many annuities, like mutual funds, also charge excessive fees, such as surrender charges of 7 percent to 20 percent if a holder cashes out their investment early, annual management fees of up to 2 percent, annual insurance fees over 1 percent,

[9] *Id.*
[10] *Id.*
[11] *Id.* at 7.
[12] Thomas Olson, *401(k) Leakage: Crafting a Solution Consistent with the Shift to Employee-Managed Retirement Accounts*, 20 ELDER L. J. 449, 483 (2013).

and various insurance riders.[13] Moreover, the shrouding of these fees and the diversity of annuity terms make comparison shopping all the more difficult. It is little wonder that the decisions of whether, with whom, and how to annuitize cause so much anxiety and reluctance.[14] With these cognitive barriers, it should come as no surprise that only a small fraction of plan participants annuitize even a portion of their savings when they retire.[15] This massive failure to annuitize means that retirees not only have to continue to manage their retirement assets, but they risk that their savings run out before they die.

In response to these inflow and outflow problems, we suggest a final reform proposal that was first put forward by Ian Ayres and Jacob Hacker.[16] It's called "Social Security Plus" and it is a public option that would allow Americans to supplement their social purchase, at an actuarially fair price, up to 200 percent of their standard benefits. The details of implementation and as well as a response to critics can be found in their article.[17] Here we focus on the ways in which their proposal simultaneously helps workers put more money aside, keep it invested, and reap the benefits of it for as long as they live.

A core attribute of the proposal is an opt-out default employee contribution of 6.2 percent to Social Security Plus. This default doubles the current mandatory employee Social Security contribution.[18] Doubling the default Social Security employee contribution (from 6.2 percent to 12.4 percent) would not double an employee's Social Security benefits, in part because the employer's contribution would not double and in part because the

[13] Timestaff, *Why Are Annuity Fees So High?*, MONEY (May 20, 2014), https://money.com/collection-post/why-are-annuity-fees-so-high/.

[14] FINANCIAL LITERACY: IMPLICATIONS FOR RETIREMENT SECURITY AND THE FINANCIAL MARKETPLACE 162 (Olivia S. Mitchell & Annamaria Lusardi eds., 2011) ("For example, the many different types of fixed and variable annuities offered in the current market might overwhelm a consumer unfamiliar with these products.").

[15] Sudipto Banerjee, *How Does the Level of Household Savings Affect Preference for Immediate Annuities?* 430 EBRI ISSUE BRIEF, (2017) ("[27] percent of new plans are adopting a lifetime income option but that less than 1 percent of participants in those plans selected it."). *See* also, Report to Congressional Requesters, *401(K) Plans: DOL Could Take Steps to Improve Retirement Income Options for Plan Participants*, United States Government Accountability Office (August 2016), www.gao.gov/assets/gao-16-433.pdf.

[16] Ian Ayres & Jacob Hacker, *Social Security Plus*, 26 ELDER L. J. 261, 286 (2019)

[17] *Id.* at 277.

[18] Social Security Press Office, *How Is Social Security Financed?*, OASDI TRUSTEES REPORT (2020), www.ssa.gov/news/press/factsheets/HowAreSocialSecurity.htm. ("Employers and employees each pay 6.2 percent of wages up to the taxable maximum of $142,800 (in 2021)").

supplemental income would be priced on an actuarially fair basis (without subsidies). Employees working for employers without plans would, by default, be enrolled at this 6.2 percent level. Employers with plans would be required to use SSP as their plan's "Enhanced Qualified Default Investment Alternative" ("EQDIA"). Hence, Social Security Plus would be every ERISA plans' default investment. All employees, with or without a 401(k), would thus make a default SSP contribution of 6.2 percent.

This opt-out contribution would powerfully respond to the coverage problem without appreciably adding to employer financial or administrative burdens. Employers – even small ones – already have systems in place for deducting Social Security contributions from employees' pay and forwarding them to the SSA.[19] Our proposal auto-enrolls anyone who works for an employer without a retirement plan. These employers, by default, would simply deduct a bit more from employees' salaries and forward it to the SSA (without any additional ERISA compliance costs or concerns).[20] Suddenly every employee in the country would by default be enrolled in a supplemental retirement program.

Of course, because it is a default, employees would have the options of opting out and reducing their contribution to 0 percent (or increasing their contribution until their total SSP purchases earned them 200 percent of standard benefits). Still, we know that default enrollments and contributions can have powerful equilibrium effects. Numerous studies have shown that default rules have an beneficially impact employee participation, contributions, and asset allocations.[21] When employees are enrolled by default in a TDA, few opt out, and most employees do not change the default contribution rate or the default allocation of assets.[22] Social Security Plus deploys both default enrollment and default contributions in ways that would almost certainly ameliorate the inflow problems. Some employees would opt to reduce or eliminate the default contribution. But the default

[19] Department of the Treasury, *Publication 15 (2018), (Circular E), Employer's Tax Guide*, IRS (2018).

[20] Jacob S. Hacker, *How to Rescue Retirement*, POLITICO (June 7, 2018), www.politico.com/agenda/story/2018/06/07/retirement-security-risk-000669, ("Step No. 2 is to automatically enroll workers and set a default contribution rate.").

[21] Brigitte C. Madrian & Dennis F. Shea, *The Power of Suggestion: Inertia in 401(k) Participation and Savings Behavior*, 116 Q. J. ECON. 1149, 1187 (2001). *See also* James Choi et al., *For Better or for Worse: Default Effect and 401(k) Savings Behavior*, NBER WORKING PAPER 8651 (2001).

[22] Esther Duflo & Emmanuel Saez, *The Role of Information and Social Interactions in Retirement Plan Decisions: Evidence from a Randomized Experiment*, 118 Q. J. ECON. 815, 842 (2003).

enrollment of the millions of workers who are currently planless, as well as the millions more who have a plan without auto-enrollment or meager contributions,[23] will spur billions of dollars of increased savings.

Moreover, SSP by default allocates these savings to a better EQDIA. The beauty of Social Security Plus is that it provides a low-risk default savings option that builds on a program that is both familiar and popular. Converting retirement investments into SSP purchases avoids all three allocation problems that have been the focus of this book: excessive fees, insufficient diversification, and inappropriate exposure to the equity premium. And it also does something that no existing QDIA can do: it transfers market risk to a superior risk bearer. Even if a defined contribution plan is optimally invested in low-cost, fully-diversified, and age-appropriate equity exposures, workers are still forced to bear the *systemic* risk that investment returns during their lifetime will fall below expectations, such as the possibility that unexpected inflation erodes the purchasing power of the retirement nest egg. Instead of making employers (with defined benefit plans) or employees (with defined contribution plans) bear the systemic risk of stock market underperformance, SSP transfers the risk to the federal government, whose unique ability to run deficits makes it a better bearer of system risk.

SSP would also ameliorate the outflow problems of the current system. It is especially well structured to reduce leakage. We respond to leakage in part by creating a default that upon job separation, any 401(k) balances would "roll into" SSP unless the employee indicates that they want to keep the funds invested in their former employer's plan or "roll over" the funds to an IRA account. SSP purchases are likely to be less subject to leakage, in part because SSP purchases would not be subject to loan defaults, post-age fifty-nine-and-a-half withdrawals, or cash-out withdrawals. Under our proposal, SSP purchases would still provide the individual with the option of hardship withdrawals, which are currently estimated to account for leakages of more than 0.3 percent a year.[24] While some of these hardship

---

[23] A 2011 analysis of Vanguard plans showed that less than a quarter of the plans had auto-enrollment and very few had default employee contributions as large as 6.2 percent. *See* Paul Schott, *Helping Working Americans Achieve a Financially Secure Retirement How the 401(k) System Is Succeeding*, INVESTMENT COMPANY INSTITUTE (July 28, 2011), https://idc.org/speeches-opinions/11_pss_ayco_401k.

[24] Olson, *supra* note 12, at 461. It would be possible to have an SSP program without the possibility of hardship withdrawals, but we worry that removing the possibility would unduly discourage SSP purchases. *See* Sylvain Catherine, Max Miller and Natasha Sarin, *Relaxing Household Liquidity Constraints through Social Security*, 189 J. PUBLIC ECON. 1, 9 (2020).

withdrawals are appropriate, employers have poorer incentives to police hardship than the SSA. Accordingly, the proposal would likely produce less leakage even while maintaining hardship withdrawals.

Finally, SSP would ameliorate the under-annuitization of retirement benefits. SSP radically simplifies the annuitization process. By default, millions of Americans would have an inflation-adjusted life annuity with the imprimatur of the United States government. Relative to the private market, the purchaser can better trust that the annuity is being offered without excess or hidden fees. What's more, SSP solves the missing market for "pre-retirement annuities."[25] Pre-retirement purchasing provides important benefits over the current system of purchasing annuities (if at all) postretirement:

> The cumulative chance of dying between ages forty and sixty-seven is roughly 20%. Because of the chance of receiving nothing, this prefunding of an annuity at forty years-old will, if you do make it, boost your return by 25% (over and above the gain from twenty-seven years of compounding).[26]

Instead of having to continually consider and recalibrate investment allocations while confronting a bewildering annuities market often filled with rapaciously self-interested actors, SSP purchasers can safely turn their attention to other pursuits of happiness – safe in the knowledge that they will have an inflation-adjusted nugget for as long as they live.

***

We end the book with this short detour into inflows and outflows in part to underscore the complexity of the regulatory problem. We also hope it will spur readers to think about how best to craft regulations that promote more robust retirement outcomes. For example, Barry Nalebuff has suggested to us that a less ambitious form of Social Security Plus would be to at least allow individuals to pre-purchase a topping-off annuity that would pay age-70 benefits to people preferring to retire at age 65. Our numerous proposals are not meant to put an end to this important discussion. We have shown that allocation errors are a substantial problem that could be ameliorated in ways that preserve substantial investor autonomy. Our task now is to summon the political will to act.

---

[25] Ian Ayres & Barry Nalebuff, *Insurance You Want to Collect*, FORBES (April 23, 2010), www.forbes.com/forbes/2010/0510/companies-annuities-investing-retirement-insurance-why-not.html#58fbe1099303.

[26] *Id.*

INDEX